GENDER AND CLIMATE CHANGE

Does gender matter in global climate change? This timely and provocative book takes readers on a guided tour of basic climate science, then holds up a gender lens to find out what has been overlooked in popular discussion, research, and policy debates. We see that, around the world, more women than men die in climate-related natural disasters; the history of science and war are intimately interwoven masculine occupations and preoccupations; and conservative men and their interests drive the climate change denial machine. We also see that climate policymakers who embrace big science approaches and solutions to climate change are predominantly male with an ideology of perpetual economic growth, and an agenda that marginalizes the interests of women and developing economies. The book uses vivid case studies to highlight the sometimes surprising differential, gendered impacts of climate changes.

Joane Nagel, Distinguished Professor of Sociology at the University of Kansas, is the author of *Race, Ethnicity, and Sexuality: Intimate Intersections, Forbidden Frontiers*.

Joane Nagel focuses her keen sociological eye on the intersection of gender and climate change, and the result is an exceptionally insightful analysis of topics such as women's greater vulnerability to a warming world, male domination of climate science and resulting blindspots, and the need for women having a greater voice in climate change policy-making. Her volume provides a superb example of the value of sociological insights into climate change.

Riley E. Dunlap, *Dresser Professor and Regents Professor of Sociology, Oklahoma State University*

We have waited a long time for a book this good—hard-hitting and analytic, amply supported empirically yet accessible to generalists, and fine-grained enough to bring these critical issues to life. What an accomplishment! Nagel deftly synthesizes a wide range of multi-disciplinary research to persuasively argue that yes, gender and climate change are connected—and why gender justice and climate justice are inextricably linked.

Elaine Enarson, *Independent Scholar*

Nagel offers an original and compelling take on climate change that will attract a major popular and scholarly audience, including teachers and students in a wide range of courses. She documents intriguing and tragic disproportionate impacts of climate on women, as well as the male-dominated profile of the fossil fuel industry and climate deniers. While her findings don't obscure the universal threat to both genders, they make clear that if you care about women you must urgently work to stop climate change, and that women will help lead resistance to the economic and military forces wreaking havoc on our environment.

Charles Derber, *author* of Greed to Green: Solving Climate Change and Remaking the Economy *and* The Disinherited Majority: Capital Questions—Piketty and Beyond

GENDER AND CLIMATE CHANGE
Impacts, Science, Policy

Joane Nagel

Routledge
Taylor & Francis Group

NEW YORK AND LONDON

First published 2016
by Routledge
711 Third Avenue, New York, NY 10017

and by Routledge
2 Park Square, Milton Park, Abingdon, Oxon, OX14 4RN

Routledge is an imprint of the Taylor & Francis Group, an informa business

© 2016 Taylor & Francis

Library of Congress Cataloging in Publication Data
Nagel, Joane.
    Gender and climate change : impacts, science, policy / by Joane Nagel.
        pages   cm
    Includes bibliographical references and index.
    1. Climatic changes–Sex differences.   2. Women and the
    environment.   3. Human beings–Effect of climate on.   I. Title.
    QC903.N34 2016
    363.738′74082–dc23   2015013606

ISBN: 978-1-61205-766-8 (hbk)
ISBN: 978-1-61205-767-5 (pbk)
ISBN: 978-1-315-67527-5 (ebk)

Typeset in Adobe Caslon Pro
by Out of House Publishing

Printed and bound in the United States of America by Publishers Graphics, LLC on sustainably sourced paper.

To Mike
From start to finish

Contents

PREFACE

In 2008, I attended a conference organized by the Kansas Insurance Commissioner on the "'what ifs' of climate change that could impact the insurance industry."[1] The meeting was attended by more than 50 Kansas insurance agents, managers, and small business insurance agency owners, as well as insurance industry association and government representatives. The speakers included a climate scientist, the research director of the National Association of Insurance Commissioners, and a senior vice president for Swiss Re, a major international reinsurance company headquartered in Zurich. The speakers discussed the risks expected from climate change (extreme weather, coastal and inland flooding, droughts and associated wildfires, crop failures) and the expected increased cost of insuring against these hazards. It was a fascinating sociological moment – local business meets global capital on an uneven landscape where the two parties had little common ground and even less shared vision, especially when it came to climate change.

The climate scientist spoke first, offering an overview of well-established findings and restrained predictions about the impacts of climate change globally and on the US Great Plains. The audience, who mainly represented a conservative industry in a conservative state, listened politely. Their lack of questions and disinterested demeanor indicated that they were not particularly impressed by the understated, but nonetheless ominous, scientific news. Even if these mainly Republican businesspeople were personally neutral on the topic of climate change, in their businesses they daily faced a clientele that was largely in denial and often hostile toward scientific pronouncements about global warming and its potential impact on their lives and livelihoods.

The conference began to engage the audience when the two speakers from industry began talking money. The insurance industry research director and the executive from the reinsurance corporation informed the conferees that increasing risks from climate change were going to result in significant rate increases in short order. These were rate increases that many members of the audience would have to pass on to their conservative, skeptical customers. Unlike switching channels when a climate change science story appears on a newscast, the rising cost of insurance against the risks of climate change was bad news the conference attendees could not easily tune out, since they were about to become its messengers. As the meeting proceeded, it became clear that these insurance businesspeople were not comfortable about carrying back home to their clients the communiqué from the multinational reinsurance industry: your insurance rates will be going up because of global warming. This news was especially unwelcome since many of them (and their customers) didn't even "believe in" climate change.

One attendee at the Kansas Insurance Commission meeting was the president of the Armed Forces Insurance Exchange at Fort Leavenworth, Kansas (home of the US Army Combined Arms Center and Command and General Staff College). He represented another conservative constituency – the military. His comments, however, revealed a surprise about the US military's institutional posture toward climate change science: "It's critical we get more informed on climate change, and this is a first step toward that. Three-fifths of our exposure is in the coastal Southeast – obviously, it's high on our radar screen."

"Three-fifths of our exposure is the coastal Southeast." Why did that particular fact lead this military insurance man to report that climate change was "high on our radar screen?" The answer is the location of large US military investments (naval bases and other military installations) in coastal regions, especially in the US southeastern seaboard and Gulf Coast – areas most vulnerable to hurricanes. Climate change models project increased intensity of storms and storm surges in coastal areas around the world, particularly hurricanes and monsoons. Models of sea level rise track the warming oceans and the melting polar ice sheets to predict that US coastlines and coastal cities face significant effects: coastal erosion, flooding of agricultural lands, residential neighborhoods, and commercial developments, and salinization of freshwater lakes, wetlands, farmlands, and drinking water supplies. The individual members of the US armed forces might hold conservative, even skeptical views of climate change since the majority are Republicans or conservative Independents.[2] The institutional stance of the US military, however, does not reflect these views. US armed service personnel may be climate skeptics, but the US armed services are not.

The Kansas Insurance Commission meeting provided me with a number of insights that are reflected in this book: the politics of skepticism; the role of gender and social class in climate change attitudes; the economic impacts of climate change, which can fly in the face of public beliefs; the importance of climate change to the US military; and the large gap between technical knowledge and popular understanding of scientific findings. I am grateful to my colleague, David Braaten, an atmospheric scientist in the University of Kansas Geography Department, for inviting me to accompany him to this meeting. I am indebted to David for other reasons as well. He helped design and served as my co-principal investigator (PI) on the five-year C-CHANGE (Climate Change Humans and Nature in the Global Environment) graduate training program for University of Kansas PhD students in the natural and social sciences and engineering (National Science Foundation (NSF0801522) IGERT (Integrative Graduate Education and Research Traineeship) award), and he led two groups of C-CHANGE trainees to Greenland as part of his graduate seminar on Climate Change in Greenland and the Arctic.[3] David's expertise and generosity are reflected in Chapter 1; his comments and corrections were critical to the chapter, but despite his best efforts, any errors remain mine.

My gratitude extends to my three other co-PIs in the NSF C-CHANGE IGERT project: Dr. Daniel Wildcat (Haskell Indian Nations University) and Drs. Leonard (Kris) Kristalka and Andrew (Town) Peterson (KU Ecology and Evolutionary Biology), for their work designing and directing C-CHANGE courses and activities. Town included C-CHANGE faculty and students in his extensive international scientific collaborations and led two groups to Mexico as part of his Climates and Borders seminar. C-CHANGE was a broadly interdisciplinary collaboration among 30 colleagues who taught or advised more than 60 graduate students who were funded and/or participated in C-CHANGE seminars and fieldwork in the US, Mexico, and Greenland. These students and colleagues were from American Studies, Anthropology, Biology, Chemical Engineering, Economics, Environmental Engineering, Environmental Studies, Geography, Geology, History, Law, Philosophy, Political Science, Psychology, Public Administration, and Sociology. This multitude of knowledges and perspectives enriched my understanding of climate change and its relationship to the natural and social world. Without the generosity of these colleagues and students, I could not have written this book.

My colleague, co-worker, and fellow traveler to almost all C-CHANGE destinations, Natalie Parker, C-CHANGE Project Coordinator, read the entire manuscript as each chapter was written. Natalie was, in many ways, my ideal intended reader: smart and educated, a non-specialist who was informed and open to argument and evidence. I benefitted from her own success and skill as an author, especially one who knows how to give supportive feedback and gentle criticism on early drafts. Natalie's influence is evident in the sections of the book marked by clarity and smoothness, but not in those places where I could not resist wading into the weeds of historical or technical detail. Our student assistant, Shaylee Vandeveer, worked tirelessly to locate data, construct summary tables, and track down citations. Several colleagues provided insightful responses to drafts of parts of the book. Ebenezer Obadare, Shannon O'Lear, and Kees van der Veen read sections and chapters on gender, science, and the military. Graduate students in my 2014 seminar on Gender and Global Environmental Change read the entire manuscript and offered a range of useful responses, even taking the risk of providing occasional critical feedback to their professor.

A number of colleagues patiently and thoughtfully answered my questions about data, literature, and ideas. Bob Brulle sent me several useful articles, leads, and ideas about climate change skepticism. Dort Daley offered thoughtful feedback to my questions about gender and policy, and gave me a great lead to International Monetary Fund (IMF) Director Christine Lagarde's thinking about women's added value. Jim Fleming responded with polite incredulity and a fountain of feedback when I asked him if and how the military's involvement in science matters. Ed Russell spent time talking and corresponding with me about the role of the military in the evolution of US chemistry as a discipline and profession, and helped me think through the implications of funding for shaping the agenda (and sometimes the bias) in science. Sharon Harlan shared literature and her own research on the effects of heat and heat waves on men's and women's health outcomes. Maril Hazlett spent an afternoon with me comparing notes on her research on Rachel Carson and the role of masculinity in science. Riley Dunlap provided insights from his research and readings on climate skepticism, and his colleague, Aaron McCright, answered my questions about gender and climate change denial. Jorge Soberón was an invaluable and gentle sounding board for me to test my hunches and claims about gender and science and the military-science complex. My colleague, Bob Antonio, supplied me with a steady stream of up-to-date research, reports, and articles on numerous aspects of climate change; I was immensely fortunate to know such a committed scholar who was so willing to share his vast knowledge of the political and economic implications of unfolding climate science. Two of my former students, now university faculty members, Lindsey Feitz and Monique Laney, were my research assistants when I and they first began learning about global climate change. I'm proud of, but not responsible for or surprised by, their successes, and grateful for their early and ongoing collegiality. The enthusiasm for this project by Dean Birkenkamp, President and Publisher of Paradigm Publishing, was critical to its completion when a major life loss left me reeling; Dean obtained careful, supportive, but also critical reviews of the book prospectus and the completed manuscript and offered invaluable advice along the way as he and the book moved to Routledge.

This book is dedicated to my dear late husband, Michael Joseph Penner. It was Mike who brought to my attention a posting about "gender and disasters" on one of several emergency management lists that he subscribed to. His enthusiasm for this project supported me throughout its writing. As a former firefighter, over the more than 30 years of our marriage, he generously shared with me countless invaluable insights into masculine culture. To the extent that I got it right about masculinity and militarism, it was because of Mike; where I got it wrong is my sole responsibility.

Notes

[1] Kansas Insurance Department. 2008. "Conference Examines Insurance Concerns about Potential Climate Change." August 28, 2008 Press Release Topeka, Kansas. Accessed on June 25, 2014 at www.ksinsurance.org/gpa/news/2008/climate_change_release8-08.pdf.

[2] A 2009 survey of 1800 active-duty troops conducted by the *Military Times* reported that 12 percent of respondents identified themselves as Democrats, 41 percent identified themselves as Republicans, and 32 percent identified as Independents; see McGarry, Brendan. 2013. "2009 Military Times Poll: In Politics, Troops Are Increasingly Independent." *Navy Times* (March 14). Accessed on June 25, 2014 at www.navytimes.com/apps/pbcs.dll/article?AID=2013303141172.

[3] For details of the NSF C-CHANGE IGERT program, see www.res.ku.edu/~crgc/IGERT/ (accessed on June 25, 2014).

INTRODUCTION
Why Gender and Climate Change?

"Say what?! Gender and climate change? Doesn't climate change affect everyone? It's a global issue, not a gender issue." These comments were made to me by a natural science colleague several years ago when I wondered aloud whether there were gendered dimensions to global climate change. His skepticism motivated the research for this book. When I began reading about gender and climate change in 2008, I found a limited scientific literature. Most of the work focused on women's vulnerabilities to climate-related disasters, mainly in developing countries. By 2015, there was a large and growing body of research on women and men and climate change. This book contributes to that research by offering a sociological analysis of gender and climate change.

Not all climate change affects women and men differently. Sometimes gender matters, sometimes it doesn't. As a point of clarification, gender refers to socially assigned roles, expectations, and positions for males and females in societies. In contrast to sex (biological and physiological differences between males and females), gender can change over time and according to social class, religion, ethnicity, region, or country. There are variations in both sex and gender in any population. While human males tend to be taller than females, some males are taller than others, and some females are taller than some males. This can be true for other physiological differences between the sexes, such as strength, endurance, or lifespan. These sexual differences are not exclusively biological; many have social origins.

For instance, nutritional differences between males and females in different countries have resulted in cross-national variations in men's and women's average height and rate of obesity. Cultural expectations of physical fitness for women can reduce inherent sexual differences in strength. Gender differences in men's and women's economic responsibilities, family duties, political rights, education, and health can make men and women more or less or equally vulnerable to the effects of climate change. These gender variations can be seen within countries and in cross-national comparisons. Gender and sexual differences and variations in gender roles across the globe have important implications for understanding whether the impacts of climate change will be similar or dissimilar for men and women, especially when climate change outcomes involve natural disasters.[1]

Gendering Natural Disasters

Most so-called "natural" disasters involve human factors, such as the collapse of inadequately designed levees that flooded parts of New Orleans during Hurricane Katrina in 2005. Whatever their causes, natural disasters affect more than 200 million people every year, and the numbers of disasters has been increasing in recent decades.[2] Disaster statistics indicate that there were three times as many natural disasters from 2000 to 2009 compared to the period from 1980 to 1989. Not all natural catastrophes are climate-related; some are geophysical (e.g. tsunamis or earthquakes). Researchers have attributed the increase in disasters from 1980 to 2009 mainly to a rise in the number of climate-related events (e.g. storms or droughts), which accounted "for nearly 80% of the increase, whereas numbers of geophysical events have remained stable."[3] Climate models suggest the trend toward stronger storms, heavier precipitation, flooding, heatwaves, and droughts causing climate-related disasters will continue as levels of carbon dioxide (CO_2) rise in the future.[4] In light of larger numbers of projected natural disasters from processes associated with climate change, it is important to understand who is at risk. Of particular interest here is whether there are gendered patterns in human risks from climate-related disasters.

In a study of 4600 natural disasters in 141 countries between 1981–2002, researchers found that natural disasters lowered the life expectancy of women more than men, killed more women than men, and/or killed women at an earlier age than men.[5] This more deadly effect of disasters on women seemed to be very much influenced by women's socioeconomic status relative to men. In many countries, women's devalued social position makes them especially vulnerable when disaster strikes. In countries where women have more equal social and economic rights, researchers found less difference in life expectancy between men and women during or after disasters. They concluded that women's equality not only improves the quality of their day-to-day lives, it can enhance their chances for survival in the face of disaster.[6]

There are several ways that gender matters in understanding global climate change. The chapters of this book will examine differences between men and women as they relate to several aspects of climate change: impacts, science, skepticism, and policy.

Gender and climate change impacts – global warming and sea level rise: Around the world not only do more women than men die in climate- and weather-related natural disasters, the disruptions following these disasters make women and adolescent girls (and sometimes boys) especially vulnerable to exploitation:

> The South Asia partnership in Barguna, Bangladesh, reported an increase in sex trafficking during times of floods, droughts and cyclones: "after cyclones Sidr and Aila, there was a lot more trafficking due to economic problems ... Indeed most of the sex workers in Dhaka, come from this part of Bangladesh."[7]

Gender and climate change science – masculinity and militarization: Climate science is a mainly male enterprise, which, in the US, is influenced by a historically male-dominated institution: the military. The US Department of Defense's interest in the security threats associated with climate change diverts funding away from mitigation measures to slow the causes of climate change and directs funding toward preparations to battle the perceived dangers arising from climate change:

> Climate change may exacerbate water scarcity and lead to sharp increases in food costs. The pressures caused by climate change will influence resource competition while placing additional burdens on economies, societies, and governance institutions around the world. These effects are threat multipliers that will aggravate stressors abroad such as poverty, environmental degradation, political instability, and social tensions – conditions that can enable terrorist activity and other forms of violence.[8]

Gender and climate change responses – skepticism and policy: Responses to climate change are shaped almost exclusively by politically-connected and/or professional men, reflecting privileged male cultural viewpoints, values, and agendas which sometimes involve denying that climate change exists or designing policies that ignore the different effects of climate change on women, people living in poverty, or other vulnerable populations:

> A recent report by the UN Food and Agriculture Organization considered the gendered effects of large-scale biofuel production, and concluded that women in particular would be adversely affected … [by] the way in which so-called marginal land, which is often used by women for household food production, is targeted for biofuel production; loss of biodiversity resulting in reduced food security; high water consumption of biofuel crops, which compete directly with household needs and increase women's workload; replacement of solid biofuel crops needed for local households; and exploitation of female biofuel plantation workers.[9]

Each chapter will examine these and other claims about gender differences in climate change impacts, science, skepticism, and politics. We will evaluate evidence in response to the question: Does gender matter? Does it matter that more women than men are affected by climate change-related disasters? Does it matter that men dominate climate science? Does it matter that men are more likely to deny climate change is a problem or that women are poorly represented in climate change policymaking?

Revealing the Gendered Face of Climate Change

It should not be surprising that climate change has a gendered face. Social science research has reported many ways that gender matters in societies: work and labor force participation, health behavior and outcomes, family dynamics, civil and human rights, crime and delinquency, political attitudes and power, discrimination, violence, poverty, consumer behavior, risk-taking, military participation, education, income, and environmental attitudes, to name a few.[10] Sociological analyses of gender in everyday social life have implications for understanding the human dimensions of global climate change. Women's and men's relative places in society, cultural definitions of masculinity and femininity, and the moral economies that define male and female worth and proper behavior all matter in the gendered aspects of climate change. These gender differences shape women's and men's vulnerability to the impacts of climate change, ability to set the scientific climate research agenda, access to resources associated with recovery from climate-related disasters, attitudes toward risks associated with climate change, and participation in the political processes that shape mitigation and adaptation policies.

There are many variations in the relative places of women and men in countries around the world. On average, across countries, women are less educated and poorer than men, but they tend to live longer. Men are more likely to hold political office, work outside the home, and be overrepresented in professional, scientific, and technical fields. Women are more likely to volunteer in their communities, work for no pay at home or for low pay in the informal economy, and be overrepresented in teaching, health care, and the service sector. Women and men not only live their private and public lives in different places in society, they occupy different cultural spaces – even when they are in the same families and communities. Most masculine cultures around the world emphasize autonomy, strength, risk-taking, and some degree of control over the women in their families. These values constitute what researchers refer to as "hegemonic masculinity."[11] While many of these characteristics might seem like dated stereotypes about men and women, they not only are typical of gender roles in the global South, they can be seen in varying degrees in the lives of women and men in the United States and other Western countries. As we shall see, the gendered aspects of climate change are a reflection of gendered aspects of social life in general. Broadly, gender inequality contributes to more unequal impacts of climate change, often making women more vulnerable than men.

In the next chapter we will review some basic climate change terms, processes, and findings. These will give us the breadth and depth of climate change knowledge that we will need to evaluate the arguments and evidence in the rest of this book about the ways that gender matters in understanding global climate change.

Notes

[1] Enarson, Elaine. 2012. *Women Confronting Natural Disaster: from Vulnerability to Resilience*. Boulder, CO: Lynne Rienner Publisher; Enarson, Elaine, and P.G. Dhar Chakrabarti (eds.). 2009. *Women, Gender, and Disaster: Global Issues and Initiatives*. Thousand Oaks, CA: Sage Publications.

[2] Guha-Sapir, Debarati, Philippe Hoyois, and Regina Below. 2013. "Annual Disaster Statistical Review, 2012: The Numbers and Trends." Centre for Research on the Epidemiology of Disasters, Université catholique de Louvain, Brussels, Belgium. Accessed on February 13, 2014 at http://reliefweb.int/sites/reliefweb.int/files/resources/ADSR_2012.pdf.

[3] Leaning, Jennifer, and Debarati Guha-Sapir. 2013. "Natural Disasters, Armed Conflict, and Public Health." *New England Journal of Medicine*, Vol. 369, No. 19:1836–42.

[4] Lau, William K.-M., H.-T. Wu, and K.-M. Kim. 2013. "A Canonical Response of Precipitation Characteristics to Global Warming from CMIP Five Models." *Geophysical Research Letters*, Vol. 40:3163–9.

[5] Neumayer, Eric, and Thomas Plumper. 2007. "The Gendered Nature of Natural Disasters: the Impact of Catastrophic Events on the Gender Gap in Life Expectancy, 1981–2002." *Annals of the American Association of Geographers*, Vol. 97, No. 3:551–566; they included 12 types of disasters in their study, all but two were weather or climate related, p. 40.

[6] Ibid.

[7] Van der Gaag, Nikki. 2014. *In Double Jeopardy: Adolescent Girls and Disasters*. Plan International, p. 66. Accessed on March 26, 2014 at https://plan-international.org/girls/reports-and-publications/index.php?lang=en; Kartiki, Katha. 2011. "Climate Change and Migration: A Case Study from Rural Bangladesh." *Gender and Development*, Vol. 19, No. 1:23–38.

[8] US Department of Defense. 2014. *Quadrennial Defense Review*, p. 8. Accessed on March 26, 2014 at www.defense.gov/pubs/2014_Quadrennial_Defense_Review.pdf.

[9] Haigh, Christine, and Bernadette Vallely. 2010. *Gender and the Climate Change Agenda: The Impacts of Climate Change on Women and Public Policy*. Women's Environmental Network, p. 27. Accessed on March 26, 2014 at www.wen.org.uk/wp-content/uploads/Gender-and-the-climate-change-agenda-21.pdf; see also Rossi, A., and Y. Lambrou 2008. *Gender and Equity Issues in Liquid Biofuels Production, Minimizing the Risks to Maximize the Opportunities*. Rome: Food and Agriculture Organization of the United Nations. Accessed on March 26, 2014 at www.fao.org/docrep/010/ai503e/ai503e00.htm.

[10] For overviews of gender matters in social science, see Anderson, Margaret, and Patricia Hill Collins. 2006. *Race, Class, and Gender: An Anthology*. Belmont, CA: Wadsworth; Marchbank, Jennifer, and Gayle Letherby. 2007. *Introduction to Gender: Social Science Perspectives*. New York: Longman; Rothenberg, Paula S. 2013. *Race, Class, and Gender in the United States: An Integrated Study*. New York: Worth Publishers.

[11] Connell, R.W. 2005. *Masculinities*. Second Edition. Berkeley, CA: University of California Press.

1
WHAT IS GLOBAL CLIMATE CHANGE?

The study of global climate change is an exciting and gloomy enterprise. The excitement comes from discoveries being made in the uncharted realm of a changing global climate. The gloom comes from the nature of many of those discoveries. Mainly, we are seeing that there's trouble on the horizon. How serious is the trouble depends on how far out we look, and on our capacity to avoid or adapt to the changes heading our way. Actually, it's less the changes *heading our way* than it is the changes *we are driving ourselves into*.

Climate Change Basics

In order to understand why researchers are increasingly troubled about the extent and direction of global climate change, we'll need to review some climate change basics. The World Meteorological Organization (WMO) distinguishes *weather* (condition of the atmosphere in a particular place over a short period of time) from *climate* (average weather over 30 years or more). Both weather and climate are variable. The difference between climate variability and climate change is the persistence of "anomalous" conditions: "events that used to be rare occur more frequently (summertime maximum air temperatures increasingly break records each year), or vice-versa (duration and thickness of seasonal lake ice are decreasing with time)."[1] Both weather and climate can be quite variable, but not constitute climate change. Climate change is when weather and climate average values shift and variability increases over at least a 30-year period, breaking records, exceeding upper and lower values, or varying in new ways from past observations: earlier or later higher highs, or lower lows, more frequent or less frequent weather events.

There has been much climate variability, but not much climate change since the end of the last Ice Age, around 10,000 years ago. Patterns of droughts, heat waves, cold spells, monsoons and hurricanes, and blizzards established a range of expected climatic variability in different regions of the world. It was during this climatically stable "interglacial" period that humans moved from exclusively hunting and gathering and began cultivating crops. Throughout these past 10 millennia, carbon dioxide (CO_2) levels in the atmosphere remained fairly constant, between 260–280 parts per million (ppm).

CO_2 is one of several greenhouse gases (GHGs) frequently cited in discussions of climate change. The other two major GHGs tracked by scientists interested in understanding climate change are methane (CH_4) and nitrous oxide (N_2O). CO_2 is the most widely used indicator of levels of GHGs in the global atmosphere partly because its effects last the longest and it makes the largest contribution to global temperatures. Stable levels of atmospheric CO_2 over the past 10,000 years started to change when the Industrial Revolution increased the use of fossil fuels in agriculture and industrial production. Work that had been done by hand or with animals until that time began to be done by machines driven by coal, oil, and gas. Burning these fossil fuels released their stored carbon in the form of CO_2 into the atmosphere, increasing levels of CO_2.

The use of machines in place of human labor not only transformed factories, it revolutionized agriculture. Fossil fuel-driven farm machinery changed small-scale farming into large-scale agriculture, factories replaced craft enterprises, roads were built, growing populations moved from farms to cities, and the United States and other industrial countries became mainly urban societies dependent on food from machine-driven agricultural production. Mechanized agriculture broke

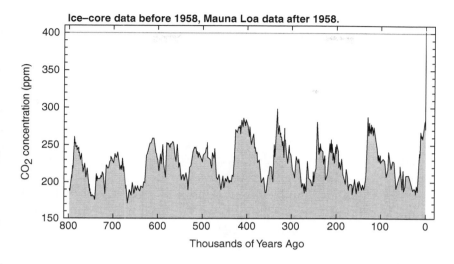

Figure 1.1 Global Carbon Dioxide Concentrations (PPM) Over the Past 800,000 Years[7]

new land, releasing carbon from the soil where it had been buried for hundreds of thousands, sometimes millions of years. Extraction and combustion of fossil fuels for heat, cooking, farming, industry, and transportation released into the atmosphere billions of tons of carbon from coal, natural gas, and oil that had been sequestered underground for hundreds of millions of years.[2]

The growth of CO_2 levels has accelerated dramatically in the last two centuries. Atmospheric CO_2 was about 280 ppm in 1850 at the start of the Industrial Revolution, and had increased only 20 ppm (7 percent) during the previous 800,000 years. In 2015, atmospheric CO_2 exceeded 400 ppm, an increase of 120 ppm (33 percent) in only the past 155 years.[3] Scientists determine CO_2 concentration using a variety of methods. Instruments such as infrared or chemical sensors directly measure atmospheric CO_2, and past atmospheres can be analyzed using air bubbles in ice cores drilled in polar ice sheets. More inferential proxy methods use marine sediments, fossil plants, or rock weathering.[4] Figure 1.1 shows data from both instruments and ice cores to chart atmospheric CO_2 levels during the past

800,000 years.[5] Before 1958 ice core data are from Greenland and Antarctica; beginning in 1958 instrument data are from Mauna Loa, Hawaii.[6]

The graph in Figure 1.1 shows the cyclical rise and decline of CO_2 levels associated with glacial minima and maxima over 800,000 years. The repeating peaks and valleys of CO_2 in the graph are initiated mainly by solar cycles and Earth's orbital changes and amplified by positive feedback processes.[8] The noticeably regular patterns in CO_2 variations over these 800 millennia are a reminder that there are many natural forces shaping Earth's planetary systems, including solar cycles and solar activity, volcanic eruptions, changes in the Earth's orbit, and major shifts in the Earth's tectonic plates. An important point to make is that human civilization does not exist throughout the vast expanse of this period, but appears on the scene far toward the right of the graph, fewer than 10,000 years ago.

In Figure 1.1, it's easy to overlook the vertical line on the right side of the chart just above year 0, a line that rises straight up from 280 to 400 ppm. That vertical line shows the increase in CO_2 in the last 165 years. It is easier to see this increase in Figure 1.2, which

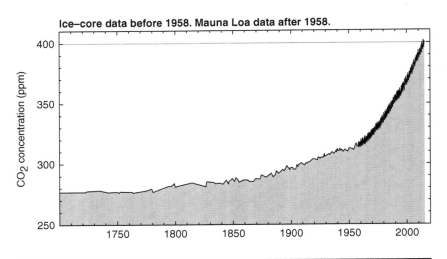

Figure 1.2 Global Carbon Dioxide Concentrations (PPM), 1700–2014[10]

charts levels of CO_2 from 1700 to 2012. Figure 1.2 shows that CO_2 levels are fairly stable until around 1850, when the upward trajectory begins, and accelerates during the second half of the 20th century. The thick lines in the graph are seasonal variations obtained from daily CO_2 measurements that Charles David Keeling began in May, 1958.[9]

With very few exceptions, scientists examining these data identify human activity as the major cause of the precipitous rise in CO_2. In particular, researchers point to our use of fossil fuels and their GHG emissions as the current most powerful driver of global climate change. The link among increased use of fossil fuels, rapidly rising CO_2 levels, and major changes in the global climate system constitute "anthropogenic" (human-caused) climate change.

Carbon Dioxide and Climate Change?

What exactly do atmospheric CO_2 levels have to do with climate change? CO_2 is critical to life on Earth. Plants use CO_2 in photosynthesis to grow and produce oxygen, and in turn, plants are a food source for other forms of life, including humans. CO_2 helps provide Earth with an atmospheric envelope, retaining the sun's heat and keeping the planet warm. The fairly constant levels of CO_2 present in Earth's atmosphere during the development of human civilization have increased dramatically. These elevated levels of CO_2 and other GHGs are raising global temperatures and warming the world's oceans. CO_2 has another effect on the oceans, which absorb about 30 percent of the CO_2 we release into the atmosphere every year. CO_2 absorption changes the chemistry of seawater, causing ocean acidification, which contributes to the decline of shellfish populations, the bleaching of corals, and threats to the species that depend on them.[11] The various changes associated with increased levels of CO_2 are producing a cascade of related, and often unpredictable, outcomes, the study of which has become climate change science.

Scientific concerns about the nature and extent of climate change underway around the planet led to the creation of the

Intergovernmental Panel on Climate Change (IPCC) in 1988. The IPCC was established by the WMO and the United Nations (UN) to provide the world with the most current and accurate available scientific information about climate change's potential environmental and socio-economic impacts to assist in formulating realistic response strategies.[12] The IPCC does not conduct research; it gathers data from scientists in UN member states. Every seven years, these scientists compile "Assessment Reports," which are reviewed and must be unanimously approved by political representatives from all countries and the reports' lead authors. In its 2013 Fifth Assessment Report (AR5), the IPCC reported:

> The atmospheric concentrations of carbon dioxide, methane, and nitrous oxide have increased to levels unprecedented in at least the last 800,000 years. Carbon dioxide concentrations have increased by 40% since pre-industrial times, primarily from fossil fuel emissions and secondarily from net land use change emissions. The ocean has absorbed about 30% of the emitted anthropogenic carbon dioxide, causing ocean acidification.[13]

Since the IPCC is not only a scientific body, but also a political one, its assessments and predictions tend to be quite moderate. In fact, the IPCC has been criticized for making predictions that proved to be too conservative and for not more loudly raising the alarm about the implications of climate change for the planet's biosphere and human societies.[14] Despite its reluctance to overstate the rate and impacts of climate change, the IPCC's AR5 lists a number of significant observed and predicted changes in Earth's atmospheric, oceanic, cryospheric, and biogeochemical systems resulting from increased GHGs. These physical system changes are listed in Table 1.1.

The IPCC qualifies its predictions in terms of their likelihood or degree of certainty, ranging from "virtually certain" (99–100 percent probability) to "exceptionally unlikely" (less than 0–1 percent probability). Most IPCC predictions fall in the range between "extremely likely" (95–100 percent probability) to "likely" (66–100 percent probability).[16] The IPCC makes only a few "virtually certain" predictions,

Table 1.1 Changes in Earth's Atmospheric, Oceanic, Cryospheric, and Biogeochemical Systems[15]

- Increases in the Earth's surface temperature such that 1983–2012 was very likely the warmest 30-year period of the last 800 years (p. 5);
- increases in ocean surface and subsurface temperature, acidity, and salinity contributing to sea level rise and significant changes in fish habitat (p. 8);
- decreases in Arctic sea ice and Greenland ice sheets contributing to alterations in atmospheric and ocean circulation systems affecting northern hemisphere weather (p.9);
- decreases in the extent of snow cover in the northern hemisphere contributing to drought (p. 9);
- increases in the rate of melting of permafrost in arctic areas contributing to increased greenhouse gas emissions (p. 9);
- increases in hot and decreases in cold temperature extremes with a trend toward warmer days and warmer nights and more frequent, longer heat waves (p. 5);
- increased likelihood of extreme precipitation events with likely increases in northern and mid-latitudes (with potential flooding) and likely decreases in the subtropics (with potential drought) (p. 5);
- increased risk of drought, especially in the Mediterranean, Southwestern US, and parts of Africa (p. 7);
- increased area affected by monsoons and a longer monsoon season (pp. 15, 23);
- increased and accelerated rate of sea level rise up to 1 meter (3 feet) during the 21st century (p. 11).

but one of several notable ones in AR5 was: "It is virtually certain that global mean sea level rise will continue beyond 2100, with sea level rise due to thermal expansion to continue for many centuries."[17] In other words, the Industrial Revolution not only transformed many human societies it also has changed the planet far into the future.

Many of the climate changes listed above have implications for the Earth's human and natural systems. Some of the effects of climate change can be beneficial. Increased temperatures can extend agricultural production into some northern regions, and an ice-free Arctic Ocean offers opportunities for resource development and shipping through a newly-opened Northern Passage. Most researchers identify far fewer benefits than costs from climate change. In 2013, the IPCC's AR5 report identified significant regional impacts of climate change on physical, natural, and human systems; most of these fall in the "likely" to "very likely" range, and are summarized in Table 1.2.

Table 1.2 Likely and Very Likely Regional Impacts on Physical, Natural, and Human Systems[18]

- **North America**: Decreasing snowpack in the western mountains; 5–20 percent increase in yields of rain-fed agriculture in some regions; increased frequency, intensity, and duration of heat waves in cities that currently experience them; monsoon precipitation will shift later in the annual cycle; increased precipitation in extratropical cyclones will lead to large increases in wintertime precipitation over the northern third of the continent; extreme precipitation increases in tropical cyclones making landfall along the western coast of the USA and Mexico, the Gulf Mexico, and the eastern coast of the USA and Canada.
- **Latin America**: Gradual replacement of tropical forest by savannah in eastern Amazonia; risk of significant biodiversity loss through species extinction in many tropical areas; significant changes in water availability for human consumption, agriculture, and energy generation; projected reduction in mean precipitation and increase in extreme precipitation; more extreme precipitation in tropical cyclones making landfall along the eastern and western coasts; increased precipitation in the southeast; decreased precipitation in central Chile and increased precipitation at the southern tip of South America.
- **Europe**: Increased risk of inland flash floods; more frequent coastal flooding and increased erosion from storms and sea level rise; glacial retreat in mountainous areas; reduced snow cover and winter tourism; extensive species losses; reduced crop productivity in southern Europe; enhanced extremes of storm-related precipitation and decreased frequency of storm-related precipitation over the eastern Mediterranean.
- **Africa**: By 2020, between 75 and 250 million people are projected to be exposed to increased water stress; yields from rain-fed agriculture could be reduced by up to 50 percent in some regions by 2020; agricultural production, including access to food, may be severely compromised; enhanced summer monsoon precipitation in West Africa; increased short rain in East Africa due to the pattern of Indian Ocean warming; increased rainfall extremes of landfall cyclones on the east coast (including Madagascar).
- **Asia**: Freshwater availability projected to decrease in Central, South, East and Southeast Asia by the 2050s; coastal areas will be at risk due to increased flooding; death rate from disease associated with floods and droughts expected to rise in some regions; enhanced summer monsoon precipitation; increased rainfall extremes of landfall typhoons on the coast; reduced midwinter suppression of extratropical cyclones; increased rainfall extremes of landfall cyclones on the Arabian Peninsula; decreased precipitation in northwest Asia; enhanced winter warming over North Asia.
- **Small islands**: Erosion of beaches and coral bleaching and decline of fisheries will reduce tourism; saltwater intrusion and storm surge flooding will threaten vital infrastructure, settlements, and freshwater resources; increased invasion by non-native species; more extreme precipitation associated with tropical cyclones.
- **Australia and New Zealand**: Reduced precipitation and increased evaporation in southern and eastern Australia and north and east New Zealand; significant loss of biodiversity by 2020 in the Great Barrier Reef and Queensland Wet Tropics; increased drought and fire in southern and eastern Australia and eastern New Zealand; reduced precipitation in northeastern Australia; increased warming and reduced precipitation in New Zealand and southern Australia; increased extreme precipitation associated with tropical and extratropical storms.

Table 1.2 (*cont.*)

- **Polar regions**: Reductions in sea ice, glaciers, and ice sheets will threaten migratory birds, mammals, higher predators, an increase in the depth of permafrost seasonal thawing; detrimental impacts on human communities include threats to infrastructure and traditional Indigenous ways of life; enhanced warming and sea ice melting; significant increase in precipitation by mid-century due mostly to enhanced precipitation in extratropical cyclones; increased warming over Antarctic Peninsula and West Antarctic.

Table 1.3 Impact of Climate Change on Earth's Physical, Natural, and Human Systems

- Increased spread of mountain pine beetles decimating forests in the Western US;[19]
- increased frequency of wildfires in the US due to plant and tree kill from insect infestations and drought;[20]
- increased heat-related illnesses and death caused by heat extremes and heat waves;[21]
- expansion of the range of mosquitoes transmitting diseases such as West Nile virus, Lyme disease, malaria, and dengue fever;[22]
- increased allergies, asthma, and other lung diseases from more pollen and mold associated with longer growing seasons;[23]
- increased flooding in coastal areas damaging property and water and sanitation systems, and increasing flood insurance;[24]
- increased plant and landcover losses from a variety of invasive plant and animal species and pests, such as insects and fungi;[25]
- decreased water resources in many semiarid areas, including the Western US and Mediterranean basin;[26]
- decreased biodiversity among plants and animals;[27]
- decreased mass and runoff from mountain glaciers reducing water supplies and hydroelectric energy production.[28]

The IPCC-identified changes in planetary climate systems are summaries of the scientific literature. Table 1.3 lists some of the specific studies leading to or supporting IPCC predictions. The research teams cited below focused on important changes in earth (including human) systems linked to various aspects of climate change.

These many projected alterations in Earth's atmosphere, landscape, marine and aquatic systems, ecology, and human societies will be felt in all regions of the world for centuries to come. Some of these alterations will be gradual and only measurable across generations. Other changes will be abrupt, in the form of disasters, or when the planetary system reaches a critical threshold – a *tipping point* – when major or unpredictable shifts occur in the climate system.[29]

The scale and scope of even the gradual earth system changes underway are staggering, and can be overwhelming when seen together. The implications of these changes are impossible to grasp at first reading. I encourage readers to try to remain engaged and review this section for a second and even third time. Familiarity will be empowering and help overcome some of the cognitive and emotional challenges of absorbing the information. It is important to present these scientific findings and projections to document the magnitude of the impacts of climate change around the world.

In the next two chapters we examine these changes as they affect human populations, especially their similar and different impacts on men and women around the world. Our focus will be on the types and locations of events where gender matters most. In some places the same type of event, such as a heat wave, flood, or drought, will have very gendered outcomes, but in other locations, the effects of the same event on men and women will be quite similar. Some climate-related events, especially those resulting in disasters, will have different outcomes for men and women, but the reasons and details can vary from case to case and country to country. Gender often matters when assessing the impacts of climate change, but it doesn't always matter in the same ways or in the same places. Some of the gender differences that we will explore in Chapters 2 and 3 are reflected in death rates from extreme weather events and disasters, such as hurricanes, wildfires, drought, and heat waves. Gender differences are not measured only in the relative number of deaths, but also in how women and men experience the consequences of climate change: displacement, opportunities, health, education, employment, power, and family relations.

Notes

1 World Meterological Organization, Commission for Climatology, Frequently Asked Questions. 2014. Accessed on May 28, 2015 at www.wmo.int/pages/prog/wcp/ccl/faqs.html.

2 Carbon is absorbed by plants during photosynthesis, making them carbon storage containers. When plants decay or are burned, their stored carbon is released into the atmosphere as CO_2. Coal, oil, and natural gas are forms of fossilized plants; when they are burned as fossil fuels, the ancient carbon becomes atmospheric CO_2. For a fuller discussion of the "carbon cycle," see the discussion on the National Aeronautics and Space Administration (NASA) Earth Observatory website at http://earthobservatory.nasa.gov/Features/CarbonCycle/.

3 Scripps Institution of Oceanography, "Carbon Dioxide Concentration at Mauna Loa Observatory." Accessed on May 27, 2015 at http://keelingcurve.ucsd.edu/; Intergovernmental Panel on Climate Change 2007. *Working Group I: The Physical Science Basis*, Table TS.2.1.1 "Changes in Atmospheric Carbon Dioxide, Methane and Nitrous Oxide." Accessed on January 8, 2014 at www.ipcc.ch/publications_and_data/ar4/wg1/en/tssts-2-1-1.html.

4 For a discussion of CO_2 measurement techniques, see National Oceanic and Atmospheric Administration, Earth System Research Laboratory Global Monitoring Division, "How We Measure Background CO_2 Levels on Mauna Loa." Accessed on January 9, 2014 at www.esrl.noaa.gov/gmd/ccgg/about/co2_measurements.html and British Antarctic Survey, Natural Environment Research Council, "Ice Cores and Climate Change." Accessed on January 9, 2014 at www.antarctica.ac.uk/bas_research/science_briefings/icecorebriefing.php.

5 Figures 1.1 and 1.2 are from Scripps Institution of Oceanography, The Keeling Curve website at: http://keelingcurve.ucsd.edu/. Accessed on May 27, 2015).

6 See pre-1958 CO_2 data from the Siple Station Ice Core in Antarctica available from the US Department of Energy's Carbon Dioxide Information Analysis Center at http://cdiac.esd.ornl.gov/ftp/trends/co2/siple2.013 and the post-1958 data from Mauna Loa at http://keelingcurve.ucsd.edu/; for a discussion of ice core data, see also Etheridge, D.M., L.P. Steele, R.L. Langenfelds, R.J. Francey, J.M. Barnola, and V.I. Morgan 1998. "Historical CO_2 Records from the Law Dome Delaware 08, Delaware 08-2, and DSS Ice Cores" in *Trends: A Compendium of Data on Global Change.* Carbon Dioxide Information Analysis Center, Oak Ridge National Laboratory, US Department of Energy. Accessed on February 6, 2014 at http://cdiac.esd.ornl.gov/trends/co2/law-dome.html.

7 Scripps Institution of Oceanography, 2015. Accessed on May 26, 2015 at http://keelingcurve.ucsd.edu/.

8 A positive feedback is a process in which an initial change brings about an additional change in the same direction. For instance, as ice begins to melt and uncover land or water, more solar radiation will be absorbed by the surface, raising temperatures and causing even more ice to melt; see National Oceanic and Atmospheric Administration. 2008. *A Paleo Perspective on Abrupt Climate Change: What Are Positive Feedbacks?.* Accessed on February 9, 2014 at www.ncdc.noaa.gov/paleo/abrupt/story2.html.

9 A weekly record of CO_2 data from 1958 to the present and a chart of seasonal variations in CO_2 levels, rising in summer and falling in winter, are available from the National Oceanic and Atmospheric Administration's Earth System

Research Laboratory at www.esrl.noaa.gov/gmd/ccgg/tren the ds/. Accessed on July 16, 2015.

[10] Scripps Institution of Oceanography, op. cit.

[11] For more information on the causes and consequences of ocean acidification, see www.pmel.noaa.gov/co2/story/Ocean+Acidification and www.whoi.edu/main/topic/ocean-acidification.

[12] Intergovernmental Panel on Climate Change (IPCC). 2013a. *History*. Accessed on January 10, 2014 at www.ipcc.ch/organization/organization_history. shtml.

[13] IPCC. 2013b. *Headline Statements from the Summary for Policymakers*. Accessed on January 10, 2014 at www.climatechange2013.org/images/uploads/WG1AR5_Headlines.pdf.

[14] Scherer, Glenn, and DailyClimate.org, 2012. "Climate Science Predictions Prove Too Conservative." *Scientific American* (December 6); Jones, Nicola. 2013. "Climate Science: Rising Tide." *Nature*, Vol. 501, No. 7467:300–302.

[15] IPCC. 2013c. Summary for Policymakers. *Climate Change 2013: The Physical Basis.* Accessed on July 6, 2015 at www.ipcc.ch/pdf/assessment-report/ar5/wg1/WG1AR5_SPM_FINAL.pdf

[16] Ibid., p. 36

[17] Ibid., p. 28.

[18] IPCC. 2013c, op. cit.

[19] Kurz, W.A., C.C. Dymond, G. Stinson, G.J. Rampley, E.T. Neilson, A.L. Carroll, T. Ebata, and L. Safranyik. 2008. "Mountain Pine Beetle and Forest Carbon Feedback Climate Change. *Nature*, Vol. 452, No. 7190:987–990.

[20] US Department of Agriculture (USDA) 2013. *Effects of Climate Variability and Change on Forest Ecosystems: A Comprehensive Science Synthesis for the US Forest Sector.* Accessed on January 10, 2014 at www.usda.gov/oce/climate_change/effects_2012/effects_forest.htm; Bhatti, J.S., R. Lal, M.J. Apps, and M.A. Price. 2006. *Climate Change and Managed Ecosystems*. Boca Raton, FL: Taylor and Frances.

[21] National Institute of Environmental Health Sciences. 2013. *Climate Change and Human Health.* Accessed on January 11, 2014 at www.niehs.nih.gov/health/materials/climate_change_and_human_health_508.pdf#search=climate change.

[22] Ibid.

[23] Ibid.

[24] US Federal Emergency Management Agency. 2013. *Flood Insurance Reform Act of 2012.* Accessed on January 11, 2014 at www.fema.gov/flood-insurance-reform-act-2012; Simpson, Andrew G. 2013. "Insurance, Tax, Climate Groups Hit Possible Delay in Flood Insurance Changes." *Insurance Journal* (October 28). Accessed on January 11, 2014 at www.insurancejournal.com/news/national/2013/10/28/309404.htm.

[25] Weed, Aaron S., Matthew P. Ayres, and Jeffrey A. Hicke. 2013. "Consequences of Climate Change for Biotic Disturbances in North American Forests." *Ecological Monographs*, Vol. 83, No. 4:441–470; USDA Forest Service. 2008, *Challenging Cheatgrass: Can Tools Like the "Black Fingers of Death" Fight*

This Formidable Invasive Species? Accessed on January 13, 2014 at www.fs.fed.us/rmrs/docs/rmrs-science/cheatgrass-challenge-2008-04.pdf.

26 IPCC. 2013c, op. cit., p. 45.

27 Warren, R., J. VanDerWal, J. Price, J.A. Welbergen, I. Atkinson, J. Ramirez-Villegas, T.J. Osborn, A. Jarvis, L.P. Shoo, S.E. Williams and J. Lowe. 2013. "Quantifying the Benefit of Early Climate Change Mitigation in Avoiding Biodiversity Loss." *Nature Climate Change*, Vol. 3, No. 7:678–82; Cox, W. Andrew, Frank R. Thompson III, Jennifer L. Reidy, and John Faaborg. 2013. "Temperature Can Interact with Landscape Factors to Affect Songbird Productivity." *Global Change Biology*, Vol. 19, No. 4:1064–1074.

28 Laghari, Javaid. 2013. "Climate Change: Melting Glaciers Bring Energy Uncertainty." *Nature*, Vol. 502, No. 7473:617–618.

29 Lenton, Timothy M., Hermann Held, Elmar Kriegler, Jim W. Hall, Wolfgang Lucht, Stefan Rahmstorf, and Hans Joachim Schellnhuber. 2008. "Tipping Elements in the Earth's Climate System." *Proceedings of the National Academy of Sciences*, Vol. 105, No. 6:1786–1793; National Research Council. 2013. *Abrupt Impacts of Climate Change: Anticipating Surprises.* Washington, DC: The National Academies Press.

2
GENDER AND GLOBAL WARMING

Changes in the Earth's atmosphere are warming the planet's lands and oceans. This warming has wide-ranging implications for Earth's biological systems, including human systems. The impact of global warming is uneven across the globe and can have different effects on women and men at different times and in different places. In this chapter we will review the climate science associated with this main driver of climate change, and then we will examine the human impacts of global warming. Our goal will be to understand when, where, and how gender matters when the heat goes up.

Climate Change and Global Warming

In its 2013 Fifth Assessment Report (AR5), the Intergovernmental Panel on Climate Change (IPCC) is explicit about the history and future trajectory of global warming:

> Warming of the climate system is unequivocal, and since the 1950s, many of the observed changes are unprecedented over decades to millennia. The atmosphere and ocean have warmed, the amounts of snow and ice have diminished, sea level has risen, and the concentrations of greenhouse gases have increased ... Each of the last three decades has been successively warmer at

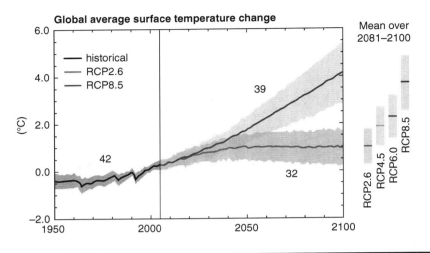

Figure 2.1 Global Mean Temperatures, 1950–2010, and Projected Temperature Increases, 2010–2100[2]

the Earth's surface than any preceding decade since 1850 ... It is *very likely* that the number of cold days and nights has decreased and the number of warm days and nights has increased on the global scale.[1]

Figure 2.1 shows past and future projected change in global annual mean surface temperature (in degrees Celsius) relative to the average during the period from 1986 to 2005.

According to IPCC estimates global mean temperatures will increase anywhere from less than 1°C to more than 5°C by 2100. These estimates are based on IPCC "scenarios" derived from Representative Concentration Pathways (RCP) climate models, each of which assumes a different level of future greenhouse gas (GHG) emissions.

As Figure 2.1 shows, in the most optimistic "peak" RCP2.6 scenario (lower line) in which GHG emissions rise and decline by the end of the century, average global temperature will increase somewhere between 0.3 and 1.7 °C (0.5–3.1°F) by 2100. The RCP2.6 scenario assumes that the reductions in GHGs after 2050 will be the result of some combination of technological advances and political policies that would replace or increase the efficiency of fossil fuel-based energy, promote significant land use changes, and find other methods of managing GHG emissions and levels.

As Figure 2.1 shows, in the "business as usual" RCP8.5 scenario (upper line), in which GHG emissions continue to increase unchecked, the mean global temperature will increase 2.6–5.4°C (5.0–9.7°F) by 2100.[3] In all scenarios, past carbon dioxide (CO_2) emissions will haunt future climates for centuries to come:

> Cumulative emissions of CO_2 largely determine global mean surface warming by the late 21st century and beyond. Most aspects of climate change will persist for many centuries even if emissions of CO_2 are stopped. This represents a substantial multi-century climate change commitment created by past, present and future emissions of CO_2.[4]

Despite this admonition about long-term planetary warming, the IPCC has been criticized for underestimating rates and levels of future global warming.[5] Citing the IPCC's low projections of fossil fuel and industrial emissions, one analyst predicted higher levels of warming than in even the most pessimistic IPCC scenarios: "We are currently on track for a rise of between 6.3°F and 13.3°F, with a high probability of an increase of 9.4°F by 2100."[6]

Although temperature rise is measured on a global scale, not all areas of the planet are warming uniformly. In all IPCC scenarios, temperatures in the northern hemisphere, especially in the Arctic, will increase the most, as will parts of Antarctica, which is the most rapidly-warming region in the southern hemisphere. In the past 50 years, mean annual temperatures on the Antarctic Peninsula have risen around 2.8°C (5°F), a rate of warming comparable to that in the Arctic.[7] The rapid warming of polar regions especially affects sea level rise, since the water released from accelerated melting of the Greenland and Antarctic ice sheets has the capacity to increase sea levels well beyond IPCC predictions.

With a predicted average global temperature increase of around 2°C, the RCP2.6 GHG emissions scenario has been labeled by some climate researchers the "2 degree world" scenario. Given the IPCC's reputation for moderate predictions, this likely is a low estimate of future global temperatures. The alternative RCP8.5 scenario doubles that prediction, and has come to be known as the "4 degree world." In a 2 degree world we can expect to see the changes catalogued in the last chapter: increased drought; extreme weather events; wildfires; heat waves; spread of pathogens and insect-borne diseases; plant pest infestations; biodiversity declines; coastal flooding and inland flash flooding; loss of glacial water supplies; threat to agricultural production in many regions leading to undernourishment and malnourishment; and threat to habitability of island nations.

The more widespread and severe outcomes predicted in a 4 degree world have alarmed even the most staid observers least likely to panic at scientific projections. For instance, in 2012, the World Bank issued a report, "Turn Down the Heat: Why a 4°C Warmer World Must be Avoided," in which authors concluded that "a 4°C world will pose unprecedented challenges to humanity ... unprecedented heat waves, severe drought, and major floods in many regions, with serious impacts on ecosystems and associated services."[8] The United Nations (UN) 2005 Millennium Ecosystem Assessment defines "ecosystem services" as:

> the benefits people obtain from ecosystems [including] provisioning services such as food and water; regulating services such as regulation of floods, drought, land degradation, and disease; supporting services such as soil formation and nutrient cycling; and cultural services such as recreational, spiritual, religious and other nonmaterial benefit.[9]

In light of the damage to important functions of ecosystems and the other losses outlined above, the World Bank report urges global cooperation and action to reduce our chances of having to face living in a 4 degree world. The report emphasizes that there is still time to act because the regional and global-scale damages will occur gradually as global temperatures increase. Since its mission is global economic development, the Bank report notes that the negative impacts of climate change will be felt more strongly in some regions and by some individuals and communities:

> While developed countries have been and are projected to be adversely affected by impacts resulting from climate change, adaptive capacities in developing regions are weaker. The burden of climate change in the future will very likely be borne differentially by those in regions already highly vulnerable to climate change and variability.[10]

Restated, the rich get warmer and inconvenienced, and the poor get hotter and incapacitated. The World Bank mentions gender only once in its 84-page report, and focuses on the health impacts likely in a 4 degree world:

> Vulnerability toward health impacts of temperature extremes varies from different subgroups of population. Mid and low income countries face more challenges compared to OECD countries. *Children and women are generally expected to be affected more severely* [italics added].[11]

The next sections describe some events that will become increasingly familiar features of the "new normal" as we turn up the global heat on the path toward a 4 degree world.

Gender, Global Warming, and Heat Waves

The summer of 2003 was the hottest recorded in Europe for five centuries. Sixteen countries were affected by the extreme temperatures, which ranged from 101°F in the United Kingdom to 118°F in Portugal.[12] In France temperatures exceeded 104°F, an unprecedented level since the French began keeping weather records in 1873.[13] These temperatures are not extraordinary in parts of the United States, but in a region of the world with no air conditioning and an environment that is not adapted to such heat, the results were devastating.

> The River Danube in Serbia fell to its lowest level in 100 years. Bombs and tanks from World War 2, which had been submerged under water for decades, were revealed, causing a danger

to people swimming in the rivers. Reservoirs and rivers used for public water supply and hydro-electric schemes either dried up or ran extremely low ... Forest fires broke out in many countries ... Extreme snow and glacier-melt in the European Alps led to increased rock and ice falls in the mountains ... some railway tracks buckled in the heat. The London Underground became unbearable. Some road surfaces melted. Low river levels prevented some boats from sailing ... [Lack of water for reactor cooling caused] two nuclear power plants to close down in Germany.[14]

The heat wave lasted for weeks and had deadly consequences for Europeans. More than 70,000 people died from the heat during the months of July and August. France was the hardest hit, with more than 15,000 dead.[15] The large number of deaths "led to a shortage of space to store dead bodies in mortuaries. Temporary mortuaries were set up in refrigeration lorries."[16]

Figure 2.2 is a National Aeronautics and Space Administration (NASA) Earth Observatory image from July 2003 that visually displays the intensity and area affected by the heat wave compared to temperatures in July 2001.

Researchers attribute the intensity and length of the heat wave to several factors associated with atmospheric and marine temperature anomalies, illustrating the interconnections of atmospheric, land, and marine systems:

[T]he Mediterranean Sea, which usually cools due to storms in normal years, did not cool down at all ... [and] a strong anticyclone persisting over the entire Euro-Mediterranean area suppressed deep convection and contributed to reduced rainfall.[18]

In order to understand the factors causing the 2003 European heat wave, a research team analyzed natural conditions, such as those described above, that were present when the heat wave occurred.[19] They then estimated the human contribution to the conditions generating the heat wave. Using risk analysis and climate modeling techniques with and without anthropogenic CO_2, they found that only by

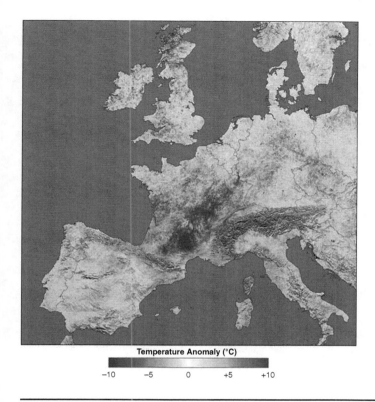

Temperature Anomaly (°C)

−10   −5   0   +5   +10

Figure 2.2 European Daytime Surface Temperatures in July 2003[17]

including anthropogenic CO_2 could they generate results like what happened in 2003 – results that were consistent across four different models. The researchers found that human influence was critical in generating the 2003 European heat wave, and concluded that 2003 quite likely marks the temperature trajectory of future summers in Europe:[20]

> Anthropogenic warming trends in Europe imply an increased probability of very hot summers ... It seems likely that past human influence has more than doubled the risk of European mean summer temperatures as hot as 2003, and with the likelihood of such events projected to increase 100-fold over the next four decades, it is difficult to avoid the conclusion that

potentially dangerous anthropogenic interference in the climate system is already underway.[21]

The 2003 European heat wave was remarkable not only for its unusually high temperatures, long duration, social and ecological disruptions, and high death rates; it also had distinct and deadly gendered outcomes. Nearly two-thirds of all those who died in Europe as a result of the heat wave were women.

> The countries most affected by ... excess summer mortality were Luxemburg, Spain, France, and Italy, where mortality increased by 14.3%, 13.7%, 11.8% and 11.6%, respectively. The female deaths represent 65% of the total number of the excess deaths during this period.[22]

The much higher female death rate in the 2003 European heat wave is consistent with other research on extreme heat events in Europe, and with research cited in an earlier chapter on women's generally greater vulnerability to all kinds of natural disasters. In a study of heat waves in nine European cities during the decade prior to 2003, researchers found that women in all age groups were more likely than men to die from the heat, but women over 65 were significantly more vulnerable than men of the same age.[23] One reason given for this difference was that older women were susceptible to respiratory and cardiovascular complications from heat exposure; other factors were the unpreparedness of European emergency response systems to cope with a heat wave of this magnitude, poorly trained and understaffed nursing homes, and the isolation of elderly women living alone in the higher floors of apartments in some European cities, in particular in Paris.[24]

Heat waves in the United States provide a more uneven gender vulnerability profile than is typically reported in Europe. In a study of extreme temperatures (hot and cold) and mortality in 50 US cities from 1989 to 2000, researchers analyzed nearly 8,000,000 deaths.[25] They found that older subjects were at higher risk when temperatures sank or soared to extremes. African-Americans, women, and those dying outside hospitals were more susceptible to extreme heat, though differences in gender were less pronounced than were those involving race and hospital access. As was the case in Europe, American women seemed most vulnerable when they suffered from some form of cardiovascular disease.[26] A study of heat-related deaths in central Arizona cities from 2000 to 2008 found similar health and gender patterns.[27]

A heat wave that occurred in one of the cities included in the above study provides an important exception to the rule of women's relatively greater risk of death during heat waves. In the city of Chicago, in July, 1995, the temperature rose above the normal high of 84°F, headed into the 90s, and continued to rise into the 100s.

> On Thursday [July 13] the temperatures hit 106 degrees and the heat index climbed to 126. Brick houses and apartment buildings baked like ovens, and indoor thermometers in high-rises topped 120 degrees even when windows were open. Thousands of cars broke down in the streets. Several roads buckled. City workers watered bridges spanning the Chicago River to prevent them from locking when their plates expanded. Train rails detached from their moorings and commuters endured long delays.[28]

After peaking at 106°F on July 13, temperatures remained high, reaching 102°F the next day, and staying in the 90s for another two days.[29] When the heat wave broke on July 17, an estimated 521 Chicagoans were dead.[30] Because of delayed physiological effects of the heat on the human body, many more died over the following days and weeks. The ultimate death count was nearly 700, and more than 3000 people were treated for symptoms of heat exhaustion and heat stroke in Chicago emergency rooms.[31]

Most deaths in the Chicago heat wave were among the elderly population. People aged 65 and older accounted for 63 percent of all deaths, 1.5 times as many Blacks as Whites died, and 55 percent of the deaths were among men: "age-adjusted death rates show that when the age factor is controlled, men were more than twice as likely as women to die."[32] Hispanics accounted for only 2 percent of heat-related mortalities, although they constituted around 23 percent of Chicago's population.[33] The explanations offered by researchers to account for the overall death rates in Chicago easily could have been written about the 2003 European heat wave:

> Risk factors for death from heat ... are living alone, living on the higher floors of buildings, living in poverty, living without air-conditioning, and using special and excessive medications ... Finally, there is the generalized impact of big cities, massive centers of heat-retaining concrete structures.[34]

All of these factors were cited as reasons for large numbers of deaths in many other heat waves, including the women who formed 65 percent of those who died in Europe in 2003. Why, then, were men twice as likely as women to die in Chicago in the summer of 1995? A researcher who conducted a "social autopsy" of the 1995 Chicago heat wave to understand who died and why, noted the paradox:

> These patterns vexed some experts on aging, because elderly women are so much more likely than their male counterparts to live by themselves that many gerontologists consider aging alone to be a women's issue. Men's relatively high death rates are even more confusing [since] women are more likely than men to report feeling lonely and isolated. The pattern begs for explanation.[35]

The explanation offered in the social autopsy emphasized the structure of neighborhoods and the atmosphere of fear that characterized the parts of the city where the most deaths occurred. These were neglected, poor areas, where residents stayed indoors, afraid to go out for supplies or help. Social institutions such as churches and the police were less present and available to residents. Complicating this socially disadvantaged environment were large numbers of men living in hotels and single-occupancy settings. These men had lost social connections with family and friends, and they tended to embrace a model of masculinity that emphasized self-reliance and avoiding trouble. When days of sustained heat wore them down, they had nowhere to turn.[36] There were other factors identified in this study that contributed to the poor quality of life in the high-death neighborhoods (lack of city services, media disregard, high crime), and while they provide insight into why so many died in Chicago in 1995, they don't entirely explain why men were at such greater risk in this particular case.

Since 1995, the city of Chicago and the state of Illinois have taken steps to address some of the deficits that cost so many lives that July. There are improvements in emergency services, heat wave aware-ness, prevention, and treatment, a program of daily contact with eld-erly, and more public cooling facilities. These measures contributed to a significantly reduced death rate during a similar Chicago heat wave four years later; in 1999 there were 103 heat-related deaths in Chicago.[37]

Gender, Global Warming, and Droughts

The IPCC 2013 AR5 reports that warmer and drier conditions are likely to persist in currently dry regions during the 21st century, specifically:

> Soil moisture drying in the Mediterranean, southwest USA, and southern African regions is consistent with projected changes in Hadley [tropical atmospheric] circulation and increased surface temperatures, so there is *high confidence* in *likely* surface drying in these regions by the end of this century under the RCP8.5 [business as usual] scenario.[38]

This prediction is consistent with the conclusions reached by research-ers cited earlier in this chapter about the future upward trajectory of summer heat in Europe.[39] Decreased soil moisture and increased tem-peratures are the ingredients for another important outcome of climate change: drought. Recurrent droughts in the southwest United States and regions of Africa fit the projections of IPCC models. In an assess-ment of climate change in the US Southwest, researchers reviewed the scientific consensus:

- warming will continue, with longer and hotter heat waves in summer;
- average precipitation will decrease in the southern Southwest;

- precipitation increases in winter will become more frequent and more intense;
- declines in river flow and soil moisture will continue;
- flooding will become more frequent and intense in some seasons in some parts of the Southwest, and less frequent and intense in other seasons and locations;
- droughts in parts of the Southwest will become hotter, more severe, and more frequent.[40]

After analyzing 14 climate models for projections of precipitation characteristics associated with global warming, researchers concluded that in many regions of the world, people can expect rainfall and drought patterns to look familiar, but magnified: "Our results are generally consistent with so-called 'the rich-getting-richer, poor-getting-poorer' paradigm for precipitation response under global warming ... [and] 'the middle-class-also-getting-poorer'."[41] Droughts that follow in the wake of extended hot and dry periods such as those described above have significant gendered consequences.

Extreme and extended droughts have cascading effects on food production, drinking and irrigation water supplies, human health, and threats to life and property. Men and women are affected by drought in many similar and different ways. The next two sections will explore two of the major gendered outcomes of droughts: water shortages and wildfires.

Gender, Drought, and Water Access

In most of the industrialized world, easy access to clean water is taken for granted. When there is drought requiring water conservation, such as in California in 1976–1977 or 2014–2015, there is no particular gendered impact – everyone conserves. To the extent that there is a gendered division of labor in the home (bathing children, cooking, and cleaning), women are more inconvenienced or, at the least, bear a greater burden in water conservation. This is in sharp contrast to the gendered impact of drought in parts of the world where water is not available in the home or even in a community well, but must be fetched from some distance and brought back to the home or garden.

> Aylito Binayo's feet know the mountain. Even at four in the morning she can run down the rocks to the river by starlight alone and climb the steep mountain back up to her village with 50 pounds of water on her back. She has made this journey three times a day for nearly all her 25 years. So has every other woman in her village of Foro, in the Konso district of southwestern Ethiopia. Binayo dropped out of school when she was eight years old, in part because she had to help her mother fetch water from the Toiro River. The water is dirty and unsafe to drink; every year that the ongoing drought continues, the once mighty river grows more exhausted … The task of fetching water defines life for Binayo … None of these jobs is as important or as consuming as the eight hours or so she spends each day fetching water.[42]

In virtually the entire global South, water work is women's work, a responsibility that often is shared by children, especially girls. Research from Guinea, Madagascar, Malawi, and Sierra Leone during the period from 2002 to 2004 found that women spent an average of 6.7 hours per week fetching water and wood, compared to 3.0 hours per week for men.[43] Even in times when water is abundant, fetching water is a time-consuming enterprise. In a 2009 study of the energy used by women to fetch water in two villages in Laos, researchers found that as much as 30 percent of women's caloric intake was used to fetch water, even when the distance was less than 1 kilometer, depending on age and the roughness and slope of the terrain.[44]

In many urban settings in developing countries, poor women are responsible for finding and obtaining water for their families. These women are faced less with geographic challenges than with high prices, limited access to water, and political landscapes that exclude them. In a study of women's quest for water in the megacities of Dhaka, Bangladesh, and Manila, Philippines, researchers found that the regulation of water access helped relieve some inequalities of class, but poor women remained outsiders to the decision-making process, and were left to depend on paternalistic water governance systems that often failed their needs.[45]

Much of the East African country of Kenya is located in a region of the continent that has a long history of intermittent droughts, some severe. Nearly half of Kenya's 41 million population lack sufficient access to safe drinking water.[46] Kenya's Turkana sector is typical of many rural communities in arid and semi-arid Africa, where desertification spreads during periods of drought and communities must cope with widespread loss of livestock, pasture, and arable agricultural land. During the recent period of extreme drought starting in the late 1990s, researchers reported childhood malnutrition, increased school dropouts, especially among girls, and a rise in human and animal diseases.[47] Interviews with local residents described the water pressures on women caused by the drought:

> Obtaining water for household use and for drinking purposes becomes very difficult during the drought period. Lack of rain means the rivers dry up. This creates competition for the available water sources that are usually so far that women and girls have to walk long distances to get to them. They walk up to 2–10 km in the Turkwell area and 30 km in the dry Kapua area. In order to beat the long queue at the water points, women have to start the trip before dawn. This poses security problems because they may be attacked by bandits or rapists on their way. To counteract this, women walk in groups. Transporting the water for long distances is also a problem because the women have to carry the water on their heads, making many trips. They have to carry the water in heavy traditional wooden troughs (ng'ageterin) that were originally meant to be carried by donkeys, before the drought killed them.[48]

Women can pay a health price for bearing the "burden of thirst," especially during droughts: spinal injury and spinal column collapse from carrying repeated heavy weight of water, pelvic deformities, spontaneous abortions and miscarriages, and chronic fatigue.[49] Beyond the direct health effects of carrying water, researchers have identified an opportunity cost (loss of income-generating activities women might be engaged in if they were not spending so much time hauling water), education cost (to girls who are forced to withdraw from school to fetch water), road casualties (water-bearing pedestrians often must share roads with vehicles and cyclists), and sexual abuse and assault (water carriers are vulnerable to sexual violence, and if attacked, often are shunned by their families and communities).[50]

Fetching water is not the only burden borne by women in developing settings that is complicated by drought. There are other personal demands placed on some women to become "drought brides":

> Prolonged drought in northern Kenya has pushed many families, like widow [Fatuma] Ahmed and her seven children, toward the outskirts of towns where they are more likely to get food and water. Aid is in short supply and people are resorting to desperate strategies. It's illegal to marry under the age of 18 in Kenya – so the phenomenon of "drought brides" is only whispered about ... "A mother will take a 14-year-old girl out of school and sell her to a man – even an old man – to get money to give the other children food," said a local chief. "Some households have 10 children and feeding those children is really hard."[51]

As this Kenyan example suggests, women are not only responsible for finding water during drought, they also have a responsibility to feed their families. In many countries both men and women bear the brunt of agricultural drought. It may be surprising to readers from industrial countries where farming is defined as men's work, even though they often have the support of women family members. Around the world, women are deeply involved in agriculture, growing significant amounts of food both for their families' consumption and for export.[52] In fact, globally, more women than men are active in the agriculture sector: 35.4 percent of agricultural workers are women, versus 30 percent of men.[53] In the global South women constitute 43 percent of the agricultural labor force, and "almost 70 percent of employed women in Southern Asia and more than 60 percent of employed women in sub-Saharan Africa work in agriculture."[54] A significant proportion of the population in the developing world, especially in rural communities, depends on women to grow the crops needed for basic nutrition, especially rice, corn, legumes, millet, and sorghum:[55]

> Women produce more than half of all the food that is grown [in the world]. In sub-Saharan Africa and the Caribbean, they produce up to 80 percent of basic foodstuffs. In Asia, they provide from 50 to 90 percent of the labour for rice cultivation. And in Southeast Asia and the Pacific as well as Latin America, women's home gardens represent some of the most complex agricultural systems known.[56]

Maize is one of the food crops widely grown in Africa. Researchers reviewed over 20,000 plantings of African maize and compared them to various climate conditions; they found the combination of increased heat and drought reduced maize crop yields nearly 2 percent. "Roughly 65% of present maize-growing areas in Africa would experience yield losses for 1°C of warming under optimal rain-fed management, with 100% of areas harmed by warming under drought conditions."[57] If such widespread basic food crop yields in Africa are reduced by a temperature increase of only 1°C, it's easier to understand the World Bank's alarm at the prospect of a 4 degree world and its implications for economic development.

When families are faced with drought, men often migrate for work so they can send money back home. In such cases, women are left to manage the household and take on primary responsibility for farming.[58] For instance, women make up 60 percent of all farmers in Mexico, where large numbers of men migrate north for work.[59] Since much of Mexico is semi-arid and rainfall is highly variable,[60] many women farmers left behind must contend with drought on their own. An example is Apolonia Alvarez, a 54-year-old farmer living near the town of Izúcar de Matamoros, in the southern central Mexican state of Puebla, where she rents around 60 square meters of a corn plot:

> "My corn almost didn't grow at all this last summer," she says. "The rain stopped when the crops were still very, very small" ... The mother of four tries to support her family with the corn she grows here, but, this past year she has only been able to harvest a

few sacks of corn ... Alvarez used to live in the state of Guerrero, but she and her family left when gun-carrying gangs made it too dangerous to stay. This state is now among the most unstable regions in the country due to gangs, who are fighting over control of the local drug trade. A few years ago, Alvarez's husband went to the US, where he now works in the construction industry.[61]

There is some relief on the horizon for women contending with the heat and drought brought on by climate variability and climate change.

In 2012, Puebla's Agricultural Ministry increased subsidies to family-run farms, to provide new irrigation systems and up-to-date farm machinery. Officials here say female farmers are a good investment for subsidies, because they tend to be more likely to pass the benefits of the subsidies on to their children and other family members.[62]

In 2013, a UN-sponsored groundwater mapping project, GRIDMAP (Groundwater Resources Investigation for Drought Mitigation in Africa Program) located two large underground aquifers in Kenya's drought-stricken Turkana region:

The Lotikipi Basin Aquifer is located west of Lake Turkana, the world's largest permanent desert lake. On its own, Lotikipi could potentially increase Kenya's strategic water reserves. The smaller Lodwar Basin Aquifer could serve as a strategic reserve for the development of Lodwar, the capital of Turkana County, provided the reserve is confirmed.[63]

If the politics of water in the United States are any indication of the likely coming battle over this new resource, as climate change continues to exert pressure on Africa's water resources, the rural population of Kenya, and especially Kenyan women, will need to mobilize to maintain access to and control of the extraction of the water from this local aquifer.

Gender, Droughts, and Wildfires

In a single year, 2013, the Australian Bureau of Meteorology reported six of the 20 hottest days in Australian recorded history. The trend toward record-breaking temperatures in the past few decades led the Bureau to add two new colors to its weather forecasting chart – deep purple and pink – to extend its temperature range to 54°C (129°F) from its previous cap of 50°C (122°F). The decision by Australian meteorologists was in line with the findings and predictions of the IPCC. Along with Europe's Mediterranean region and the US Southwest, Australia is one of the regions of the world that the IPCC AR5 reported likely to have experienced statistically-significant increased heat waves since the 1950s, and very likely to see continued warm spells and heat waves of increasing frequency and duration during the 21st century.[64] The IPCC identifies Australia's eastern and southern regions as most vulnerable to rising temperatures. With warm spells and heat waves come drought and an increased likelihood of wildfires.

During the period from 2001 to 2007 Australia averaged 52,000 wildfires or "bushfires" per year.[65] During the same period, the US averaged 76,500 wildfires per year.[66] The landmass of Australia is about 80 percent the size of the United States, but Australia's population is less than 7 percent of the US population. That would appear to reduce Australians' risk from wildfire. However, most Australians live in coastal regions, especially in the southeastern states of South Australia, New South Wales, and Victoria – all three are located in a part of the country that already is dry and warm, and expected to get drier and warmer during the next century.[67] In many areas of both the US and Australia, suburban residential growth has pushed further and further into rural spaces at the "wildland-urban interface" (WUI), where homes and associated structures are built among forests, shrubs, or grasslands as people seek privacy, space, and nature.[68] Americans and Australians living in WUI areas are at risk from wildfire, but especially Australians, because so many live in the highest-risk region of the country.

Australia's wildfire danger became deadly apparent on February 7, 2009, when a prolonged drought and weeks of high temperatures created conditions for what were described as the worst bushfires in the nation's history. The date became known as "Black Saturday," as the fire raged across 4500 square kilometers in Australia's southern Victoria state, destroying more than 2000 homes, killing countless animals, and injuring 5000 people.[69] One hundred men and 73 women died in the fires of Black Saturday. Two-thirds of the deaths occurred in a single firestorm, when it was too late for people to evacuate. Not long after Black Saturday's fires, researchers began to investigate the factors that led some people to evacuate to safety and others to stay at their peril, in particular what the role of gender might have been in determining the death rate.

The book *Gender and Wildfire* compares the responses of men and women to the danger of wildfire in two high-risk regions: Australia's state of Victoria and Southern California in the US. The author compares Australia's 2009 Black Saturday with the Station Fire that occurred in Southern California in the same year. Two male fire-fighters died in the Station Fire, but there were no civilian deaths reported. Interviews of Australians and Californians revealed some similarities in attitudes about who is responsible to fight wildfires and how that responsibility fits into notions of masculinity. One Australian woman emphasized the links among wildfire, manhood, and nationhood:

> The mythical building up of the bushfire volunteer ... It's very important that we always have that mythical icon. It has to be male ... Look at who they talk about in the newspaper articles. It's about men. [Bushfire] gives us that connection to that myth-ical, mythologized hero that we have not had in Australia due to our lack of war ... Bushfire gives us all of that. Gives us commu-nity. It gives us heroes.[70]

An American woman was asked about her role in supporting her hus-band during a wildfire:

> I stayed because I didn't have the kids [who were with their grandmother] ... And see my husband wasn't going to leave no matter what because my husband was raised here, up the street, so he goes, "Well, I'm going to stay" and then I'm the kind of wife that says "If you're going to fight, we're going to fight together!".[71]

The decision to stay or leave in Australia's Victoria state on Black Saturday was a negotiation that illustrates how existing gender relations can shape outcomes in disasters:

> There is evidence of disagreements as the fire approached. In virtually all cases this was between women who wanted to leave and take the men with them and men who either wanted to stay and defend or who felt they had to support others in that role. In some cases it appears that the difference in opinion was long standing, in other cases it was only acknowledged at the last minute. This led to some people changing their plans at the last minute. This appears particularly the case for couples. There are instances where women who fled under these circumstances survived. Conversely, there is also evidence of such disagreements where males refused to leave, but relatives decided to stay, leading to additional fatalities.[72]

Although cultural beliefs can be deeply held, Black Saturday changed Australian men's and women's opinions about whether or not to evacuate from a dangerous wildfire area. In 2008, a year before the deadly fires, 75 percent of Australian men and 48 percent of Australian women interviewed said they would "stay and defend" rather than evacuate or leave early. In 2013, four years after the fires, the figures had changed: 60 percent of men and 23 percent of women said they would stay. Many more Australian women who had been undecided in 2008 (35 percent), reported in 2013 that they would evacuate (60 percent).[73]

In the US both men and women were more likely to report that they would evacuate in the face of a dangerous wildfire. In 2011, 38 percent of American men and 20 percent of American women said they would "stay and defend," and like their Australian female counterparts, far more US women than men reported that they would evacuate or leave early.[74] The gendered culture of men to defend the home and the ambivalence of women about whether to leave or stand by their men combined with the fast-moving fires on Black Saturday to contribute to the high death rate in Australia. California's policy of "mandatory evacuation" in dangerous fire situations likely played a role in helping residents make up their minds to leave, and thus eliminated civilian deaths in the Station Fire.[75] To the extent that mandatory evacuation rules shaped the different outcomes in the two 2009 fire disasters, the comparison underlines the importance of public emergency preparedness policies in preventing deadly disasters.

Another similarity between wildfires in the US and Australia, and many other countries, is the structure of professional firefighting. Firefighting in both the US and Australia often involves large-scale military-style, often aerial assaults on wildfires and the major focus is on "fighting" fire rather than preventing it. Firefighting is an almost exclusively male domain with a paramilitary command structure and a culture that emphasizes loyalty, bravery, informed risk-taking, and facing danger.[76] In the United States fewer than 4 percent of paid firefighters are women.[77] A variety of organizations fight wildfires: municipal fire departments, National Guard crews, the US National Park and Forest Service and other federal agencies, wildfire "hotshot" teams, as well as volunteer groups. These firefighters also are overwhelmingly male, with a few exceptions, such as the all-women "Apache 8" White Mountain-Fort Apache hotshot team.[78]

Given the gender imbalance in firefighting, it is not surprising that far more men than women are killed and injured fighting wildfires. The Wildland Firefighter Foundation acknowledged 37 line-of-duty firefighter deaths in 2013; only one woman was on the list of those killed in the line of duty.[79] The International Association of Fire Fighters (IAFF) established an IAFF Fallen Fire Fighter Memorial in 2003. On its website, the IAFF lists the names of firefighters and emergency medical personnel who died in the line of duty and whose names are on the Memorial's Wall of Honor. A review of 1400 names posted found that 1.6 percent were women.[80] Like war fighting, firefighting is a gendered arena, where men test their courage and, more often than women, give their lives. The gender integration of the fire service, expansion of cities into wildfire areas, and increased likelihood of drought-driven wildfires in many parts of the world may slowly erode the gender imbalance in deaths from climate change-related wildfires. But at present, more men than women are at risk of injury and death from wildfires, though women more often must deal with the many disruptions to daily life in wildfire-ravaged communities: reestablishing and managing households, enrolling and transporting children to alternative schools, providing care to stressed or injured family members, handling the paperwork associated with insurance claims, and establishing safety procedures for children and pets in the event of future fires.

In the next chapter we will explore some similar and opposite gendered impacts of perhaps one of the most immediately dangerous aspects of climate change: sea level rise. Specifically, we'll focus on the gendered dimensions of two of the main effects on men, women, and social systems of rising sea levels: flooding and storm surges.

Notes

[1] Intergovernmental Panel on Climate Change (IPCC), 2013. *Climate Change 2013: The Physical Science Basis*. New York: Cambridge University Press, pp. 4–5. Accessed on February 5, 2014 at www.ipcc.ch/report/ar5/wg1/.

[2] Ibid., p. 21.

[3] Ibid., p. 18. An increase of 1 °C equals an increase of 1.8 °F.

[4] Ibid., p. 27.

[5] Rahmstorf, Stefan. 2010. "A New View on Sea Level Rise." *Nature Reports: Climate Change*, Vol. 464, No. 7290:44045. Accessed on January 27, 2014 at www.nature.com/climate/2010/1004/full/climate.2010.29.html.

[6] Scherer, Glenn. 2012. "How the IPCC Underestimated Climate Change." *Scientific American* (December 6). Accessed on February 14, 2014 at www.scientificamerican.com/article/climate-science-predictions-prove-too-conservative/; see also Peters, Glen P., Robbie M. Andrew, Tom Boden, Josep G. Canadell, Philippe Ciais, Corinne Le Quéré, Gregg Marland, Michael R. Raupach, and Charlie Wilson. 2013. "The Challenge to Keep Global Warming Below 2°C." *Nature Climate Change*, Vol. 3, No. 1:4–6.

[7] Vaughan, David G. "Antarctic Peninsula: Rapid Warming." *British Antarctic Survey*. Accessed on January 27, 2014 at www.antarctica.ac.uk/bas_research/science/climate/antarctic_peninsula.php.

[8] World Bank. 2012. *Turn Down the Heat: Why a 4°C Warmer World Must be Avoided*, pp. xiii, 64. Accessed on January 17, 2014 at http://climatechange.worldbank.org/sites/default/files/Turn_Down_the_heat_Why_a_4_degree_centrigrade_warmer_world_must_be_avoided.pdf.

[9] United Nations. 2005. *Millennium Ecosystem Assessment*, p. 27. Accessed on February 5, 2014 at www.maweb.org/documents/document.765.aspx.pdf.

[10] World Bank, op. cit., p. 64.

[11] Ibid., p. 56.

[12] Met Office (United Kingdom's national weather service). "August 2003 – Hot Spell." Accessed on February 17, 2014 at http://web.archive.org/web/20070306095012/www.metoffice.gov.uk/climate/uk/interesting/aug-03maxtemps.html.

[13] Poumadere, Marc, Claire Mays, Sophie Le Mer, and Russell Blong. 2005. "The 2003 Heat Wave in France: Dangerous Climate Change Here and Now." *Risk Analysis*, Vol. 25, No. 6:1483–1494, p. 1485.

[14] Ibid., "The Heat Wave of 2003." Accessed on February 17, 2014 at www.metoffice.gov.uk/education/teens/case-studies/heatwave; deBeer Brendan. 2013. "High Temperatures to Ease, but Remain High." *Portugal News Online* (July 5). Accessed on February 17, 2014 at http://theportugalnews.com/news/portugal-facing-record-high-temperatures/28802.

[15] Robine, Jean-Marie, Siu Lan K. Cheung, Sophie Le Roy, Herman Van Oyen, Clare Griffiths, Jean-Pierre Michel, François Richard Herrmann. 2008. "Death Toll Exceeded 70,000 in Europe during the Summer of 2003." *Comptes Rendus Biologies*, Vol. 331, No. 2:171–178.

[16] Met Office, op. cit.

[17] National Aeronautics and Space Administration Earth Observatory. "European Heat Wave, August 16, 2003." Accessed on February 17, 2014 at http://earth-observatory.nasa.gov/IOTD/view.php?id=3714.

[18] Feudale, Laura, and Jagadish Shukla. 2011. "Influence of Sea Surface Temperature on the European Heat Wave of 2003 Summer. Part One: An Observational Study." *Climate Dynamics,* Vol. 36, Nos. 9–10:1691–1703, p. 1696; for a detailed overview of the meteorological conditions that generated the heat wave, see Black, Emily, Mike Blackburn, Giles Harrison, Brian Hoskins, and John Methven. 2004. "Factors Contributing to the Summer 2003 European Heatwave." *Weather*, Vol. 59, No. 8:217–223.

[19] Stott, Peter A., D.A. Stone, and M.R. Allen. 2004. "Human Contribution to the European Heatwave of 2003." *Nature*, Vol. 432, No. 7017:610–613.

[20] An example is the European heatwave in 2015 which broke many previous records. Rice, Doyle. 2015. "Dangerous Heat Wave Scorching Europe." USA Today (July 1). Accessed on July 6, 2015 at www.usatoday.com/story/weather/2015/07/01/heat-wave-europe/29565161/.

[21] Ibid., p. 613. The 2010 Russian heat wave, blamed for 50,000–70,000 deaths, fits these predictions.

[22] Robine *et al.*, op. cit., p. 175; Epidemiologists calculate "excess" death rates as the number or percent of deaths in excess of a baseline, non-crisis death rate.

[23] D'Ippoliti, Daniela, Paola Michelozzi, Claudia Marino, Francesca de'Donato, Bettina Menne, Klea Katsouyanni, Ursula Kirchmayer, Antonis Analitis, Mercedes Medina-Ramón, Anna Paldy, Richard Atkinson, Sari Kovats, Luigi Bisanti, Alexandra Schneider, Agnès Lefranc, Carmen Iñiguez, and Carlo A. Perucci. 2010. "The Impact of Heat Waves on Mortality in Nine European Cities: Results from the EuroHEAT Project." *Environmental Health,* Vol. 9:37–45.

[24] Toulemon, Laurent, and Magali Barbieri. 2006. "The Mortality Impact of the August 2003 Heat Wave in France." Paper presented at the 2006 Population

of America Association Meeting, Los Angeles, March 30–April 1. Accessed on February 17, 2014 at http://paa2006.princeton.edu/papers/60411; Codot, Emmanuelle, Victor G. Rodwin, and Alfred Spira. 2007. "In the Heat of the Summer: Lessons from the Heat Waves in Paris." *Journal of Urban Health*, Vol. 84, No. 4:466–468.

[25] Medina-Ramó, Mercedes, Antonella Zanobetti, David Paul Cavanagh, and Joel Schwartz. 2006. "Extreme Temperatures and Mortality: Assessing Effect Modification by Personal Characteristics and Specific Cause of Death in a Multi-City Case-Only Analysis" *Environmental Health Perspectives*, Vol. 114, No. 9:1331–1336.

[26] Ibid., p. 1335.

[27] Harlan, Sharon L., Gerardo Chowell, Shuo Yang, Diana B. Petitti, Emmanuel J. Morales Butler, Benjamin L. Ruddell, and Darren M. Ruddell. 2014. "Heat Related Deaths in Hot Cities: Estimates of Human Tolerance to High Temperature Thresholds." *International Journal of Environmental Research and Public Health*, Vol. 11, No. 3:3304–3326.

[28] Klinenberg, Eric. 2002. *Heat Wave: A Social Autopsy of Disaster in Chicago*. Chicago, IL: University of Chicago Press, p. 1.

[29] Angel, Jim. 2009. "The 1995 Heat Wave in Chicago, Illinois." Illinois State Water Survey, State Climatologist Office for Illinois. Accessed on February 18, 2014 at www.isws.illinois.edu/atmos/statecli/general/1995chicago.htm.

[30] Klinenberg, op. cit., p. 9.

[31] Harmon, Katherine. 2010. "How Does a Heat Wave Affect the Human Body?" *Scientific American* (July 23). Accessed on February 18, 2014 at www.scientific-american.com/article/heat-wave-health/.

[32] Klinenberg, op. cit., p. 20.

[33] Whitman, S., G. Good, E.R. Donoghue, N. Benbow, W. Shou, and S. Mou. 1997. "Mortality in Chicago Attributed to the July 1995 Heat Wave." *American Journal of Public Health*, Vol. 87, No. 9:1515–1518, p. 1516.

[34] Ibid., p. 1518.

[35] Klinenberg, op. cit.

[36] Ibid.

[37] Centers for Disease Control. 2003. "Heat Related Deaths – Chicago, Illinois, 1996–2001, and United States, 1979–1999." *Morbidity and Mortality Weekly Report*, Vol. 52, No. 26, July 4:610–613.

[38] IPCC, op. cit., p. 5.

[39] Stott *et al.*, op. cit.

[40] Jardine, Angela, Robert Merideth, Mary Black, and Sarah LeRoy. 2013. *Assessment of Climate Change in the Southwest United States*. Washington, DC: Island Press, pp. 5–6.

[41] Lau, William K.-M., H.-T. Wu, and K.-M. Kim. 2013. "A Canonical Response of Precipitation Characteristics to Global Warming from CMIP5 Models." *Geophysical Research Letters*, Vol. 40, No. 12:3163–3169, p. 3169.

[42] Rosenberg, Tina. 2010. "The Burden of Thirst." *National Geographic Magazine* (April). Accessed on February 20, 2014 at http://ngm.nationalgeographic.com/print/2010/04/water-slaves/rosenberg-text.

43 United Nations Development Programme. 2011. "Tracing the Effects – Understanding the Relations," pp. 45–66 in *Human Development Report 2011: Sustainability and Equity: A Better Future for All*, p. 58. Accessed on March 1, 2014 at www.unis.unvienna.org/unis/en/news/2011/human-development-report-2011.html.

44 LaFrenierre, Jeff. 2009. *The Burden of Fetching Water: Using Caloric Expenditure as an Indicator of Access to Safe Drinking Water – A Case Study from Xieng Khouang Province, Lao PDR*. M.A. Thesis, University of Denver, p. 44.

45 Ahmed, Sayeed Iftekhar. 2013. *Water for Poor Women: Quest for an Alternative Paradigm*. New York: Lexington Books.

46 United Nations Educational, Scientific, and Cultural Organization (UNESCO). 2013. "Strategic groundwater reserves found in Northern Kenya." Accessed on February 20, 2014 at www.unesco.org/new/en/media-services/single-view/news/strategic_groundwater_reserves_found_in_northern_kenya/.

47 Wawire, Violet K. 2003. "Gender and the Social and Economic Impact of Drought on the Residents of Turkana District in Kenya." *Gender Issues Research Report Series*, No. 21, Organisation for Social Science Research in Eastern and Southern Africa, Nairobi, Kenya.

48 Ibid., p. 13.

49 Rosenberg, op. cit.; see also *Facts about Women and Water*. Scientific-Information Center of the Interstate Coordination Water Commission of the Central Asia. Accessed on February 20, 2014 at www.gender.cawater-info.net/what_is/facts_e.htm.

50 Sorenson, Susan B., Christiaan Morssink, and Paola Abril Campos. 2011. "Safe Access to Safe Water in Low Income Countries: Water Fetching in Current Times." *Social Science and Medicine*, Vol. 72, No. 9:1522–26, p. 1525.

51 Migiro, Katy. 2011. "Child 'Drought Brides" Sold Secretly in Kenya" (August 4). London: Thomson Reuters Foundation. Accessed on July 16, 2015 at www.trust.org/item/?map=feature-child-drought-brides-sold-secretly-in-kenya/.

52 United Nations Food and Agricultural Organization (FAO). 2014. *Men and Women in Agriculture*. Accessed on February 20, 2014 at www.fao.org/gender/gender-home/gender-why/did-you-know/en/.

53 FAO, 2011. *Gender*. Accessed on February 20, 2014 at www.ifc.org/wps/wcm/connect/1b175a804f7ce0a9b82dfe0098cb14b9/chapter9.pdf?MOD=AJPERES.

54 FAO, 2014, op. cit.

55 Doss, Cheryl R. 2002. "Men's Crops? Women's Crops? The Gender Patterns of Cropping in Ghana." *World Development*, Vol. 30, No. 11:1987–2000.

56 Ibid.; see also FAO. 1996. "Women Feed the World." World Food Summit: Food for All, Rome, November 13–17. Accessed on February 20, 2014 at www.fao.org/docrep/x0262e/x0262e16.htm.

57 Lobell, David B., Marianne Bänziger, Cosmos Magorokosho, and Bindiganavile Vivek. 2011. "Nonlinear Heat Effects on African Maize As Evidenced by Historical Yield Trials." *Nature Climate Change*, Vol. 1, No. 1:42–45, p. 42.

58 For an examination of women's sometimes desperate drought-coping strategies in Zimbabwe, see Tichagwa, Wilfred. 1994. "The Effects of Drought on the Condition of Women." *Focus on Gender*, Vol. 2, No. 1:20–25.

59 Deutsche Velle. 2013. "Mexico's Rural Women Fight Drought." August 3. Accessed on February 20, 2014 at www.dw.de/mexicos-rural-women-fight-drought/a-16653191.

60 Liverman, Diana M. 1999. "Vulnerability and Adaptation to Drought in Mexico." *Natural Resources Journal*, Vol. 39, pp. 99–115, p. 99.

61 Deutsche Velle, op. cit.

62 Ibid.

63 UNESCO, op. cit.

64 IPCC, op. cit. pp. 5, 106, 204; see also Fischer, E.M., and C. Schar. 2010. "Consistent Geographical Patterns of Changes in High-Impact European Heatwaves." *Nature Geoscience*, Vol. 3, No 6:398–403.

65 Australia officially refers to wildfires as "bushfires"; Australian Institute of Criminology. 2009. "The Number of Fires and Who Lights Them." Accessed on February 19, 2014 at www.Aic.gov.au/Publications/Current% 20 Series/Bfab/41 to 60/Bfab 059.html.

66 National Interagency Fire Center. 2013. "Total Wildland Fires and Acres." Accessed on July 16, 2015 at www.aic.gov.au/publications/current%20series/bfab/41-60/bfab059.htm.

67 IPCC, op. cit., p. 211.

68 Radeloff, V.C., R.B. Hammer, S.I. Stewart, J.S. Fried, S.S. Holcomb, and J.E. McKeefry. 2005. "The Wildland-Urban Interface in the United States." *Ecological Applications*, Vol. 15, No. 3:799–805, p. 799.

69 Australian Broadcasting Company. 2009. "Black Saturday." Accessed on February 19, 2014 at www.abc.net.au/innovation/blacksaturday/.

70 Eriksen, Christine. 2014. *Gender and Wildfire: Landscapes of Uncertainty*. New York: Routledge, p. 4.

71 Ibid., p. 31.

72 Tyler, Meagan. 2013. "Gender, Masculinity and Bushfire: Australia in an International Context." *Australian Journal of Emergency Management*, Vol. 28, No. 2:20–27, p. 24; see also Haynes, K., J. Handmer, J. McAneney, A. Tibbits, and L. Coates 2010. "Australian Bushfire Fatalities, 1900–2008: Exploring Trends in Relation to the 'Prepare, Stay and Defend or Leave Early' Policy." *Environmental Science and Policy*, Vol. 13, No. 3:185–194.

73 Eriksen, op. cit., p. 28.

74 Ibid. See also Zara, Claire, and Debra Parkinson. 2013. *Men on Black Saturday: Risks and Opportunities for Change*. Women's Health Goulburn North East and Monash University. Accessed on February 19, 2014 at www.whealth.com.au/documents/work/about-men/FINAL-REPORT-Vol-1.pdf.

75 Op. cit., p. 29.

76 Hinds-Aldrich, Matthew I. 2012. *The Way of the Smoke Eater: Rethinking Firefighter Culture in the Field of Structural Fire Protection*. PhD dissertation, Sociology, University of Kent, UK. I can speak personally about masculinity and firefighting culture from my own experience of being married for over 30 years to a professional firefighter.

[77] US Bureau of Labor Statistics. 2014. *Labor Force Statistics from the Current Population Survey*. "Table 11: Employed Persons by Detailed Occupation, Sex, Race, and Hispanic or Latino Ethnicity." Accessed on February 27, 2014 at www.bls.gov/cps/cpsaat11.htm.

[78] Dejong, David H. 2004. "Fire Warriors: American Indian Firefighters in the Southwest." *Forest History Today* (Spring/Fall). In 2011 a film was made by Sande Zeig about the Apache 8 hot shot crew: www.apache8.com/; see also "Apache Eight, Documentary about All Female Fire Crew." *Wildfire Today* (March 29, 2011). Accessed on February 18, 2014 at http://wildfiretoday. com/2011/03/29/apache-8-documentary-about-all-female-fire-crew/. For a first-hand account of a woman wildfire fighter posted in 2010, see "True Story: I'm a Female Wildfire Fighter." Accessed on February 20, 2014 at www.yesandyes.org/2010/04/true-story-im-female-wildfire-fighter.html.

[79] Wildland Firefighter Foundation. 2013. Accessed on February 18, 2014 at www.wffoundation.org/; the International Association of Women in Fire and Emergency Services has posted a list of dozens of women firefighters who died in the line of duty with dates of death going back to the 1980s. Accessed on February 18, 2014 at www.i-women.org/in_memoriam.php.

[80] International Association of Fire Fighters, 2014. *Wall of Honor*. Accessed on February 18, 2014 at www.iaff.org/hs/ffm/wall/index.aspx. My thanks to Natalie Parker for her assistance with this analysis.

3
GENDER AND SEA LEVEL RISE

In this chapter we will examine the gendered dimensions of one of the major consequences of global warming: sea level rise. First, we will review the climate science associated with predictions of sea level rise, and then we will examine its human impacts. Our goal will be to understand the times and places that gender matters when the oceans rise and the storms surge.

Climate Change and Sea Level Rise

In its 2013 Fifth Assessment Report (AR5), the Intergovernmental Panel on Climate Change (IPCC) identifies sea level rise as a "virtually certain" outcome of climate change, and that the oceans will continue to rise for centuries into the future, even if we immediately halt the increase in the global production of greenhouse gases (GHGs).

> It is *virtually certain* that global mean sea level rise will continue beyond 2100, with sea level rise due to thermal expansion to continue for many centuries ... Sustained mass loss by ice sheets would cause larger sea level rise, and some part of the mass loss might be irreversible. There is *high confidence* that sustained warming greater than some threshold [1–4°C or 1.8–7.2°F] would lead to the near-complete loss of the Greenland ice sheet over a millennium or more ... Abrupt and irreversible ice

loss from a potential instability of marine-based sectors of the Antarctic ice sheet in response to climate forcing is possible, but current evidence and understanding is insufficient to make a quantitative assessment.[1]

Global sea levels rose between 0.17 and 0.21 meters (about 8 inches) in the period from 1901 to 2010.[2] Even this seemingly small increase in sea level rise already is being felt around the world in stronger storm surges, tidal flooding, and coastal erosion.[3] The IPCC predicts sea levels will rise between 0.25 meters and 1 meter (roughly 1 to 3 feet) by the end of the 21st century. How quickly and how much sea levels rise by 2100 depends on the rate of GHG emissions that are warming the planet. Global warming increases ocean volume and leads to sea level rise primarily in two ways: by increasing ocean temperatures causing thermal expansion of sea water (warm water takes up more space than cold water) and by adding water from melting polar ice sheets.[4]

> Together, the Antarctic and Greenland ice sheets contain more than 99 percent of the freshwater ice on Earth. The Antarctic Ice Sheet … is roughly the area of the contiguous United States and Mexico combined … The Greenland Ice Sheet … is three times the size of Texas … If the Greenland Ice Sheet melted, scientists estimate that sea level would rise about 6 meters (20 feet). If the Antarctic Ice Sheet melted, sea level would rise by about 60 meters (200 feet).[5]

Although the Greenland ice sheet is melting much more rapidly than the Antarctic ice sheet, it would take centuries for both of these ice sheets to release all of their stored freshwater into the oceans.[6] Even at the modest rates of ice sheet decline projected by the IPCC (rates which have been criticized by some scientists as too conservative),[7] the ice sheets' capacity to affect sea level rise makes estimating their melt rate an important task for researchers.

Whether sea levels rise 1–3 feet or more during the next century, unlike water in a bathtub, sea levels do not rise uniformly around the world.[8] Coastal regions in the Pacific, including island nations like Tuvalu and Kiribati, as well as the state of Hawaii and the country of

Bangladesh, are likely to see some of the highest increases in sea level, while northern Europe likely will experience below-average increases.[9] There are several reasons for this unevenness, including marine and atmospheric circulation systems, coastal sea depths, and shifts in land-mass related to melting ice sheets.[10] The degree of the threat from sea level rise is related to coastal land elevation and the extent of development along coastlines.

The Maldives, an island republic in the Indian Ocean, is one of the lowest-lying countries on Earth. In 2009, Mohamed Nasheed, president of the Maldives, along with his ministers, dressed up in full scuba gear and held a cabinet meeting underwater to dramatize the threat of sea level rise to the island's habitability. In a letter to Ban Ki-moon, Secretary-General of the United Nations, he outlined the impact of climate change on his country:

> The threats posed to the Maldives from climate change are well-known. Every beach lost to rising seas, every house lost to storm surges, every reef lost to the increasingly warm waters, every job lost as fish stocks dwindle, and every life lost to more frequent extreme weather events will make it harder and harder to govern the country until a point is reached when we must consider abandoning our homeland.[11]

It is not only in the Pacific that sea level rise is changing landscapes and threatening coastal populations. Sea levels along the US East Coast are rising faster than the global average, and constitute a sea level rise "hotspot" extending from Cape Hatteras in North Carolina to north of Boston, Massachusetts.[12] An example is the coastal city of Norfolk, Virginia. This "hotspot" community has been dealing with increasing episodes of frequent flooding of coastal properties in the last few decades. On some high-tide days the salt waters invade, flooding buildings, submerging roads, and killing plants and trees. In vulnerable neighborhoods lawns are dying and being replaced with marsh grass.

> Sharon McDonald, the city's tax commissioner, says she has seen a dramatic change in her Larchmont neighborhood since 1986, when her family bought a gracious colonial facing the Lafayette

River. In August 2011, for the first time, a storm hurled water into the crawlspace, damaging the ductwork. Now [in 2013], her street regularly floods at each end. She once tried to drive a Volvo through the seemingly shallow water, but the car died midstream. "If high tide's in the morning, and you need to go to work, you need to park your car somewhere else," she says, noting her husband, David, keeps sandbags by the back door of his business downtown.[13]

Norfolk residents whose homes and neighborhoods are being inundated by climate change-related sea level rise do not need to look far to see one of the major reasons why. One third of global carbon dioxide (CO_2) emissions come from burning coal, which is a leading contributor to sea level rise. In 2012, coal-fired power plants generated approximately 37 percent of US electricity, and 9 percent of the world's exported coal came from the United States.[14] Lamberts Point Coal Terminal, in Norfolk, Virginia, is the "largest and fastest coal loading pier in the northern hemisphere."[15] As one conservationist noted:

> "There is a bit of an irony that Norfolk has the largest coal export facility in North America and we've also got the highest rate of sea level rise on the East Coast," says Skip Stiles of Wetlands Watch. "Can't escape that irony."[16]

The waters lapping higher and higher on the shores of Virginia might be inconveniencing residents and businesses, but they don't seem to be causing much alarm. In *High Tide on Main Street: Rising Sea Level and the Coming Coastal Crisis*, an oceanographer argues that the gradual rise in sea levels are deceiving to many coastal property owners. He predicts that at some point, these homeowners will find that while they are still standing on relatively dry ground, their home values are submarining: "Property values will likely go underwater long before the property does."[17] By his analysis, coastal communities like those in Virginia, New Jersey, North Carolina, and South Florida are building on borrowed time. Florida's massive and expanding beachfront development is resting on low-lying land, an eroding coastline, and exposure to hurricanes. Added to these is the slow but relentless rise of the sea, making

South Florida's ongoing real estate boom unsustainable. When will it crash? Investors note that there is no sign that anyone in Florida is discounting the price of coastal real estate.[18] But a recent hurricane may represent a turning point in US public awareness of coastal risk.

Hurricane Sandy moved up the Eastern seaboard of the United States in late 2012, causing extensive flooding, especially in New York and New Jersey, when the lower Manhattan subway and New Jersey Transit operations center were flooded by as much as 9 feet of water.[19] The storm resulted in nearly 150 deaths, damaged an estimated 650,000 homes, and left 8.5 million customers without power for weeks and even months in some areas. Sandy destroyed $75 billion in buildings and infrastructure, caused property values to fall by $5 billion, and reduced local tax revenues by $77 million.[20] The National Hurricane Center expected Sandy to rank as the second-costliest cyclone on record, after Hurricane Katrina.[21] Thousands of people lost their jobs temporarily, some permanently, when businesses were destroyed; schools were closed for a week or more for hundreds of thousands of schoolchildren. In the immediate aftermath of the storm, many housing sales were suspended or settled for greatly reduced prices. But not all.

> Two days after the storm, Joseph Zisa, the city attorney of Hackensack, N.J., called his real estate agent to meet him at the house on the bay in Manahawkin that he was closing on, to see whether it had survived. The porches were gone, and a 107-foot telephone pole lay across the yard, having missed the house by inches. He closed that week at the pre-storm price. "The view of the water," he explained. "It's so special."[22]

Zisa's experience was not typical. In neighborhoods where residents were unable or unwilling to sell their storm-damaged homes, rebuilt homes sat on streets next to or across from abandoned properties. In 2013, a year after the storm, New York Governor Andrew Cuomo proposed a $400 million plan to pay pre-Sandy prices for storm-damaged homes in flood-prone areas like Staten Island. The houses would then be demolished, and the land turned into wetlands or undeveloped coastal buffer zones. Some homeowners seemed poised to accept the offer:

On the eastern shore of Staten Island, virtually an entire neighborhood, the Fox Beach section of Oakwood Beach, has decided it wants to move. In the neighborhood, which has long been tormented by routine flooding as well as brush fires, 133 of 165 households have signed up to take a buyout if one is offered, according to Joseph Tirone, Jr., the leader of the Oakwood Beach Buyout Committee ... Staten Island borough president, James P. Molinaro, said his office had received calls from scores of homeowners seeking information on buyouts ... "Some people have said, 'We've had floods in the last 10 years maybe three or four times ... We want to get out of here. We're afraid.'"[23]

The enthusiasm to sell and move was not universal.

"The only place where more than just a small handful want to relocate is a couple of communities on Staten Island," Senator Charles E. Schumer, Democrat of New York, said at [a] news conference. "Otherwise, just about everybody – you take Nassau, Suffolk, Queens – they all want to rebuild and come back, and I think that's great. That shows the spirit of New York."[24]

Only time will tell how long the spirit of New York can protect residents and their property values against the encroaching waters and storm surges associated with sea level rise. But whether they are located in areas with the highest expected sea level rise, or in areas with average or below average predicted sea level rise, coastal areas around the world are vulnerable to the rising oceans. The question is how fast and how high will the seas rise?

Figure 3.1 shows estimated and measured sea levels from 1700 to 2100. Historical data (1700–2010) are based on paleo sea level data, tide gauge data, and altimeter data. Future projections (2010–2100) are IPCC estimates of the extent and timing of sea level rise during the 21st century.

The IPCC's most optimistic future sea level rise scenario (RCP2.6) is the lower line in Figure 3.1 and presumes a combination of technology, shifts to renewable energy sources, and energy efficiency will stop the rise in GHGs by the mid-21st century, resulting in predicted sea

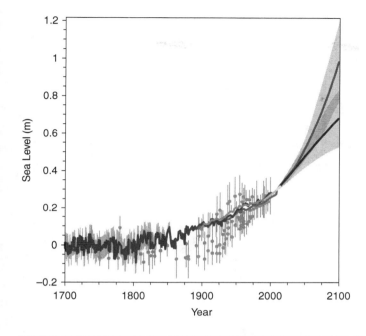

Figure 3.1 Global Mean Sea Levels, 1700–2010, and Projected Sea Level Rise, 2010–2100[25]

level rise 1-2 feet (.3-.6 meters) by 2100. The least optimistic ("business as usual") IPCC scenario (RCP8.5) is the upper line in Figure 3.1. In RCP8.5 emissions continue to increase at the present rate, with CO_2 reaching 936 ppm by the end of the century and sea levels rising to a global average of 2-3 feet (.5-1.0 meters). Scientists expect that this kind of increase in sea levels would lead to "the real risk of the forced displacement of up to 187 million people over the century (up to 2.4% of global population)."[26]

Most of the world's population lives in coastal areas, but not everyone will experience sea level rise in the same way. Rising coastal waters represent a slow-moving series of small-scale inconveniences and large-scale disasters, some gradual and others abrupt, including shoreline erosion; flood-related property damage; increased flood insurance rates; infrastructure deterioration; intrusion of salt water into fresh drinking water and irrigation supplies; salinization of coastal farmland and fishing ponds; destruction of vegetation; higher tides; and stronger storm surges. A number of these results of sea level rise affect women and men in different ways: employment and unemployment, displacement, mental and physical health, and death. The next two sections explore the gendered impacts of storm surges and flooding associated with sea level rise. The two examples to follow do not themselves constitute conclusive evidence of climate change, but they represent the kinds of events we can expect to see more often in the future.

Gender, Sea Level Rise, and Storm Surges

The most direct impact of sea level rise is flooding. Floods from tropical storm surges are the most dangerous and costly of the flooding threats from sea level rise. One of the highest documented storm surges in the US peaked at 25–28 feet during Hurricane Katrina in 2005.[27] Researchers predict that storm surges that previously occurred once every century are likely to become once-a-decade events by mid-century.[28] Severe tropical storms, labeled hurricanes, cyclones, or typhoons, depending on where they occur, are among the world's most deadly disasters.[29] At the moment, the science is inconclusive about the exact extent to which climate change will generate greater numbers of hurricanes and cyclones.[30] Researchers expect that continued data collection will clarify the relationship between climate change and the frequency of tropical storms: "We stand on the cusp of potentially large changes to Atlantic hurricane activity."[31]

There is more scientific confidence about the likely increase in the intensity of tropical storms since intensity is related to ocean temperatures, which are warming. Climate models suggest that we can expect stronger storms, with intensity increases of 2 to 11 percent by 2100.[32] Stronger storms mean stronger storm surges,[33] and the flooding produced by storm surges inflicts tremendous damage to property and infrastructure and causes most deaths in hurricanes. The impacts of hurricanes and their associated storm surges are not uniform within countries or around the world. There is a great deal of variation in how storm surges affect human populations in terms of displacement, distress, and death. Some of that variation is gendered. The next two sections describe two major storms – in Bangladesh (Cyclone Marian) and the US (Hurricane Katrina). These storms occurred in very different times, places, and cultural systems. What they have in common is the importance of gender in understanding the consequences of the storms.

Cyclone Marian, Bangladesh, 1991

The country of Bangladesh is on the Bay of Bengal, one of the most active tropical cyclone regions in the world.[34] Bangladesh is densely populated and poor, with a population of 155 million people and an annual gross domestic product (GDP) per capita of approximately $830.[35] Nearly half of Bangladeshis live in concentrated coastal communities situated near or at sea level that flood seasonally due to storms, cyclones, and high tidal waves. Seven percent of the country's surface is comprised of rivers, streams, and canals, and most of the country is connected by a series of navigation waterways that expand during the typhoon season and shrink during the dry season.[36] All of these topographical and demographic features make Bangladesh particularly vulnerable to the gradual effects of sea level rise, such as the increasing salinization of agricultural soil and drinking water and abrupt disasters, such as storm surges and flooding during monsoon season.[37]

The deadliest tropical storm in Bangladesh's history occurred in April, 1991, when a Category 4 cyclone, "Marian," with winds up to 210 kilometers per hour, struck its southern coastline. An estimated quarter of a million homes were completely destroyed, and another million were damaged. Up to 80 percent of crops, livestock, and poultry in the affected area were destroyed and several hundred thousand acres of agricultural lands were exposed to salt water intrusion. The total economic impact of the cyclone was estimated to be around $2 billion.[38] Marian displaced millions of people who faced a plethora of dangers in the storm and its aftermath: drowning, illnesses from waterborne diseases, injuries from snake bites and collapsed large trees and structures, lack of food, contaminated drinking water, limited medical assistance, and few proper sanitation facilities.[39]

The International Federation of Red Cross and Red Crescent Societies estimated that approximately 140,000 were killed in the cyclone, and 90 percent were women and children.[40] In order to understand this startling imbalance in mortality between women and men, we need to examine the gendered social and cultural context within which these deaths occurred. In most countries, including poor countries, female life expectancy exceeds that of males. Bangladesh is one of the few countries in the world in which men live longer than women.[41] This is in part due to cultural attitudes toward women reflected in their disadvantaged position in Bangladesh's social and economic system. Both their cultural devaluation and material hardship make Bangladeshi women considerably more vulnerable than men when disaster strikes.

Starting at an early age, Bangladeshi females have less access to healthcare and nutrition than males. As in most countries, women in Bangladesh earn less than men, and many more live in poverty, especially when they are in female-headed households. Less food, poorer healthcare, lower incomes, higher poverty all combine to make women less resilient when sickness or disaster occur. Cultural expectations for women's modesty further limit their options. For instance, Bangladeshi women are not taught to swim, and some are in "purdah," where either they do not leave the home or are not to be seen uncovered by men outside the family. Since storms are so frequent in Bangladesh, "both women and men [tend to be] sceptical of the validity and meaning of cyclone warnings."[42] Because of their relative isolation, women at home were left unaware when news of Cyclone Marian's severity was passed among men in public places. When the storm waters surged in April, 1991, thousands of Bangladeshi women and their children drowned.

> Begum, from Kolubari village of Sapleza union, Mothbaria Upazila, tied herself to a tree trunk to survive on the night of the cyclone. She was pregnant and suffering from malnutrition. After a while, she was unable to stand due to pain in her lower abdomen. The child in her womb stopped moving. She did not have any money to go to a doctor. She was panicked, doubting whether her unborn child would see the light of the world, even if she herself survived.[43]

Some women did not seek shelter because they were responsible for the home – caring for children, finding food, water, and fuel, cooking meals, growing crops, tending livestock – duties which tied poor women to low-lying residences. Their mobility was limited by cultural definitions of women's proper dress, demeanor, and public visibility – their long, loose clothing restricted movement; they were ashamed to seek higher ground occupied by unrelated men; shelters did not provide separate, secure space for women; medical teams were predominantly male. Interviews with Bangladeshi women confirmed these constraints:

> During these tense moments, women cannot manage their clothing and hair because of the wind. On top of that, they head towards shelter with their children in one hand and household goods in the other, all of which becomes difficult to manage and, in many cases, becomes the cause of their deaths. Many children cannot run because they refuse to get down from their mothers arms, as a result of which the mothers cannot run either. That's why women and children suffer more.[44]

During the storm, some women were abandoned by their families to look after property, and some poor women had limited family support and were solely responsible for their homes and families. In some rescue situations, differential evaluations of boys and girls contributed to the gender imbalance in death rates:

> Abul Kalam had five daughters and one son. He was a poor share cropper. He was holding his children together and fighting against the wind – fearful of the rising water. In his struggle to survive, Abul Kalam released his daughters one after the other so his son could survive.[45]

Bangladeshi women's lesser nutritional, cultural, social, and economic position relative to men left them more exposed to the storm. The result was that the death rate for women aged 20–44 was nearly five times higher than for men: 71 per 1000 for women compared to 15 per 1000 for men.[46]

The intertwining of sea level rise, storm surges, and socially-defined notions of gender shaped a particular set of outcomes in Bangladesh. Since 1991 the Bangladeshi government has expanded the availability of storm shelters, including some exclusively for women or with sections for women separate from men, instituted more early warning systems, undertook some coastal improvements such as embankments and mangrove restoration projects designed to absorb some of the power of storm surges, and included more women's voices and concerns in storm response planning. The World Health Organization reports that the death rate from severe cyclones in Bangladesh has dramatically declined since 1991. Bangladesh was hit by eight Category 3 or above cyclones during the period between 1992 and 2009. The average death rate was 747, and while gender breakdown data were not reported, the reduced death rate necessarily would have resulted in the deaths of many fewer women and children despite their likely continued higher risk of death compared to that of their countrymen.[47]

Research on the impact of hurricanes and storm surges in other countries emphasizes not only the relative impact on women from the immediate effects of flooding, but the longer-term consequences for women's health, livelihoods, and vulnerability to domestic violence and sex trafficking. Typhoon Haiyan, a Category 5 storm, hit the Philippines in 2013, affecting an estimated 90,000 pregnant women. The destruction and disorganization of medical delivery systems in the storm's aftermath increased the risks for these women and their newborns as well as those for whom they served as main caregivers: children, injured, and elderly. In addition to pregnant women's healthcare and medical needs in the aftermath of the storm, emergency planners emphasized women's post-storm needs for sexually transmitted diseases (STD) prevention and treatment, contraception and menstrual hygiene supplies, shelter from sexual violence and exploitation – especially for girls and adolescents – and ways to incorporate women into recovery planning.[48] These kinds of gender-specific post-disaster needs are not unique to hurricanes or to women living in relatively poor countries, nor are they news to emergency planners and responders. Virtually identical lists of girls' and women's needs for menstruation, STD prevention, and contraception supplies, prenatal, pregnancy, and newborn assistance, caregiver support, and protection from sexual predation are repeatedly noted as often absent, but nonetheless critical relief supplies.[49]

Hurricane Katrina, United States, 2005

It is not only in the global South that gender dynamics shape vulnerabilities to disasters. Even in countries where women are in positions of relatively greater social and economic status, inequalities of race and class can shape chances of recovery or survival. Disaster vulnerabilities are not always measured in death rates. For instance, Hurricane Katrina, a Category 5 storm, hit the coast of Louisiana in August, 2005, leaving an estimated 1464 people dead.[50] The storm killed roughly equal numbers of men and women, but 55 percent of those killed were African Americans.[51] In New Orleans, there were raced and gendered dimensions to who had the resources and capacity to evacuate the city in the face of Katrina:

> Poverty combines with race and ideologies about gender to produce a metric of deep disadvantage in terms of mobility: even in a country as awash in cars as the United States, women are less likely to have a car or a driver's license than their male counterparts.[52]

New Orleans' Ninth Ward and surrounding areas sustained most of the damage when the levees ruptured during the storm. Major New Orleans public housing apartments were in the most devastated parts of the city and flooded during and after the storm when the levees failed. Even when the storm didn't destroy them completely, the buildings were demolished afterward to make way for new development. Three-quarters of New Orleans' public housing was occupied by African-American women and their children whose low incomes qualified them for housing assistance. Many of these women and their families had no access to a car to evacuate the city, and they became part of the estimated 40,000 who took refuge from the rising waters in the Superdome and Convention Center.[53]

Like women in Bangladesh and around the world, many of the female residents of New Orleans' Ninth Ward were responsible for the health and safety of their children and extended family. Of the 233,284 women and girls who accounted for more than half of the city's population in 2005, approximately one-quarter were girls under 10 years of age or women over 65.[54] Because of their limited resources, these families relied on public transportation, local food networks, and restricted access to healthcare and disability services. When the storm struck, these New Orleans women found themselves alone with their neighbors and dependent families.

> I stood [stayed] for the hurricane. Me and my family. My momma, my five sisters, and all their kids … My momma [didn't] want to leave so, we stood … there a couple of days … Mom decided we [would] leave because the water [was] rising, and the toilets were backing up. So we walked from the project to the Superdome … We had an air mattress for the kids. I'm short, and the water was higher than me. So I'm panicking. I don't want to go out there. So I had my baby … she was six months, and I had a little niece that was like nine months. We put them two on the air mattress and the other kids on the air mattress. Got under a bridge where [there was] no water, and we set the air mattress down. The air mattress busted. So they had some people pushing file cabinets … we decided to get the file cabinet and put it in the water and put all the children in there so we put all the older kids in the cabinets and the two little ones in a cooler.[55]

In the days immediately following the storm reporters and officials described New Orleans as a "war zone" where "anarchy" reigned. Reports quickly emerged about rapes, murders, and gangs of armed young men terrorizing the city, and especially those trapped in the Superdome. New Orleans was described by reporters and local politicians as in a state of anarchy.[56] New Orleans Mayor Ray Nagin expressed his frustration outside the Superdome and Convention Center several days after the hurricane struck: "They have people standing out there, have been in that frickin' superdome for five days, watching dead bodies, watching hooligans killing people, raping people."[57] As the *Houston Chronicle* summarized, "The ugliest reports – children with slit throats, women dragged off and raped, corpses piling up in the basement – soon became a searing image of post-Katrina New Orleans."[58]

This image was both gendered and raced, and largely untrue. It also was widely unquestioned because the images resonated with racial and gender stereotypes. The initial reports painted a picture of dangerous Black men sniping, looting, and raping.[59] Many observers expressed little sympathy for the presumed victims of this crime wave, Black women, who were depicted as "culprits in their own misfortune" because of their presumed laziness, promiscuity, and irresponsibility, rather than because of low pay, lack of jobs, lack of affordable housing, lack of transportation out of flooded areas, and poor city, state, and federal disaster relief.[60] Few reports focused on the damage done to the resiliency of those whose lives were disrupted by Hurricane Katrina, including the destruction of pre-Katrina support networks and mutual aid systems on which many of New Orleans' most vulnerable residents depended. Little attention was paid to the bravery and generosity of the displaced toward one another.

> Three women reported that … individuals unexpectedly helped them. One pregnant woman said: "A lady I knew … paid a deposit down [on] an apartment for us in Houston. And that was like before they started doing the voucher." A postpartum woman described how a security man helped them by buying "some Pampers for the baby and stuff," then took off early from work to drive them to a relative's house: "So the man drove us all the way to the other side of Houston, to their house." Another pregnant woman related being befriended by a young couple at a shelter in Baton Rouge: "A young couple … saw us, we were sitting outside the shelter. They invited us to their home for a couple of days … They drove us to Houston, where they paid for a hotel for a week or so.[61]

Depictions of Katrina's victims not as heroic and generous but rather as violent and degenerate played into existing US racial and gender stereotypes. The assumptions on which they were built began to crumble in the aftermath of the storm. During the next month investigative reporters began challenging both the war zone and anarchy images. The *Los Angeles Times* reported that state officials confirmed there was only one verified homicide inside the Convention Center, and no murders inside the Superdome. Ten bodies were recovered from the Superdome, six inside and four outside, and of those inside four died of natural causes, one overdosed, and one jumped to his death; four bodies were recovered from the Convention Center.[62] There was little substantiated evidence of rapes. The *Seattle Times* reported that Louisiana National Guard Lieutenant Colonel Jacques Thibodeaux was at the Convention Center and Superdome: "I've heard of situations and rumors of rapes and murders and complete lawlessness in both the Superdome and the Convention Center, and I can tell you that I was at both those locations and those are just false, those things didn't happen."[63] Mayor Nagin later recanted his earlier statements.[64]

Reports about post-Katrina New Orleans reveal a moral economy of raced and gendered valuations of worth, credibility, and dangerousness that reflects not only a unique American narrative, but also extends to disasters around the world. Who merits sympathy and help after climate-related disasters like storm surges, heat waves, droughts, wildfires, floods, epidemics, or torrential rains? Is it we fortunate and deserving people in wealthy countries whose consumption and comfortable way of life are contributing to the rise in GHGs that are driving many of these disasters? Is it those simply unlucky people in poor neighborhoods or in the global South whose lives and landscapes are being transformed into often unrecognizable, sometimes uninhabitable futures? These questions raise issues of environmental justice that we will explore in later chapters.

Opinions about blame and deservingness aside, the reality of Katrina and its impact on New Orleans women was lost income, lost housing, and lost support systems. Some women permanently left the area, some lived in Federal Emergency Management Agency (FEMA) trailers for months, even years, and some found housing elsewhere in the city. In the three years after the storm, rental prices in New Orleans increased 39 percent, and many of those who were displaced found themselves closed out of the housing market.[65] Fourteen months after the storm only 51 percent of displaced Black residents had returned to New Orleans, compared to 71 percent of other displaced residents.[66] Who returned to New Orleans after Katrina was not only a matter of race but a matter of gender. A year after the storm, in the most damaged sections of the city, 56.8 percent of those who still had not returned were women.[67] Two years after the storm, there remained a gender gap in returnees: the female population of New Orleans dropped by 45.2 percent from 2005 to 2007; the male population declined by 40.2 percent.[68]

Women and men had different experiences after Hurricane Katrina, and not only in terms of who was displaced, blamed for post-storm violence, or more likely to be able to return to their homes in New Orleans. Six months after the storm, a research team analyzed data from a sample of 1043 individuals living in New Orleans at the time of the storm. They found that women were nearly three times more likely than men to report symptoms of post-traumatic stress disorder.[69] Especially hard hit were primary caregivers, most of whom are women.[70] Researchers interviewed Michelle Castillo two years after the hurricane as she cared for her elderly diabetic father and two teenaged children:

> Every family member – including Michelle – exhibits symptoms of mental stress and the physical symptoms that can accompany it … "I've never seen him [her father] so unwilling to even try to do things for himself" … "My kids are not secure, they're clingy and scared in a way I've never seen them. They just can't seem to get a foothold in this place we're trying to call home." Both children spent the bulk of their summer vacation inside Castillo's rented house watching television, gaining weight and largely refusing to go outside to engage in summer activities. "I wish I had more family or friends here. Every day I begin knowing that it's going to be a struggle and I just feel as though I'm wrecked, like I can't go on, can't keep doing this all by myself."[71]

Rates of domestic violence against women also increased in the year following the hurricane. A 2006 survey of Katrina displacees living in FEMA trailers in Louisiana found that gender-based violence against women had increased more than three-fold (from 4.6 per 100,000 to 16.3 per 100,000) since the storm, and remained high, though declined to two-fold a year later in 2007.[72]

As women tried to deal with the stresses of caregiving and sometimes violent tensions at home, they also faced a struggle to find a place in the post-Katrina economy. Accommodations and food service, healthcare and social assistance, and education services were the hardest-hit employment sectors in Louisiana; together these sectors lost 58,000 jobs. More women than men are employed in these jobs, so women suffered disproportionate job loss compared to men.[73] In all disasters, jobs created in the aftermath favor male workers. In New Orleans after the storm, demolition and construction jobs to clear debris and rebuild the city were far more available to men than to women, since fewer than 3 percent of workers in the construction trades are women.[74] Even outside the construction occupational sector, the discrepancy between male and female income after Katrina was stark:

> New Orleans women have returned to help rebuild the city, comprising more than half the workforce in 2006 and 2007. Those efforts, however, have not been rewarded. The income of Black/African American women, who make up the largest demographic group of workers, declined by 3 percent while the wages of White women dropped by 5 percent between 2005 and 2007. In contrast, the wages of men increased on average by 19 percent. The largest recorded increase in wages was not among construction workers, as might have been expected, but among White males in professional and managerial positions. And while the average earnings of men in managerial and professional occupations increased by 22 percent, the earnings of women in those occupations decreased by 5 percent.[75]

Climate change did not cause Cyclone Marian in Bangladesh or Hurricane Katrina in the United States. The 8-inch rise in sea level during the past century no doubt contributed to the size of their storm surges, though how much isn't calculable. In light of predicted increased sea levels, these two hurricanes serve as harbingers of future storms. They also serve to illustrate the different impacts these storms had on the women and men living in their paths. In the case of Marian, we saw not only destruction, but also disproportionate numbers of women's deaths. In the case of Katrina, men and women experienced different rates of displacement, mental health outcomes, employment losses and opportunities, and changes in income. The extreme deadliness to women of Cyclone Marian is not as common as the less lethal psychological, social, and economic injuries inflicted by Hurricane Katrina on its female victims. In each case, both the realities and the cosmologies of gender shaped the different outcomes experienced by men and women.

Gendered impacts are not the only ways in which gender matters for understanding global climate change. The next two chapters examine the role of gender in science and the influence on climate science of a dominant masculine institution – the military. Our focus will be to understand how male overrepresentation in science generally, and climate science specifically, intersects with science funded by militarily-organized masculinity to create a "military-science complex" with important consequences for climate change research and responses.

Notes

[1] Intergovernmental Panel on Climate Change (IPCC), 2013. *Climate Change 2013: The Physical Science Basis.* New York: Cambridge University Press, pp. 26–27. Accessed on February 5, 2014 at //www.ipcc.ch/report/ar5/wg1/.
[2] Ibid.
[3] Ibid., p. 5.
[4] Ibid.
[5] US National Snow and Ice Data Center. *Quick Facts on Ice Sheets.* Accessed on February 14, 2014 at http://nsidc.org/cryosphere/quickfacts/icesheets.html.
[6] There is some evidence that North Atlantic ocean warming and freshwater addition might produce abrupt changes in deep ocean circulations that "in the most extreme cases would as much as double the sea level increases projected by 2100 AD for densely populated circum-North Atlantic regions," Galaasen, Eirik Vinje, Ulysses S. Ninnemann, Nil Irvalı, Helga (Kikki) F. Kleiven, Yair Rosenthal, Catherine Kissel, and David A. Hodell. 2014. "Rapid Reductions

and North Atlantic Deep Water during the Peak of the Last Interglacial Period." *Science* (February 20). Accessed on February 28, 2014 at www.sciencemag.org/content/early/2014/02/19/science.1248667.full.

[7] Rahmstorf, Stefan. 2010. "A New View on Sea Level Rise." *Nature Reports: Climate Change*, Vol. 464, No. 7290:44045. Accessed on January 27, 2014 at www.nature.com/climate/2010/1004/full/climate.2010.29.html.

[8] IPCC, op. cit., p. 24; new measurements of Greenland ice sheet dynamics in 2014 indicated "that the outlet glaciers of Greenland, and the ice sheet as a whole, are probably more vulnerable to ocean thermal forcing and peripheral thinning than inferred previously from existing numerical ice-sheet models." Morlighem, M., E. Rignot, J. Mouginot, H. Seroussi, and E. Larour. 2014. "Deeply Incised Submarine Glacial Valleys beneath the Greenland Ice Sheet." *Nature Geoscience*, Vol. 7, No. 6:418–422.

[9] Kirby, Alex. 2013. "Ice Melt Means Uneven Sea Level Rise around the World." *Climate Central* (February 22). Accessed on January 21, 2014 at www.climatecentral.org/news/ice-melt-means-uneven-sea-level-rise-around-the-world-15640.

[10] Spada, G., J.L. Bamber, and R.T.W.L. Hurkmans. 2013. "The Gravitationally Consistent Sea-level Fingerprint of Future Terrestrial Ice Loss." *Geophysical Research Letters*, Vol. 40, No. 3:482–486.

[11] Statement by His Excellency Mohamed Nasheed, President of the Republic of Maldives to the General Debate of the General Assembly, September 24, 2009. Accessed on January 23, 2014 at www.un.org/ga/64/generaldebate/pdf/MV_en.pdf.

[12] Marshall, Michael. 2012. "Sea-level Rise Accelerates Faster on US East Coast." *New Scientist Environment* (June 24). Accessed on January 21, 2014 at www.newscientist.com/article/dn21969-sealevel-rise-accelerates-faster-on-us-east-coast.html.

[13] Koch, Wendy. 2013. "Rising Sea Levels Torment Norfolk, Virginia, and Coastal US." *USA Today* (December 18). Accessed on January 21, 2014 at www.usatoday.com/story/news/nation/2013/12/17/sea-level-rise-swamps-norfolk-us-coasts/3893825/.

[14] US Energy Information Administration. 2013. Frequently Asked Questions. Accessed on June 10, 2014 at www.eia.gov/tools/faqs/faq.cfm?id=427&t=3.

[15] Hutchins, Reynolds. 2014. "Local Reaction to EPA Proposal to Reduce Carbon Emissions Less Heated Than DC Rhetoric." *Inside Business* (June 5). Accessed on June 10, 2014 at http://insidebiz.com/news/local-reaction-epa-proposal-reduce-carbon-emissions-less-heated-dc-rhetoric.

[16] Naylor, Brian. 2014. "How Coal Industry Jobs Coexist with Rising Sea Levels in Virginia." National Public Radio (June 10). Accessed on June 10, 2014 at www.npr.org/2014/06/10/320051737/how-coal-industry-jobs-coexist-with-rising-sea-levels-in-virginia.

[17] Englander, John. 2012. *High Tide on Main Street: Rising Sea Level and the Coming Coastal Crisis*. Ames, Iowa: The Science Bookshelf, p. 142; see also Madigan, Nick. 2013. "South Florida Faces Ominous Prospects for Rising Waters."

New York Times (November 10). Accessed on February 5, 2014 at www.nytimes.com/2013/11/11/us/south-florida-faces-ominous-prospects-from-rising-waters.html?_r=0.

[18] Miller, John E. 2013. "If You're Looking for a Real Estate Boom, Head to the Coasts." *Business Insider*, (January 8). Accessed on January 1, 2014 at www.businessinsider.com/real-estate-market-booming-on-coast-2013-1.

[19] National Center for Atmospheric Research. 2012. "Dissecting Sandy's Surge: What Made the High Water so High?" Accessed on January 24, 2014 at www2.ucar.edu/atmosnews/opinion/8585/dissecting-sandys-surge.

[20] Maxfield, John. 2013. "Hurricane Sandy, One Year Later: Assessing the Economic Cost." *Daily Finance* (October 26, 2013). Accessed on January 16, 2014 at www.dailyfinance.com/on/hurricane-sandy-anniversary-economic-cost/.

[21] National Hurricane Center. 2013. *Tropical Cyclone Report: Hurricane Sandy* (February 12), p. 15. Accessed on January 30, 2014 at www.nhc.noaa.gov/data/tcr/AL182012_Sandy.pdf.

[22] Nir, Sarah Maslin. 2012. "Along Coast, Hurricane Left Housing Market in Turmoil." *New York Times* (December 27). Accessed on January 24, 2014 at www.nytimes.com/2012/12/28/nyregion/real-estate-market-along-coast-upended-by-hurricane.html.

[23] Kaplan, Thomas. 2013a. "Cuomo Seeking Home Buyouts in Flood Zones." *New York Times* (February 3). Accessed on January 24, 2014 at www.nytimes.com/2013/02/04/nyregion/cuomo-seeking-home-buyouts-in-flood-zones.html?pagewanted=all; see also, Fox Beach 165; Oakwood Beach Buyout at http://foxbeach165.com/.

[24] Kaplan, Thomas. 2013b. "Home Owners in Flood Zones Opt to Rebuild, Not Move." *New York Times* (April 26). Accessed on January 24, 2014 at www.nytimes.com/2013/04/27/nyregion/new-yorks-storm-recovery-plan-gets-federal-approval.html.

[25] IPCC, op. cit. p. 26, Figure SPM 9.

[26] Nicholls, Robert J., Natasha Marinova, Jason A. Lowe, Sally Brown, Pier Vellinga, Diogo de Gusmão, Jochen Hinkel and Richard S.J. Tol. 2011. "Sea-level Rise and Its Possible Impacts Given a 'beyond 4°C World' in the Twenty-first Century." *Philosophical Transactions of the Royal Society*, Vol. 369, No. 1934: 161–181.

[27] National Hurricane Center. 2013. *Storm Surge Overview*. Accessed on February 4, 2014 at www.nhc.noaa.gov/surge/.

[28] Tebaldi, C., B.H. Strauss, and C.E. Zervas (2012). "Modelling Sea Level Rise Impacts on Storm Surges along US Coasts." *Environmental Research Letters*, Vol. 7, No. 1:014032.

[29] According to the US National Oceanic and Atmospheric Administration, "Hurricanes, cyclones, and typhoons are all the same weather phenomenon; we just use different names for these storms in different places. In the Atlantic and Northeast Pacific, the term 'hurricane' is used. The same type of disturbance in the Northwest Pacific is called a 'typhoon' and 'cyclones' occur in the

South Pacific and Indian Ocean. In the Atlantic, hurricane season officially runs June 1 to November 30. In the Pacific, typhoons and cyclones occur more frequently between May and October." US National Oceanic and Atmospheric Administration. *Ocean Facts*. Accessed on January 15, 2014 at http://ocean service.noaa.gov/facts/cyclone.html.

30   Grinsted, Aslak, John C. Moore, and Swetlana Jevrejeva. 2013. "Projected Atlantic Hurricane Surge Threat from Rising Temperatures." *Proceedings of the National Academy of Sciences*, Vol. 110, No. 14:5369–5373; Greene, Charles H., Jennifer A. Francis, and Bruce C. Monger. 2013. "Superstorm Sandy: A Series of Unfortunate Events?" *Oceanography*, Vol. 26, No. 1:8–9.

31   Vecchi, Gabriel A., Kyle L. Swanson, and Brian J. Soden. 2008. "Whither Hurricane Activity?" *Science*, Vol. 322, No. 5902:687–689, p. 688; see also NOAA. 2013. *Global Warming and Hurricanes*. Accessed on January 21, 2014 at www.gfdl.noaa.gov/global-warming-and-hurricanes.

32   Knutson, Thomas R., John L. McBride, Johnny Chan, Kerry Emanuel, Greg Holland, Chris Landsea, Isaac Held, James P. Kossin, A.K. Srivastava, and Masato Sugi. 2010. "Tropical Cyclones and Climate Change." *Nature Geoscience*, Vol. 3, No. 3:157–163.

33   Tebaldi *et al.*, op. cit.

34   Bern, C., J. Sniezek, G.M. Mathbor, M.S. Siddiqi, and C. Ronsmans. 1993. "Risk Factors for Mortality in the Bangladesh Cyclone of 1991." *Bulletin of the World Health Organization*, Vol. 71, No. 1:73–78.

35   World Bank. 2014. "Bangladesh at a Glance." Accessed on July 29, 2014 at http://devdata.worldbank.org/AAG/bgd_aag.pdf.

36   Mondal, Abdul Matin. 2001. "Sea Level Rise along the Coast of Bangladesh." *Bangladesh Inland Water Transport Authority*, Ministry of Shipping. Accessed on January 30, 2014 at www.gloss-sealevel.org/publications/documents/bangladesh_2001.pdf; Shamsuddoha, Md., and Rezaul Karim Chowdhury. 2007. *Climate Change Impact and Disaster Vulnerabilities in the Coastal Areas of Bangladesh*. Accessed on January 30, 2014 at www.preventionweb.net/files/4032_DisasterBD.pdf.

37   Parvin, Gulsan Ara, and S.M. Reazul Ahsan. 2013. "Impacts of Climate Change on Food Security of Rural Poor Women in Bangladesh." *Management of Environmental Quality*, Vol. 24, No. 6:8802–8814.

38   USAID. nd. "The Bangladesh Cyclone of 1991." Accessed on January 30, 2014 at http://pdf.usaid.gov/pdf_docs/PNADG744.pdf.

39   Alam, Khurshid, Naureen Fatema, and Wahida Bashar Ahmed. 2008. "Case Study: Gender, Human Security and Climate Change in Bangladesh." In Dankelman, Irene, Khurshid Alam, Wahida Bashar Ahmed, Yacine Diagne Gueye, Naureen Fatema, AND Rose Mensah-Kutin, 2008, *Gender, Climate Change and Human Security: Lessons from Bangladesh, Ghana, and Senegal.* Women's Environment and Development Organization. Accessed on January 30, 2014 at www.wedo.org/wp-content/uploads/hsn-study-final-may-20-2008.pdf; Chowdhury, A.M.R., A.E. Choudhury, K. Islam, M. Bennish, E. Noji, and R.I. Glass. 1993. "Risk Factors for Mortality in the 1991 Bangladesh Cyclone." *World Health Organization Bulletin*, Vol. 71:73–78.

[40] Schmuck, Hannah. 2002. "Empowering Women in Bangladesh." *International Federation of Red Cross and Red Crescent Societies* (February 25). Accessed on April 11, 2009 at www.reliefweb.int/rw/rwb.nsf/AllDocsByUNID/570056eb0 ae62524c1256b6b00587224.

[41] Baden, Sally, Cathy Green, Anne Marie Goetz, and Meghna Guhathakurta. 1994. "Background Report on Gender Issues in Bangladesh." *Briefings on Development and Gender, Institute for Development Studies.* Accessed on January 30, 2014 at www.bridge.ids.ac.uk/reports/re26c.pdf.

[42] Karim, Nehal. 2006. "Options for Cyclone Protection: Bangladesh Context." *Climate Institute.* Accessed on February 10, 2014 at www.climate.org/PDF/Bangladesh.pdf.

[43] Alam *et al.*, op. cit., p. 6.

[44] Ibid., p. 12.

[45] Akhter, Farida. 1992. "Women, Not Only Victims," pp. 59–65. In Hossain, Hameeda, Cole P. Dodge, and F.H. Abed (eds). *From Crisis to Development: Coping with Disasters in Bangladesh.* Dhaka, Bangladesh: University Press Limited, p. 64.

[46] Baden *et al.*, op. cit.

[47] Haque, Ubydul, Masahiro Hashizume, Korine N. Kolivras, Hans J. Overgaard, Bivash Das, and Taro Yamamoto. 2012. "Reduced Death Rates from Cyclones in Bangladesh: What More Needs to Be Done?" *Bulletin of the World Health Organization*, Vol. 90, No. 2:150–156.

[48] Inter-Agency Working Group on Reproductive Health in Crises. 2013. "Addressing the Needs of Women and Girls in the Philippines Typhoon Haiyan Response and Recovery." Accessed on July 29, 2014 at http://iawg.net/2013/philippines/IAWG_Advocacy_Statement_for_the_Philippines_November-15_2013.pdf.

[49] Enarson, Elaine, and P.G. Dhar Chakrabarti. 2009. *Women, Gender and Disaster: Global Issues and Initiatives.* Thousand Oaks, CA: Sage Publications.

[50] National Hurricane Center. 2012. *Hurricanes in History.* Accessed on February 17, 2014 at www.nhc.noaa.gov/outreach/history/; Olsen, Lise. 2010. "5 Years after Katrina, Storm's Death Toll Remains a Mystery." *Houston Chronicle* (August 30). Accessed on February 3, 2014 at www.chron.com/news/nation-world/artic le/5-years-after-Katrina-storm-s-death-toll-remains-1589464.php.

[51] Jonkman, Sebastiaan N., Bob Maaskant, Ezra Boyd, and Marc Lloyd Levitan. 2009. "Loss of Life Caused by the Flooding of New Orleans After Hurricane Katrina: Analysis of the Relationship between Flood Characteristics and Mortality." *Risk Analysis,* Vol. 29, No. 5:676–698; see also Sharkey, Patrick. 2007. "Survival and Death in New Orleans: An Empirical Look at the Human Impact of Katrina." *Journal of Black Studies*, Vol. 37, No. 4:482–501.

[52] Seager, Joni. 2006. "Noticing Gender (or not) in Disasters." *Geoforum*, Vol. 37, No. 1:2–3

[53] Duncan, Jeff. 2013. "Shelter from the Storm: Doug Thornton Reflects on the Superdome in Katrina." *The Times-Picayune* (January 29). Accessed on February 4, 2014 at www.nola.com/superbowl/index.ssf/2013/01/superdome_series_catching_Up_w_2.html.

[54] Willinger, Beth, and Janna Knight. 2012. "Setting the Stage for Disaster: Women in New Orleans before and after Katrina." In David, E., and E. Enarson (eds.), *The Women of Katrina: How Gender, Race, and Class Matter in an American Disaster*, pp. 55–75. Nashville: Vanderbilt University Press, p. 55.

[55] Zotti, Marianne E., Van T. Tong, Lyn Kieltyka, and Renee Brown-Bryant. 2012. "Factors Influencing Evacuation Decisions among High-Risk Pregnant and Post-Partum Women." In David, E., and E. Enarson (eds.), *The Women of Katrina: How Gender, Race, and Class Matter in an American Disaster*, pp. 90–104. Nashville: Vanderbilt University Press, pp. 94–96.

[56] Stock, Paul. 2007. "Katrina and Anarchy: A Content Analysis of a New Disaster Myth." *Sociological Spectrum*, Vol. 27, No. 6:705–26.

[57] Roberts, Michelle. 2005. "Superdome Crime More Urban Myth Than Real." *Houston Chronicle* (September 28). Accessed on February 4, 2014 at www.chron.com/news/hurricanes/article/Superdome-crime-more-urban-myth-than-real-1479934.php.

[58] Ibid.

[59] Tierney, Kathleen, Christine Bevc, and Erica Kuligowski. 2006. "Metaphors Matter: Disaster Myths, Media Frames, and Their Consequences in Hurricane Katrina." *The Annals of the American Academy of Political and Social Science*, Vol. 604, No. 1:57–81.

[60] Ransby, Barbara. 2006. "Katrina, Black Women, and the Deadly Discourse on Black Poverty in America." *Du Bois Review*, Vol. 3, No. 1:215–222, p. 218; Giroux, Henry. 2006. *Stormy Weather: Katrina and the Politics of Disposability*. Boulder, CO: Paradigm Books; Read, Chris. 2009. "His and Her Katrina." Paper presented at the annual meeting of the Midwest Sociological Society, Des Moines.

[61] Zotti *et al.*, op. cit., pp. 97–98.

[62] Rosenblatt, Susannah, and James Rainey. 2005. "Katrina Takes a Toll on Truth, News Accuracy." *Los Angeles Times* (September 27). Accessed on April 10, 2009 at http://articles.latimes.com/2005/sep/27/nation/na-rumors27.

[63] Thevenot, Brian, and Gordon Russell. 2005. "Reports of Anarchy at Superdome Overstated." *Seattle Times*, September 26. Accessed on April 10, 2009 at http://seattletimes.nwsource.com/html/nationworld/2002520986_katmyth26.html.

[64] Roberts, op. cit. Joni Seager is not so sanguine about dismissing the veracity of sexual violence reports: "The lack of curiosity about the rapes in the midst of the New Orleans disaster is … particularly disturbing … no interviews with police officials about the magnitude of rape, no curiosity about the nature of masculinity that contemplates rape even in conditions of extreme human suffering, no disaster experts assuring us that rape-support teams are included in the rescue teams, no discussion about the medical and psychological resources that women who have survived unimaginable tragedy and stress and have also been raped will need." Seager, op. cit., p. 3.

[65] Fernandes, Rhea, Allison Suppan Helmuth, and Jane M. Henrici. 2010. *Mounting Losses: Women and Public Housing after Hurricane Katrina*. Washington, DC: Institute for Women's Policy Research, August. Accessed

on February 3, 2014 at www.iwpr.org/publications/pubs/mounting-losses-women-and-public-housing-after-hurricane-katrina.

[66] Fussell, Elizabeth, Narayan Sastry, and Mark Van Landingham. 2010. "Race, Socioeconomic Status, and Return Migration to New Orleans after Hurricane Katrina." *Population and Environment*, Vol. 31, Nos. 1–3:20–42; see also Elizabeth Fussell. 2007. "Constructing New Orleans, Constructing Race: A Population History of New Orleans." *The Journal of American History*, Vol. 94, No. 3:846–855.

[67] Groen, Jeffrey A., and Anne E. Polivka. 2010. "Going Home after Hurricane Katrina: Determinants of Return Migration and Changes in Affected Areas." *Demography*, Vol. 47, No. 4:821–844.

[68] Willinger, Beth, with Jessica Gerson. 2008. "Demographic and Socioeconomic Change in Relation to Gender and Katrina." In B. Willinger (ed.), Katrina and the Women of New Orleans. New Orleans: Tulane University, Newcomb College Center for Research on Women, pp. 25-31, p. 25. Accessed on July 16, 2015 at https://tulane.edu/newcomb/upload/NCCROWreport08.pdf

[69] Galea, S., C.R. Brewin, M. Gruber, R.T. Jones, D.W. King, L.A. King, R.J. McNally, R.J. Ursano, M. Petukhova, and R.C. Kessler. 2007. "Exposure to Hurricane-related Stressors and Mental Illness after Hurricane Katrina." *Archives of General Psychiatry*, Vol. 64, No. 12:1427–1434; see also Chia-Chen Chen, Angela, Verna M. Keith, Chris Airriess, Wei Li, and Karen J. Leong. 2007. "Economic Vulnerability, Discrimination, and Hurricane Katrina: Health among Black Katrina Survivors in Eastern New Orleans." *Journal of the American Psychiatric Nurses Association*, Vol. 13, No. 5:257–266; Adeola, Francis O. 2009. "Mental Health and Psychosocial Distress Sequelae of Katrina: An Empirical Study of Survivors." *Human Ecology Review*, Vol. 16, No. 2:195–210; and Kronenberg, Mindy E., Tonya Cross Hansel, Adrianne M. Brennan, Howard J. Osofsky, Joy D. Osofsky, and Beverly Lawrason. 2010. "Children of Katrina: Lessons Learned About Post-disaster Symptoms and Recovery Patterns." *Child Development*, Vol. 81, No. 4:1241–1259; researchers found a similar gendered post-traumatic stress disorder (PTSD) response a year after Hurricane Mitch hit Nicaragua: Caldera, T., L. Palma, U. Penayo, and G. Kullgren. 2001. "Psychological Impact of the Hurricane Mitch in Nicaragua in a One-Year Perspective." *Social Psychiatry and Psychiatric Epidemiology*, Vol. 36, No. 3:108–114.

[70] Abramson, D., R. Garfield, and I. Redlener. 2007. *The Recovery Divide: Poverty and the Widening Gap among Mississippi Children and Families Affected by Hurricane Katrina.* New York: National Center for Disaster Preparedness; see also Overstreet, Stacy, and Berre Burch. 2008. "Mental Health Status of Women and Children Following Hurricane Katrina." In Willinger, 2008. op. cit., pp. 59–64. Accessed on February 3, 2014 at http://tulane.edu/nccrow/upload/NCCROWreport08.pdf.

[71] Terzieff, Juliette. 2006. "Katrina Survivors Lashed by Emotional Tailwinds." *Women's eNews* (August 13). Accessed on July 29, 2014 at http://womensenews.org/story/060813/katrina-survivors-lashed-emotional-tailwinds.

72 Anastario, Michael, Nadine Shehab, and Lynn Lawry. 2009. "Increased Gender-based Violence among Women Internally Displaced in Mississippi 2 Years Post-Hurricane Katrina." *Disaster Medicine and Public Health Preparedness*, Vol. 3, No. 1:18–26; for a general discussion of Women's vulnerability in Disasters, see Enarson, Elaine. 1999. "Violence against Women in Disasters: A Study of Domestic Violence Programs in the United States and Canada." *Violence Against Women*, Vol. 5, No. 7:742–768.

73 US Department of Labor. 2012. *Leading Occupations for Women*. Accessed on February 4, 2014 at www.dol.gov/wb/stats/Occupations.htm#Lofw. *Women's Participation in Selected Occupations (1985–2012)*. Accessed on February 4, 2014 at www.dol.gov/wb/stats/facts_over_time.htm#wilf.

74 National Women's Law Center. 2012. *Women in Construction: 6.9 Percent Is Not Enough*. Accessed on February 3, 2014 at www.nwlc.org/sites/default/files/pdfs/womeninconstructionfactsheet.pdf; see also Jones-DeWeever, Avis. 2008. *Women in the Wake of the Storm: Examining the Post-Katrina Realities of the Women of New Orleans and the Gulf Coast*. Washington, DC: Institute for Women's Policy Research. Accessed on January 20, 2014 at www.iwpr.org/publications/pubs/women-in-the-wake-of-the-storm-examining-the-post-katrina-realities-of-the-women-of-new-orleans-and-the-gulf-coast.

75 Willinger, 2008, op. cit.

4
GENDER AND CLIMATE CHANGE SCIENCE

Gender matters not only for climate change impacts. Contemporary US climate science has a gendered face reflecting the history of science, a mainly male enterprise that emphasizes technological advance, is rooted in the military interests of the US, and seeks not only to understand, but to control and alter the natural world.[1] Feminist critics contend that the scale and dimensions of climate change are adequately understood. They fault climate scientists for spending too much time and money measuring and modeling the geophysical characteristics of climate change and giving too little attention to the social impacts, especially the gendered causes and consequences of climate change. They argue that research efforts should be focused on documenting the effects of a changing climate on vulnerable populations and designing ways to reduce its threat.[2] Critics further maintain that the past and present priorities of climate science funding agencies and researchers are shaped by elitist institutional and personal interests, noting that mainly male researchers' highly technical findings are inaccessible to non-specialists, especially those whose interests and perspectives seldom are represented in scientific labs.[3] It was only after a quarter-century of these critiques that the leading international climate change organization, the United Nations Framework Convention on Climate Change (UNFCCC), recognized the need for gender balance in its decision-making and expert bodies and directed its scientific research group, the Intergovernmental Panel on Climate Change (IPCC), to include consideration of gender in its 2013 Fifth Assessment Report (AR5).[4]

Despite the UNFCCC's and IPCC's recent awakening to the ways their policies have privileged male scientists and policymakers, the gendered and social justice implications of climate change remain marginal concerns that rarely are addressed in leading scientific journals where climate research is published. This results from widely-held assumptions about what is a legitimate scientific question. Social and gendered aspects of scientific phenomena are considered by many scientists as irrelevant to the investigation of natural phenomena, at best, and "politically correct" distractions, at worst. In part to address this bias, in 1997 the US National Science Foundation (NSF) began requiring researchers not only to outline the "scientific merit" of their proposed investigations, but also to address the "broader impacts" of their research. Scientists were expected to specify how their research would advance scientific education, public outreach, and/or benefit society.[5] There was immediate resistance from scientists and engineers to the "Broader Impacts Criterion" on the grounds that research should be judged only on its technical merit, and scientists are not trained to address social impacts.[6]

It has been nearly two decades since NSF introduced the Broader Impacts Criterion, but the multitude of scientific articles detailing the effects of rising atmospheric and ocean temperatures and acidity on corals, plants, fish, marine mammals, and other natural systems still seldom explore the human consequences of these changes, much less the gendered causes or impacts of climate change. For instance, countless publications on the dynamics of Greenland's ice sheet and glaciers set their sights firmly on geophysics and hydrology, scarcely noting the cultural, social, economic, or gendered aspects of life in Arctic communities whose lives and livelihoods are being reshaped along with the ice and the coastline. Voluminous research on climate change disruptions of plant and animal habitats almost never mentions the men and women whose rural and urban homes are eroding into the sea, flooding more frequently and severely, or heating up and burning. Studies of the displacement of biological species by climate change tend to focus only on the natural world, as if humans – women or men – exist in a separate realm irrelevant to research questions. Proposed plans to respond to climate change by storing carbon in forests or underground typically are described in terms of their technical dimensions, which rarely include detailed considerations of the women and men who live there and who are not at the table when carbon sequestration schemes are designed and decided.

Even when human aspects of climate change are the subject of scientific inquiry, researchers generally fail to delve into distinctions of gender, race, class, or age. An example is research on the effects of climate change on food production. The world's commodity food crops (wheat, corn, sorghum, rice) increasingly are grown in large-scale farming enterprises using patented hybrid seeds that evoke the common image of a man driving an industrial agricultural machine. A good deal of research on the effects of climate change on food crops is geared toward the development of seeds and techniques to benefit this kind of mainly male-dominated large-scale agricultural production.[7] Far fewer food science resources are directed toward women agricultural workers who constitute a much larger percentage of farmers in countries where agriculture is not mechanized.[8] Smallholder women farmers produce a significant amount of the food eaten by their families and sold in small markets. These women and other small-scale producers are of relatively little or no interest to agribusiness or the scientists who work for them.[9] In Chapters 2 and 3 we saw examples of the importance of deconstructing the concept of "human" into its gendered, classed, raced, and aged components when considering the impacts of rising average temperatures and sea levels. For instance, there is a large literature on the effects of elevated temperatures on the human body, and researchers recognize that men and women respond differently to heat exertion and heat waves. Despite this recognition, there is little scientific research on why there are different medical outcomes from heat exposure for men and women.

Men at Work

The feminist critique of science as masculine in its personnel and perspective reflects the fact that, in many ways, the history of science is the history of men. Prominent 19th- and 20th-century women scientists are the rare female exceptions that prove the men-only rule: Lise Meitner, Maria Skłodowska-Curie, Rosalind Franklin, Rachel Carson.[10] Until the 20th century, the exclusion of women scientists from male-only scientific and medical societies was nearly universal. The US National Academy of Sciences (NAS) elected its first woman member, Florence R. Sabin, MD, in 1925.[11] The British Royal Society (equivalent to the US National Academy) did not admit a woman until 1945.[12] Only recently did the doors of the boys' and men's science clubs slowly open to girls and women, and when females walked in, what they found inside the clubhouse was far from gender friendly or even gender neutral.[13] In 2007 the European Molecular Biology Organization surveyed male and female members of two gender-progressive research networks containing at least 40 percent women scientists. Despite their apparent commitment to including women, the survey found that male scientists were nearly twice as likely to hold permanent and/or leadership positions and less than half as likely to recognize gender inequalities in scientific research settings:

> The overwhelming majority of women (76.6%) agreed with the strong statement that "research is ruled by men", compared with 47.3% of the men. In addition, more than 75% of female interviewees believed that women are too often relegated to administrative or subordinate roles, whereas only around 33% of their male colleagues shared this opinion. These notable differences in perceptions could be because men either find it difficult to recognize an imbalance between themselves and their female colleagues, or they prefer not to admit the problem.[14]

The findings of this study illustrate that even today, with increased numbers of women working in science, scientific organizational cultures and practices are slow to evolve, especially when the men who benefit from ongoing inequalities are in charge of change. The focus of this chapter is not simply to document historical and contemporary gender discrimination in science. Our goal is to explore the impact of past and present male domination of science on the production of scientific knowledge generally and in the specific case of climate science.

This chapter begins by spotlighting some gender cornerstones of 20th-century environmental and natural science upon which rests 21st-century climate science. The gendered history of science has left an imprint on the scientific study of climate change. While not all climate science research priorities, approaches, and findings reflect male domination, the next two chapters are an attempt to build a case for the importance of seeing gender in climate science. Some sections will focus on science generally, not just climate science. In this chapter, we will examine the gender structure of science and engineering in general, in environmental science, and in climate science. The next chapter explores the implications of a gendered institution – the military – and the masculine military substructure of climate change science, especially the influence of US science's largest source of public funding: the Department of Defense.

Gender and Polar Science

The Arctic is a good place to locate a discussion of gender and climate science. Temperatures are rising the fastest in the Arctic, with several important consequences. Scientists predict that before mid-century melting sea ice will open a northern passage for ships traveling between Europe and Asia during summer months.[15] Sea level rise will alter coastlines as water held in land-based glaciers and polar ice sheets melts into the oceans. Melting permafrost and retreating land ice offer increasing opportunities to develop oil, gas, and mineral resources in the far North. Changes in Arctic geography, resource transport, and development have implications for geopolitics in a region marked historically by both competition and cooperation and controlled by member countries of the Arctic Council: Canada, Denmark, Finland, Iceland, Norway, Russia, Sweden, and the United States.[16]

The Arctic has been home to humans for thousands of years, including migrating Indigenous peoples, Viking voyagers, various settler populations, and European explorers. Despite its harsh conditions and remote location, the Arctic has a significant scientific and gendered history. Most Western polar exploration was undertaken by men who were officers in or supported by their country's militaries.[17] For the most part, these polar explorers' primary motivation was to achieve personal and national recognition, not to pursue military advantage. Nevertheless, descriptions of European polar exploration in the early 20th century often sound like military campaigns and victories in which the men and their deeds are described as "heroic," and part of "the heroic age of polar exploration."[18] Reports of the Arctic and Antarctic adventures of Europeans and North American explorers such as Roald Amundsen, Robert Peary, and Ernest Shackleton typically have been framed in the language of colonial expansion and domination – discovery, conquest, and triumph – and recounted with respect and admiration in many books, biographies, films, and television series.[19] Public and historical celebrations of these male explorers' bravery and resolve in the face of dangerous and isolated polar landscapes disregard the fact that, in the case of the Arctic, the landscape had been populated for centuries, and the explorers extensively used the technologies and knowledge of the Indigenous people living there, including Native women.[20]

The life of Vilhjalmur Stefansson, an early 20th-century Canadian Arctic explorer, embodies both the self-discipline and self-indulgence that typified the lives of most polar explorers. Stefansson's background was less military and more scholarly than other explorers, and he wrote several books about his travels which were motivated, in part, by a search for exotic, so-called "Copper Inuits" (blond-haired, blue-eyed Arctic Natives).[21] During his expeditions, Stefansson formed close relationships with a number of Inuits, both men and women, whose skills at hunting, fishing, navigating, and living in the Arctic led him to conclude that "the costs of an expedition could be significantly reduced if one was prepared to live as the Inuit did."[22] In his 1964 autobiography, *Discovery*, Stefansson recounts the start of the ill-fated 1913–1916 Canadian Arctic expedition in which four young companions perished: "I boarded the Karluk with a widowed Eskimo woman, Pannigabluk ... from Alaska. She was an excellent seamstress, something no party wintering on the arctic coast can afford to be without."[23] Stefansson's seamstress, Pannigabluk, could not save the expedition for him, but they had a son together, Alex. After his final expedition, Stefansson returned to North America, leaving Alex and Pannigabluk behind.[24] He resumed a comfortable and privileged life built on his reputation as an explorer and eventually married Evelyn Schwartz. Together they went on to establish the Stefansson Collection on Polar Exploration at Dartmouth College.[25]

Rear Admiral Robert E. Peary was a model for Stefansson's strategy of living like the Inuits. During his Arctic expeditions he developed close relationships with Native guides, hunters, dogsled drivers, and women.[26] There was no comparable fame for Peary's African American "aide" and fellow explorer, Matthew Henson, but both men depended on the skills of their Inuit colleagues, and both men fathered children with Greenlandic Inuit women.[27] Despite his extramarital liaisons, Peary's wife, Josephine Peary, was a loyal supporter and partner in several of his later expeditions.

> [Josephine Peary] called herself a "nineteenth century woman" accepting a supporting role to her husband, quietly enduring his infidelity with Inuit women, and fiercely defending his claim to have reached the North Pole ... Yet Josephine also challenged traditional attitudes about gender. At a time when Americans had come to view the Arctic as a stage for manly endeavor, she joined Robert on his Greenland expedition of 1891–92. She returned with him to the Arctic again in 1893, giving birth to her daughter Marie Ahnighito Peary. In her book about Marie's birth and infancy, *The Snow Baby*, girls and women emerge as the heroines of Arctic life while men, including Robert, are almost entirely absent.[28]

Josephine Peary's recounting was not designed to challenge the awe that the saga of Arctic exploration was intended to inspire; she simply included herself and her daughter in the narrative. Her story of heroines rather than heroes was an intrusive anomaly – a family adventure, not a tale of solitary manly triumph and domination. The often hidden history of the role of wives and lovers in the work of European polar explorers betrays a feminine side of the chronicle of intrepid men singlehandedly overcoming Arctic perils.

The Military-Science Partnership

Polar exploration's tales of victorious masculinity notwithstanding, and despite the military connections of most explorers, the Arctic's actual military potential was not developed until the Second World War, when it was a critical route for weapons and supplies sent from the United States, United Kingdom, and Iceland to their ally, the Soviet Union.[29] When the war ended, the US and the USSR dissolved their alliance and entered into four decades of Cold War. Each power used the Arctic strategically, taking advantage of Second World War-era bases to position military personnel, equipment, and resources, setting up polar-based radar systems to spy on one another, deploying submarines in cat-and-mouse patrols under the Arctic sea ice, and pointing nuclear missiles at each other over the North Pole – the shortest line of attack.

The history of the weapons and technology used by military powers during the 20th century – the First World War, Second World War, Cold War, Korean War, and Vietnam War – is central in the history of 20th-century science and engineering. Examples of militarized science and scientific militarization include, but are not limited to, chemistry (to design and test chemical and incendiary weapons and defoliants);[30] meteorology (to track the global path of radiation from nuclear weapons and testing and to predict battlefield weather conditions);[31] oceanography (to map the ocean floor and the currents for military submarines and surface vessels);[32] physics (to design, test, and produce nuclear weapons) and astronomy (to explore military uses of space);[33] microbiology (to design and test biological weapons and provide medical intelligence about battlefield diseases);[34] geography (to design maps and topographic models to support military campaigns);[35] electrical engineering (to design radar for tracking enemy activity and control systems for military vehicles);[36] and aerospace engineering (to design and build military aircraft, rockets, and satellites).[37]

These and other scientific and engineering fields were largely male enterprises on both the military and civilian sides. Once again, the few female exceptions prove the mainly male rule: Navy Commander Mary Sears, founding figure in oceanography, Marie Tharp, who mapped the ocean floor, Chien-Shiung Wu, Manhattan Project physicist, and Myrtle C. Bachelder, Manhattan Project chemist.[38] These female scientists, along with their male counterparts, not only provided important knowledge to military decisionmakers; the development of their disciplines was shaped, in part, by their participation in major military operations. The book *War and Nature: Fighting Humans and Insects with Chemicals from World War I to Silent Spring* traces the military-scientific collaboration that led to the growth of US chemistry as a prominent scientific discipline and one of the biggest businesses in the world.[39] The book's title provides a lead in to our next section, which examines one of the most famous chapters in environmental science history. It begins as a woman scientist challenges the chemical industry and the male scientists working in it.

"Silence, Miss Carson!"

The modern environmental movement is widely attributed to the publication of *Silent Spring* in 1962 by Rachel Carson, then editor-in-chief of all US Department of Fish and Wildlife publications. Carson had a Master's degree in zoology from Johns Hopkins University and was a successful science writer, with three best-selling, award-winning books before *Silent Spring*.[40] Even before its publication, *Silent Spring* was serialized in *New Yorker* magazine and selected by the Book-of-the-Month club. Carson intended *Silent Spring* to sound an alarm about dangers associated with the widespread use of chemicals, in particular the pesticide DDT, in post-Second World War America:

> Since the mid-1940's over 200 basic chemicals have been created for use in killing insects, weeds, rodents, and other organisms described in the modern vernacular as "pests"; and they are sold under several thousand different brand names. These sprays, dusts, and aerosols are now applied almost universally to farms, gardens, forests, and homes – nonselective chemicals that have the power to kill every insect, the "good" and the "bad," to still the song of birds and the leaping of fish in the streams, to coat the leaves with a deadly film, and to linger on

in soil – all this though the intended target may be only a few weeds or insects. Can anyone believe it is possible to lay down such a barrage of poisons on the surface of the earth without making it unfit for all life? They should not be called "insecticides," but "biocides."[41]

Carson did not advocate the elimination of insecticides and other chemicals, but she called for a retreat from what she saw as humanity's wholesale "war on nature":

All this is not to say there is no insect problem and no need of control. I am saying, rather, that control must be geared to realities, not to mythical situations, and that the methods employed must be such that they do not destroy us along with the insects.[42]

Silent Spring sold 40,000 advance sales before its publication on September 27, 1962, 600,000 by the end of the year, and over a million copies before Carson's death from breast cancer in 1964.[43] The book's message captured the attention of the public, including President John Kennedy, who ordered the President's Science Advisory Committee (PSAC) to issue a report on pesticides, and directed Senator Abraham Ribicoff to chair committee hearings on environmental pollution and regulation of pesticides. Carson's book not only shocked her readers and sympathetic politicians, it propelled the chemical industry into re-action. The president of Monsanto Corporation attacked Carson as "a fanatic defender of the cult of the balance of nature," and the Veliscol Corporation, a leading manufacturer of the pesticide chlordane, threatened to sue Carson's publisher, Houghton-Mifflin, if they published the book, and to take legal action against the Audubon Society if they published excerpts from the book in their magazine.[44] John Vosburgh, editor of *Audubon Magazine*, counterpunched in an editorial accompanying the magazine's first excerpt of *Silent Spring*:

Seldom has a book ruffled the feelings of an American industry to such an extent as Rachel Carson's *Silent Spring* has done in the ranks of the chemical manufacturers. Apparently, a $300,000,000-a-year business doesn't like being sprayed with

Figure 4.1 *Farm Chemicals* Magazine, October, 1963[47]

facts on the heedless use of its poisons any more than many people like being sprayed with insecticides.[45]

The uproar surrounding *Silent Spring* and its author intensified after it was published. An October 1962 review in *Chemical & Engineering News*, entitled, "Silence, Miss Carson," drew attention to both her gender and her unmarried status, and put Carson in her place among "the organic gardeners, the antiflouride leaguers, the worshipers of "natural foods," those who cling to the philosophy of a vital principal, and pseudo-scientists and faddists."[46] The October 1963 cover of the trade journal *Farm Chemicals* featured a drawing of three industry representatives forcefully testifying before the Ribicoff Senate committee with Carson depicted as a witch on a broomstick flying overhead in the background (Figure 4.1).

A biological weapons pioneer who reviewed the book for the leading journal *Science* dismissed Carson's analysis as one-sided, sarcastic, melodramatic, and old news to responsible and qualified scientists whose work properly acknowledged modern chemistry's important contributions:

> [Their] reports are not dramatically written, and they were not intended to be best sellers. They are, however, the result of careful study by a wide group of scientists, and they represent balanced judgments in areas in which emotional appeals tend to over-balance sound judgment based on facts ... it is my hope that some equally gifted writer will be willing to do the necessary research and to write the even more dramatic story of the values conferred on mankind by the chemical revolution of the last two decades.[48]

Carson and her work stood up to the onslaught from the chemical industry and scientists who felt under attack by their participation in efforts to control nature. The PSAC issued its report in the spring of 1963, and the journal *Science* retreated from its reviewer's earlier critique, commending the PSAC report as "a temperate document, even in tone, and carefully balanced in its assessments of risks versus benefits, it adds up to a fairly thorough-going vindication of Rachel

Carson's *Silent Spring* thesis."[49] *Science* even acknowledged the necessity for Carson's alleged hyperbole: "Prior to her shouting, virtually no one was paying attention, and it is a fact that the PSAC study itself, though previously contemplated, finally got under way only after she aroused a public furor."[50]

At about the same time, another leading scientific journal, *Nature*, also came to Carson's defense in a review of *Silent Spring*, although the author spotlighted her gender with the title, "An American Prophetess."

> Rachel Carson has made a frontal assault on powerful vested interest, and "these animals are very cruel; when one attacks them they defend themselves". But they must not do so by impugning her scientific quality. The fact that she writes lucidly, and with the punch that must provoke the envy of the manufacturers' advertising staff, does not mean that she is not a scientist ... She rests her case not on vague generalizations but on concrete instances, and authenticates it with forty-eight pages of references to scientific literature.[51]

The mobilization against Carson and *Silent Spring* was not only industrial chemistry's defense of its economic interests, it also reflected a worldview that placed "man" above nature and embraced science as universal, objective, and unimpeachable. *Silent Spring* was published at a time of continued atomic and hydrogen bomb testing and growing popular awareness of the effects of radiation.[52] The anxious reaction caused by the book revealed a public that was losing confidence in the unimpeachable wisdom of all scientific undertakings. The environmental movement that followed on the heels of *Silent Spring's* publication continues to reflect this atmosphere of uneasiness about the trustworthiness of science, especially industrial science.[53]

The controversy surrounding *Silent Spring* was not only about its message; it was about the messenger herself. Carson was documenting the dangers of indiscriminate and widespread use of pesticides, and she was calling for the public to get involved in science and the regulation of its products. She was also a woman, one of very few working in science. In 1960 fewer than 9 percent of chemists were women, and less than 1 percent of chemical engineers were women.[54] Carson was the wrong gender in the wrong field with the wrong attitude toward science and nature.

Gender Disparities and Bias in Science, Engineering, and Medicine

More than 50 years after the publication of *Silent Spring*, women remain in the minority in natural science and engineering fields, but their numbers have grown. In 2011 women comprised 39.6 percent of chemists and materials scientists and 12.6 percent of chemical engineers. In the physical and atmospheric science fields most closely associated with climate change, women are much less represented in comparison to biological, medical, and social sciences. Women comprised 16.6 percent of atmospheric and space scientists, 20.3 percent of conservation and forestry scientists, and 30.4 percent of environmental scientists and geoscientists, compared to 46.9 percent of biological scientists, 52.9 percent of medical and life scientists, and 61.2 percent of social scientists. Women remain substantially underrepresented in the ranks of engineers, constituting only 13.2 percent of all engineers, with no area of engineering higher than 20.2 percent female (environmental engineering).[55] Women are notably underrepresented in the geosciences – the fields most involved in climate science.[56] A 2009 study by the American Geological Institute found that:

> In the geosciences, women currently earn 43 percent of all geoscience degrees [and 38 percent of geoscience PhD degrees], but comprise only 4.2 percent of tenure track geoscience faculty and 8.6 percent of non-tenure-track geoscience faculty. In comparison, women comprise 28 percent of all science and engineering tenure track faculty positions.[57]

These data show the continued gender imbalance (what one research team termed the gender "brain drain") in the natural sciences and engineering, especially in climate science fields and in science higher education.[58] Does it matter that these fields are primarily the domain of men? Does research by these mainly male scientists and engineers, whether on climate change or any other topic, ever reflect a gendered bias? Perhaps the best documented evidence of gender disparities is in the medical and pharmaceutical sciences and suggests that gender can indeed matter in the conduct of science. Investigations into gender bias in medical research have documented the role of gendered perspectives and interests in determining what questions are asked, which scientific procedures are followed, how the data are analyzed, and, ultimately, what knowledge is produced. The gender bias in medical research being discussed here does not refer to discrimination against women scientists, though there is a large literature on discrimination against women in science, technology, engineering, and mathematics (STEM) education and employment.[59] Rather, the bias being explored here refers to assumptions about gender that researchers bring to their investigations and professional roles. Those gender biases can be held by men or women, since neither is inoculated against the cultural forces that shape gender assumptions and expectations, which, in turn, can produce bias in science.

An example of gender mattering in medicine is treatment for depression. Only half as many men as women are diagnosed with major depression, but men are four times more likely to commit suicide and twice as likely to abuse drugs and alcohol. Since suicide and substance abuse often are associated with depression, researchers reviewing these data conclude that stereotypes of "typical" masculinity and "normal" male behavior tend to make both patients and clinicians (male or female) less likely to recognize depression among men.[60] An even more common example of gender bias in medicine can be seen in research that asks scientific questions about men's health to the exclusion of questions about women's health, includes only male subjects in research on the safety and efficacy of treatments, designs drugs and protocols based on knowledge about their usefulness for men, but not women, and makes recommendations for all patients based on research conducted only on men.

The origins of the gender bias in medical science can be attributed to several factors: the scientific adoption of the male model as the universal "human" model, the tendency of mainly male researchers to identify the important questions and design the studies and treatments for diseases and conditions in which they are personally interested as men, male pharmaceutical corporation executives, scientists, and politicians who direct funding for research into conditions and diseases that they believe affect them as men, and unexamined attitudes held by both male and female medical professionals about which diseases are more likely to affect men or women.[61]

Perhaps the most notorious example of gender bias in medical science and practice involves research and treatment of heart disease. Although cardiac disease is the leading killer of women, historically it has been viewed as primarily a man's disease. In the late 1980s researchers began documenting gender disparities in heart disease diagnosis and care:

> Women have long been excluded from the population considered at high risk for cardiovascular disease. In fact, myocardial infarction is the primary cause of death for women who are more than 40 years of age, and women's risk of dying during the first 2 weeks after a heart attack is double that of men. Cardiovascular disease kills approximately 500,000 women each year and about 450,000 men. All forms of cancer, the second leading cause of death, kill approximately 237,000 women per year. Clinical studies historically have used men as subjects, so much of what is known currently about diagnosing and treating coronary heart disease is known about men.[62]

The major reasons for women's higher death rates from heart attack include late diagnosis (neither patients nor their doctors expected women to have heart problems), unsuitability of diagnostic instruments for women's bodies (smaller blood vessels made cannulation difficult), less aggressive treatment for women diagnosed with heart attacks (later angioplasties and fewer pacemakers and heart transplantations), and limited knowledge of the effects of various treatments on women (most cardiac research on treatment and drugs was conducted on men).[63] Despite recognition of women's higher death rates resulting from inadequate treatment for heart disease, the gender disparities have persisted up to the present. In the mid-2000s, leading medical journals noted the continuing gender gap in cardiac care:

Differences in cardiac care according to gender have now been described for 20 years. As early as 1987, Tobin et al. reported that 40% of male patients with abnormal exercise radionuclide scans were referred for cardiac catheterization, whereas only 4% of the female patients were referred for future testing. Since then, many investigations have continued to describe a less aggressive management strategy for coronary artery disease (CAD) in women than in men in a variety of settings, but predominantly in patients with acute coronary syndromes.[64]

Just as *Silent Spring* galvanized public and political attention on the consequences of the widespread use of pesticides, a growing awareness of gender health disparities during the 1990s caught the attention of women members of Congress. In 1994, in an atmosphere of public and congressional indignation, the National Institutes of Health issued guidelines for the inclusion of women and minorities as subjects in clinical research to address gender disparities in the federal funding of medical testing, research, and clinical trials.[65] Three years later, in response to reports of insurance companies refusing to pay for hospital stays following breast surgery, requiring instead so-called "drive-through mastectomies," Connecticut Representative Rosa DeLauro sponsored H.R. 135, the Breast Cancer Patient Protection Act of 1997, to require medical managed-care programs to allow women to stay in hospital for up to two days after a mastectomy. The bill did not pass Congress, and has been reintroduced multiple times, most recently in 2013 when it was referred to committee.[66]

Advances in the science associated with women's health have led to increased inclusion of women in clinical trials and treatment protocol research, expanded funding for investigations of diseases affecting primarily women, like breast cancer, and broadened awareness of gender disparities in medical science and practice.[67] That researchers continue to find gender biases in pharmaceutical trials, medical research, and medical treatments illustrates how difficult it is to change deep-seated gendered assumptions about women and men – about what kinds of likely diseases each faces or types of appropriate treatment for each.[68]

A Gender Critique of Climate Change Science

If gender matters in some medical research, does it matter in all medical research, or all scientific research, especially climate science? Various critics of the research findings of the IPCC have focused on its reliance on large-scale general circulation models (GCMs).[69] Feminist scholars argue that GCMs reflect a classically masculine approach which minimizes knowledge gained from human lived experience in favor of abstract mathematical representations of reality.[70] Climate change skeptics charge that the models are "alarmist" social constructions that generate "phantom threats" designed to satisfy environmental pressure groups and to promote scientists' self-interest in fame and funding.[71] Beyond their negative evaluations of GCMs, there is little other common ground for proponents of these two critiques, though both likely would agree that:

> [I]t is difficult to imagine an environmental phenomenon less directly observable, more remote from everyday experience, and more dependent on the technical apparatus of science for constructing its apparent "reality" than the so-called greenhouse effect.[72]

Although GCMs are acknowledged by their designers to be complex, inaccurate, and incomplete representations of the actual global climate system, they are the backbone of the IPCC reports.[73] Climate models rest on the prestige of their mainly male designers (prominent scientists and engineers), advanced technology used to create them (supercomputers), technical language (Navier-Stokes equations and computationally intensive numerical models), and elevated status of the institutions where they are refined and tested (national laboratories, scientific agencies, leading universities).

The work of climate scientists and the IPCC has been and remains essential to understanding the physical processes associated with climate change and sounding the alarm about its seriousness. The predictions of these models and the science that supported them were the basis of our discussion of climate change and its impacts in the previous three chapters. In fact, we spent the last two entire chapters examining the impacts of climate change on men and women, relying largely on the findings associated with GCMs reported in the 2013 IPCC's AR5, *Climate Change 2013: The Physical Science Basis.* Despite the importance of this research, there have been major blind spots in climate science and the work of the IPCC, particularly in the area of climate justice, and especially with regard to gender inequalities related to climate change.

In the first three chapters of this book on gender and climate change we depended on the 1552-page IPCC Working Group I report on *Climate Change 2013 – The Physical Science Basis* to estimate the gendered implications of its predictions, though the words "gender" or "women" never appear in its pages. A word search of the report does, however, generate dozens of entries for "human," mostly referring to human influence on the climate system. Apparently the IPCC's AR5 of Working Group I is interested in humans, but not men or women. A similar search of the IPCC AR5 of Working Group II's "Summary for Policymakers," which focused on climate change "impacts, adaptation, and vulnerability," yields similar results – no men or women, only humans. The same absence of references to "gender" or "women" characterized IPCC AR5 of Working Group III's "Summary for Policymakers," which focused on "mitigation of climate change." Some of the chapters of the full Working Group II and III reports do reference gender and women, but they do not discuss men, and few readers look beyond the more succinct "Summary" documents, since presumably that is what is important for policymakers and non-specialists to know.[74]

The disjuncture between "human" causes and impacts of climate change and the gender causes and impacts, or the class or racial or regional or age-related causes and impacts of climate change, reflects the level of generality of much climate change science, including climate models. Climate science depicts the causes and impacts of climate change as a universal process in which human distinctions are irrelevant. This emphasis on "human" obscures differences between men and women, rich and poor, young and old, educated and uneducated, urban and rural, or global North and global South as they relate to the causes and consequences of climate change. "Human" implies a common and equal contribution to and fate in the face of climate change. "Human" ignores unequal inputs as well as unequal impacts within and across populations. A critique of this universalism is that while we all may be human, and we all may be in this together, we do not all equally contribute to the problem, nor are we all going to have the same experience of climate change. The IPCC acknowledges that historically most greenhouse gas (GHG) emissions originated in the global North with increasingly catastrophic effects in the global South. Its failure to deconstruct "anthropogenic" climate change, however, obscures the raced, classed, and gendered nature of both its causes and consequences.

The focus of GCMs and IPCC reports on "humans" creates a comfortable "objectivity" and distance for the model makers – a safe space that equalizes blame for the problem being studied by the mostly male climate scientists from developed countries. By emphasizing the "human contribution" to climate change, researchers can ignore exactly which groups of humans are doing the causing and paper over who is responsible for climate injustices and inequalities. How should we understand climate modelers' difference-erasing focus on the universal "human" aspects of climate change? The study of gender inequalities in European molecular biology cited above offers two possible explanations: the emphasis on "human" is because male scientists do not see any significant differences among humans, or because they prefer not to acknowledge differences that are an indictment of the system in which they have not only an investment, but a controlling interest.[75] Critics make a direct connection between the overrepresentation of men in climate science and policy and the gender biases and blind spots in both climate science and climate policy.

> Men dominate the issue at all levels, as scientific and economic experts, entrepreneurs, policy makers and spokespeople. Since the 1970s climate change had been identified and explained by natural scientists ... It is not irrelevant that the majority of climate scientists are men. The Intergovernmental Panel on

Climate Change (IPCC) is mostly made up of male scientists, with "chairman" Rajendra Pachauri leading at the global level. Men also dominate in the climate policy arena … The most prominent politicians associated with the issue are male … In 2007 an Internet survey of "global consumers" in 47 countries conducted by The Nielsen Company and Oxford University found that 18 out of the 22 "most influential spokespeople on climate change" are men.[76]

Invisible Gender Hands

If climate scientists see only humans, what do we find when we look behind that genderless curtain? There has been some research directed toward a gender analysis of the "human" contribution to GHG emissions.

> The impact of gender inequalities is absent from the notion of ecological footprint that has been used in an essentialist way, as it differentiates humanity only in terms of Northern or Southern location. This ignores the gendered qualities of paid and unpaid work and of transport and energy use and the feminisation of poverty … these inequalities mean that both the causes and consequences of global warming are gendered.[77]

A 2014 study of "gendered emissions and ecological footprints" in developed countries used mainly Canadian data to calculate men's and women's GHG emissions arising from their participation in three broad areas of life: employment, transportation, and residential consumption. Among sectors employing men and women, men represented 72–90 percent of workers in industries with the highest GHG emissions (e.g. electricity and heat, fossil fuel production, mining, agriculture, construction, manufacturing), and women represented 56 percent of workers in industries with the lowest GHG emissions (commercial, institutional, service), the result being that the male share of GHG emissions from employment was 76 percent. In the transportation sector, men were found to drive more miles and heavier road vehicles than women, the result being that the male share of GHG from vehicular transportation was 89 percent. Women and men were each assigned 50 percent in the residential consumption category; the ecological footprint from energy use, food, and other consumption increases with household income, but was not seen to vary by gender. The overall conclusion of the research was that men produced 76.5 percent of GHG emissions in Canada, which was considered typical for wealthy countries.[78]

These results parallel findings of a 2007 Swedish study of women's and men's ecological footprints, which concluded that men's greater GHG production resulted from their employment, transportation use, and masculine lifestyles, including their "risk-taking, aggressiveness, and violence," which were seen to have implications "for sustainability and resource use."[79] The study concluded with more than two dozen gender-specific recommendations, including:

- take action to prevent men from using resources "in the name of all," but in reality for themselves by means of high-level policy statements and guidelines for funding distribution without conducting gender impact analyses;
- work actively to ensure that a disproportionately large share of public resources does not continue to benefit a small group of comparatively rich men – for instance in terms of influence, transportation etc. – by such means as gender budgeting and auditing;
- make clear how women live more sustainably to the benefit of others but often at the cost of ill-health to themselves – and take action to remedy the situation.[80]

The last point is consistent with research findings that environmental work is women's work: organizing community cleanups, managing household recycling, educating children to be environmentally aware, and learning about and practicing green consumerism. For instance, the US EcoMom Alliance "pushes all the right buttons of hegemonic femininity ... to convince women that it is their duty as mothers to save the planet [by inviting] women to 'take the ecomom challenge'" to do the women's work of green household practices and consumer decisions.[81] Men as well as women are aware of the gendered nature of "green" consumption, as a *Los Angeles Times* reporter noted in 2012:

> At the LA auto show, each year I watch men ogle performance cars, 4-wheel drive trucks and imported luxury sedans. Overwhelmingly, auto industry data show men purchase these vehicles, though they consistently rank among the lowest-mileage vehicles on the road. One day at the show, a fellow from Murrieta [California] examining new electric vehicle models told me, in a not uncommon refrain, "Sure, I like these cars, they make sense for the environment. Would I buy one? Yeah, for my wife."[82]

Efforts to dissect "human" contributions to GHG emissions and sustainable consumption by separating men's and women's differential contributions have been met with indifference by most climate researchers, if they are even aware of the research, and with derision from some in science. In an op-ed comment about the Swedish study whose recommendations are partially listed above, the journal *New Scientist* asked, "Are men to blame for global warming?" and concluded, "Even climate change cannot escape the gender wars."[83]

This disdain is articulated in the absence of much interest in gender issues in environmental science, even environmental social science. Researchers surveyed articles published in the top five environmental social science journals from 1980 to 2005, and "turned up references to the terms 'sex,' 'gender,' or 'feminism' in just 3.9% of citations."[84] One prominent sociologist's 2009 book, *The Politics of Climate Change*, focuses mainly on class-based and regional impacts of climate change, and as one reader noted, "he does not mention gender as the relevant category, nor does he mention women other than to remind us that they too drive SUVs."[85]

Global climate models are not the only target in the so-called "gender wars" associated with critiques of climate change science. Critics of "remote sensing" (by land-based, aerial, and space-based photographic, radar, and other surveillance systems) have contrasted this distant, technology-dependent approach to environmental monitoring with "local sensing" (by on-the-ground observers, especially those living in an area for years or generations).[86]

> A critical approach to remote sensing reveals some of the unquestioned assumptions that undergird the celebratory discourse surrounding Earth remote sensing, giving preference to those voices that are least likely to be heard. Because programs like EOS [Earth Observing System] and EOSDIS [EOS Data and Information System], relying as they do upon aerospace and electronics technologies, are primarily the domain of white [or privileged non-white] men in the wealthiest countries, [a more critical approach] means looking at the matter from the perspective of women and the disempowered.[87]

According to this critique mainly privileged men are likely to do the remote sensing and use the remotely sensed data to advance their studies of the global environmental and climate systems emphasizing human universals and nearly universal disinterest in questions of environmental or climate justice. Does it matter that men are doing the sensing, remotely or otherwise? The critics continue by arguing that remote sensing is only one of many technologies used by mainly male scientists whose interests are not only to understand, but also to control nature. That viewpoint is imbedded in the highly technical tools and detached perspective associated with remote sensing, especially satellite sensing systems like EOS:

> In the discourse surrounding global environmental monitoring programs like the USGCRP [US Global Change Research Program] … terms like "managing the planet" and "global management" abound. The [earth as a] "blue marble" image fosters the notion that the earth is [both knowable and] manageable … To manage means to control, to handle, to direct, to be in charge. The remote sensing project functions simultaneously as symptom, expression, and reinforcement of modernity's dream of knowledge as power.[88]

By this argument, the technologies that are used to study and "solve" the problem of climate change are part of its causes. It is an act of faith that a problem which resulted from the quest to control nature and intervene in earth systems from a position of superior knowledge can be solved by the same techniques and assumptions. In the language of some ecofeminists: "In order to do violence to Mother Nature ... *homo scientificus* had to set himself apart from, or rather above, nature."[89] As the problems from climate change multiply and intensify, how long can the willful disregard of the gendered or raced or classed or regional injustices be expected to stand unchallenged?

Gender! Science! Action!

The feminist critiques of environmental and climate science summarized above are not simply attacks on men and masculinity. Researchers posit that when data from global climate models and remote sensing programs are used to guide policy – turning gendered science into action – they can ride roughshod over local rights and interests to become tools of oppression wielded in the name of neutral scientific resource management. Carbon offset schemes are among those most commonly cited as examples of the costs to locals, often women, in poor countries, to address the problem of carbon dioxide (CO_2) produced by rich countries. Sometimes referred to as "carbon colonialism" or "environmental colonialism" (when rich polluting countries purchase or control land in poor countries in order to relocate their unwanted carbon or waste), many of these schemes involve creating plantations of carbon-consuming trees, restricting the removal of existing forests, or limiting local use of forests designated as carbon sinks (storage containers).[90]

One major international carbon management forestry program is the United Nations REDD+ (Reducing Emissions from Deforestation and Forest Degradation) program.[91] Originally conceived as a means of forest conservation, REDD+ now contains a carbon offset dimension in which carbon-polluting countries like the US and China make payments to less polluting countries, such as Vietnam, Zambia, and Papua New Guinea to "deposit" carbon in their forests. In some countries, local and Indigenous groups have objected to having their traditional lands and forests restricted to them, and have begun to organize in opposition to REDD+:

The UN "forest deal" [REDD+] jeopardizes the human future by serving to further entrench fossil fuel use – the major cause of the climate crisis – while at the same time failing to safeguard the future of forest and the rights of Indigenous Peoples and forest-dependent communities over their territories and knowledge. Further, there is a disregard from Northern countries to address the high levels of consumption in those countries as a driver of deforestation.[92]

Remote sensing of landcover is used to keep track of forests in REDD+ deposit countries, but the data do not reflect the gendered consequences of REDD+ forestry management regimes. The implementation of REDD+ policies have exposed women in particular to gradual resource loss and disrupted lifeways. In many traditional and developing settings, women use forests for gathering wild foods, medicines, and fuel wood; they often have deep knowledge of forest ecology that is intimately intertwined with gendered and cultural practices. Such women seldom have formal rights in natural resource governance, and so have little influence on large-scale national and international decisions over resources important to them and their communities.

The Tanzania Natural Resources Forum noted the gender inequalities faced by women in REDD+ projects:

[W]omen face wide discrimination, and are thus more vulnerable to bearing the costs of REDD and losing out on its benefits. Because of these and other differences, "gender-blind" PFM [participatory forest management] and REDD+ programmes can exacerbate existing inequalities and exclusions.[93]

Recognition of such gendered consequences of globally designed, locally implemented projects, have led the UN-REDD+ organization to recognize the need for "designing and implementing gender-responsive REDD+ strategies," though there are no currently-enforced guidelines, nor any clear plan for how to use technologies such as remote sensing to benefit women.[94]

The deforestation of poor countries caused by wealthy countries' hunger for meat, wood products, and land, as well as the incremental loss of access to forest resources by local communities, are examples of what one researcher calls "slow violence."[95] Environmental slow violence is not the spectacular devastation caused by a storm surge or wildfire; rather it is the incremental, almost invisible process of delayed destruction: global warming, soil erosion, ocean acidification, and bio-diversity loss. Because of its gradualness, slow violence is difficult to document, identify the causes of, or mobilize against. When slow violence results from science-informed global resource management policies such as the creation of conservation areas, watershed changes, or carbon sinks, both the men and women affected must adapt, move, or die. After all, it's no one's fault, they simply are the "unfortunate victims" of the invisible hand of coastal erosion, desertification, or salt water intrusion into farmland or drinking water supplies.

This recognition of inequalities in the global system brings us full circle to the melting Arctic and the Indigenous male and female descendants of some of the Inuit communities that supported the efforts of European and North American polar explorers a century ago. These Arctic men and women now face forced relocation resulting from the destruction of their homes, hunting grounds, and cultures by melting permafrost and coastal collapse, all legacies of a century of heroic empire.[96]

There have been some calls for a "reconstruction of climate science in which climate models and their projection maps [are] one form (among many) of technologically mediated, embodied, and situated knowledge about the climate."[97] Such a revised approach would include distinctions among "human" populations in order to understand the causes and impacts of climate change and to design mitigation and adaptation strategies. As one researcher argues:

> I make the case for feminist social research on climate change with the following argument: shedding light on the gender dimensions of climate change will enable a more accurate diagnosis and a more promising "cure" than is possible with a gender neutral approach. My argument is that any attempt to tackle climate change that excludes a gender analysis will be insufficient, unjust and therefore unsustainable.[98]

That said, most researchers, even those with an interest in addressing serious social problems arising from global climate change, remain gender blind. And even when they recognize that there are regional inequalities in climate change-related problems, they strongly prefer global-scale data and models despite their limited usefulness. A 2013 study of food security published in *Science* illustrates both researchers' preference for limited-utility global models and their disregard for gender as an important social variable. These researchers published results using large-scale global data, though they were fully aware of the need for "much finer resolution information."[99] They justified using their global models because "at much finer grid scales of 5 to 20 km there are even greater limits to the skill of predictive crop science than at the global level." They lamented the loss of important social information (e.g. economic, demographic, political, and social responses to climate change) when modeling with such macro-scale data, but seemed unaware of the role of "gender" in climate change adaptation:

> [Local data gathering] approaches tend to capture more adaptation capabilities than macro-models, such as asset-drawdown, job-switching, migration, social policy responses, and collective action for adaptation and assistance. But it is difficult to appropriately capture with micro-level studies the covariate risks of climate change that cut across broad regions.[100]

This study of food "security" provides a segue to our next chapter, where we explore another gendered aspect of science – its militarization – which is characterized, in part, by increasingly common descriptions of climate change as a security threat. Chapter 5 examines the extent of the US Department of Defense's funding of US science, and discusses some of the implications for climate change research resulting from this masculine militarization of science.

Notes

[1] For a broad set of feminist critiques emphasizing these and other masculinist characteristics of science, see Bartsch, Ingrid, and Muriel Lederman. 2000. *Gender and Science Reader*. New York: Routledge.

2 Israel, Andrei L., and Carolyn Sachs. 2012. "A Climate for Feminist Intervention: Feminist Science Studies and Climate Change." In Alston, M. and K. Whittenbury (eds.), *Research, Action and Policy: Addressing the Gendered Impacts of Climate Change.* Dortdrecht, Netherlands: Springer Netherlands, pp. 33–51.

3 Hart, David M., and David G. Victor. 1993. "Scientific Elites and the Making of US Policy for Climate Change Research, 1957–1974." *Social Studies of Science*, Vol. 23, No. 4:643–680; Backstrand, Karin. 2004. "Scientisation vs. Civic Expertise in Environmental Governance: Eco-feminist, Eco-modern and Post-modern Responses." *Environmental Politics*, Vol 13, No. 4:695–714; *The Economist*. 2013. "How Science Goes Wrong." *The Economist* (October 19). Accessed on August 3, 2014 at www.economist.com/news/leaders/21588069-scientific-research-has-changed-world-now-it-needs-change-itself-how-science-goes-wrong.

4 United Nations. 2013. "Gender and Climate Change." United Nations Framework Convention on Climate Change, Warsaw Conference of Parties (November 11–16). Accessed on August 3, 2014 at http://unfccc.int/resource/docs/2013/sbi/eng/l16.pdf; the Bixby Center on Population and Reproductive Health. 2014. "Invitation to Bring Gender to the Global Climate and Health Discussion – IPCC Report and Global Discussion." Accessed on August 3, 2014 at http://bixby.ucla.edu/2014/04/02/bixby-invitation-to-bring-gender-to-the-global-climate-and-health-discussion-ipcc-report-and-global-discussion-april-3rd/.

5 Holbrook, J. Brit. 2005. "Assessing the Science – Society Relation: The Case of the US National Science Foundation's Second Merit Review Criterion." *Technology in Society*, Vol. 27, No. 4:437–451; see also the articles in *Social Epistemology: A Journal of Knowledge, Culture and Policy*, Vol. 23, Nos. 3–4, 2009.

6 American Physical Society. 2007. "NSF's 'Broader Impacts' Criterion Gets Mixed Reviews." *APS News*, Vol. 16, No. 6. Accessed on August 3, 2014 at www.aps.org/publications/apsnews/200706/nsf.cfm.

7 Food and Agriculture Organization of the United Nations. 2001. "The Seed Sector and Food Security. Seed Production and Improvement: Assessment for the CEEC, CIS and Other Countries in Transition." Accessed on July 29, 2014 at ftp://ftp.fao.org/docrep/fao/005/y2722E/y2722E00.pdf; see also Okali, Christine, and Lars Otto Naess. 2013. "Making Sense of Gender, Climate Change and Agriculture in Sub-Saharan Africa: Creating Gender-Responsive Climate Adaptation Policy." *Future Agricultures*, Working Paper 057. Accessed on July 30, 2014 at www.future-agricultures.org/component/docman/doc_details/1727-making-sense-of-gender-climate-change-and-agriculture-in-sub-saharan-africa#.U9mYlvldXh4.

8 Raney, Terri, Gustavo Anriquez, Andre Croppenstedt, Stefano Gerosa, Sarah Lowder, Ira Matuscke, Jakob Skoet, and Cheryl Doss. 2011. "The Role of Women in Agriculture." Food and Agriculture Organization of the United Nations, ESA Working Paper No.11-02. Accessed on August 3, 2014 at www.fao.org/docrep/013/am307e/am307e00.pdf.

9   Gronski, Robert, and Leland Glenna. 2009. "The World Trade, Farm Policy and Agribusiness Accountability: The Role of Reflexive Modernization in Constructing a Democratic Food System." *Southern Rural Sociology*, Vol. 24, No. 2:130–148.

10 Lee, Jane J. 2013. "6 Women Scientists Who Were Snubbed Due to Sexism." *National Geographic Daily News* (May 19). Accessed on April 8, 2014 at http://news.nationalgeographic.com/news/2013/13/130519-women-scientists-overlooked-dna-history-science/?rptregcta=reg_free_np&rptregcampaign=20131016_rw_membership_n1p_us_se_w#finished; Sime, Ruth Lewin. 1997. *Lise Meitner: A Life in Physics*. Berkeley, CA: University of California Press; Maddox, Brenda. 2003. *Rosalind Franklin: The Dark Lady of DNA*. New York: Harper; Lear, Linda. 1997. *Rachel Carson: Witness for Nature*. New York: Henry Holt and Co.; Nobel Foundation. 1903. *The Nobel Prize in Physics: Marie Curie*. Accessed on April 9, 2014 at www.nobelprize.org/nobel_prizes/physics/laureates/1903/marie-curie-bio.html.

11 National Academy of Sciences. 2005. "Florence R. Sabin." Accessed on April 8, 2014 at www.nas.edu/history/members/sabin.html.

12 Notes and Records of the Royal Society of London. 1946. "Admission of Women into the Fellowship of the Royal Society." *Royal Society Journal of the History of Science* (April 1), Vol. 4, No. 1:39–40. Accessed on April 8, 2014 at http://rsnr.royalsocietypublishing.org/content/4/1/39.

13 For a discussion of the exclusionary history and contemporary state of affairs for women in science and engineering, see National Research Council. 2013. Committee on Women in Science, Engineering, and Medicine. Accessed on April 8, 2014 at http://sites.nationalacademies.org/PGA/cwsem/index.htm; McNutt, Marcia. 2013. "Leveling the Playing Field." *Science*, Vol. 341, No. 6144:317.

14 European Molecular Biology Organization. 2008. "Gender and Science." *EMBO Reports*, Vol. 9, No. 5:494–495.

15 Smith, Laurence C., and Scott R. Stephenson. 2013. "New Trans-Arctic Shipping Routes Navigable by Midcentury." *Proceedings of the National Academy of Sciences*, Vol. 110, No. 13:4855–4856.

16 Greenland is a semiautonomous country with colonial links to Denmark, so it is at present an observer state. Accessed on March 10, 2014 at www.arctic-council.org/index.php/en/.

17 Karner, Julie. 2006. *Roald Amundsen: The Conquest of the South Pole*. New York: Crabtree Publishing Company; Rear Admiral Robert E. Peary, US Navy. 1964. *Biographies in Naval History, Naval History and Heritage Command*. Accessed on March 10, 2014 at www.history.navy.mil/bios/peary_roberte.htm; Lansing, Alfred. 2014. *Endurance: Shackleton's Incredible Voyage*. New York: Basic Books.

18 Solomon, Susan. 2013. "To the Ends of the Earth: The Historic Age of Polar Exploration." *Scientific American*, January 17, 2013. Accessed on March 10, 2014 at www.scientificamerican.com/article/to-the-ends-of-the-earth-polar-exploration/; Maxtone-Graham, John. 2000. *Safe Return Doubtful: The Heroic Age of Polar Exploration*. London: Constable and Robinson; Wilkinson, Alec. 2013. *The Ice Balloon: SA Andree and the*

Heroic Age of Arctic Exploration. New York: Vintage; for a more critical view, see Pegg, Barry. 1993. "Nature and Nation and Popular Scientific Narratives of Polar Exploration." In McRae, M.W. (ed.), *The Literature of Science: Perspectives on Popular Scientific Writing*. Athens, GA: University of Georgia Press.

[19] In 2013, the "Shackleton Epic" team set out to re-create Ernest Shackleton's successful effort to reach help for his stranded crew. The trip was documented in a three-part US public television program, "Chasing Shackleton," aired in January 2013, and was chronicled in *Scientific American* magazine, see Solomon, op. cit.

[20] McGhee, Robert. 2007. *The Last Imaginary Place: A Human History of the Arctic World*. Chicago, IL: University of Chicago Press; Damas, David. 2002. *Arctic Migrants/Arctic Villagers: The Transformation of Inuit Settlement in the Central Arctic*. Montréal: McGill-Queen's University Press.

[21] Stefansson, Vilhjalmur. 1913. *My Life with the Eskimo*. New York: Macmillan Company; for a list of Stefansson's books and a summary of his life and travels, see Pálsson, Gísli. 2000. *The Legacy of Vilhjalmur Stefansson. The Arctic*. Accessed on March 12, 2014 at www.thearctic.is/PDF/G%C3%ADsli%20um%20 Vilj%C3%A1lm.pdf.

[22] Pálsson, 2000, op. cit.

[23] Stefansson, Vilhjalmur. 1964. *Discovery: The Autobiography of Vilhjalmur Stefansson*. New York: McGraw-Hill, p. 105.

[24] Pálsson, Gísli. 2003. *Travelling Passions: The Hidden Life of Vilhjalmur Stefansson*. Winnipeg, Canada: University of Manitoba Press.

[25] Henighan, Tom. 2009. *Vilhjalmur Stefansson: Arctic Adventurer*. Toronto: Dundurn; Pálsson, Gísli. 2004, "Race and the Intimate in Arctic Exploration," *Ethnos*, Vol. 69, No. 3:363–386; Pálsson, Gísli. 2008. "Hot Bodies in Cold Zones: Arctic Exploration." *The Scholar and Feminist Online*, Vol. 7, No. 1. Accessed on March 10, 2014 at http://sfonline.barnard.edu/ice/print_palsson.htm.

[26] For an illustrated discussion and literature review, see Roche, Rebecca. 2010. "Peary, Henson and their Inuit Women." Accessed on March 10, 2014 at http://eskimowives.blogspot.com/.

[27] Counter, S. Allen. 2002. *North Pole Legacy: Black, White, and Eskimo*. Montpelier, VT: Invisible Cities Press; Julien Staffan made a documentary film, *Prize of the Pole*, about the journey of Hivshu Peary (a.k.a. Robert E. Peary II), "to reconcile his ties to his great-grandfather." Accessed on March 11, 2014 at http://filmcatalog.nmai.si.edu/title/2337/; see also Erikson, Patricia Pierce. 2011. "Meet The Other Pearys." *Portland Monthly*, Winterguide. Accessed on March 11, 2014 at www.portlandmonthly.com/portmag/2010/12/meet-the-other-pearys/.

[28] Robinson, Michael. 2009. *The Coldest Crucible: Arctic Exploration and American Culture*. Chicago, IL: University of Chicago Press; for quote see Osher Map Library Exhibit, *The Pearys*. Accessed on March 10, 2014 at http://oshermaps.org/exhibitions/the-coldest-crucible/v-pearys; the Pearys' daughter's middle name, "Ahnighito," is an Inuit word referring to a large meteorite that had landed in Greenland thousands of years earlier; in what one researcher called "a

spectacular act of vandalism," after several attempts, Peary succeeded in removing the 30-ton meteorite, which had significant meaning and utility to local people, and the Pearys sold it to the American Museum of Natural History. See Mitchinson, John, and John Lloyd. 2010. *The Book of the Dead: Lives of the Justly Famous and the Undeservedly Obscure.* New York: Random House; see also Peary, Josephine. 1901. *The Snow Baby.* New York: Frederick A. Stokes Company; and Rizzo, Johnna. 2013. "Meteorite on Board." *National Geographic Daily News,* February 15. Accessed on March 11, 2014 at http://news.nationalgeographic.com/news/2013/13/pictures/130215-meteorite-earth-hit-science-space-peary-american-museum-natural-history/.

29 Woodman, Richard. 2004. *Arctic Convoys, 1941–1944.* London: John Murray; for a discussion of the transition of Arctic science from masculine heroic exploration to (still) male-dominated modern scientific methods and infrastructures, see Zeller, Suzanne, and Christopher Jacob Ries. 2014. "Wild Men in and Out of Science: Finding a Place in the Disciplinary Borderlands of Arctic Canada and Greenland." *Journal of Historical Geography,* Vol. 44 (April):31–43.

30 Russell, Edmund. 2001. *War and Nature: Fighting Humans and Insects with Chemicals from World War I to Silent Spring.* New York: Cambridge University Press; Pechura, Constance M. and David P. Rall. 1993. *Veterans at Risk: The Health Effects of Mustard Gas and Lewisite.* Washington, DC: National Academy Press.

31 Fleming, James Roger. 2010. *Fixing the Sky: The Checkered History of Weather and Climate Control.* New York: Columbia University Press; Conway, Erik M. 2007. "The World According to Garp: Scientific Internationalism and the Construction of Global Meteorology, 1961–1980." In Vining, Margaret and Barton C. Hacker, (eds.), *Science in Uniform, Uniforms in Science: Historical Studies of American Military and Scientific Interactions,* pp, 131–147. Lanham, MD: Scarecrow Press.

32 National Research Council. 2000. *Oceanography and Mine Warfare.* Washington, DC: National Academy Press. Accessed on March 17, 2014 at www.nap.edu/catalog.php?record_id=9773; Hamblin, Jacob D. 2005. *Oceanographers and the Cold War: Disciples of Marine Science.* Seattle, WA: University of Washington Press.

33 Baggott, Jim. 2009. *Atomic: The First War of Physics and the Secret History of the Atom Bomb: 1939–49.* London: Icon Books; Kevles, Daniel J. 1977. *The Physicists: The History of a Scientific Community in Modern America.* New York: Knopf; Fleming, James Rodger. 2011. "Iowa Enters the Space Age: James Van Allen, Earth's Radiation Belts, and Experiments to Disrupt Them." *The Annals of Iowa,* Vol. 70, No. 4:301–324.

34 Washington, M., M. Brown, T. Palys, S. Tyner, and R. Bowden. 2009. "Clinical Microbiology during the Vietnam War." *Military Medicine,* Vol. 174, No. 11:1209–1214; my thanks to Town Peterson for pointing out to me the military dimensions and history of microbiology.

35 Pearson, Alastair W. 2002. "Allied Military Model Making during World War II." *Cartography and Geographic Information Science,* Vol. 29, No. 3:227–241;

Palka, Eugene J. 2011. "Military Geography in the US: History Scope and Recent Developments." In Galgano, Francis, and Eugene J. Palka, (eds.), *Modern Military Geography*, pp. 5–20. New York: Routledge; La Rocque, Alex J. 2008. "The Role of Geography in Military Planning." *The Canadian Geographer*, Vol. 1, No. 3:69–72.

36   Guerlac, Henry E. 1987. *Radar in World War II*. New York: American Institute of Physics; Winkler, David F., and Julie L. Webster. 1997. *Searching the Skies: The Legacy of the United States Cold War Defense Radar Program*. Langley, VA: United States Air Force Air Combat Command. Accessed on March 17, 2014 at www.dtic.mil/dtic/tr/fulltext/u2/a331231.pdf; Buderi, Robert. 1996. *The Invention That Changed the World: How a Small Group of Radar Pioneers Won the Second World War and Launched a Technological Revolution*. New York: Simon & Schuster.

37   Leslie, Stuart W. 1993. *The Cold War and American Science: The Military-Industrial-Academic Complex at MIT and Stanford*. New York: Columbia University Press; Ferguson, Robert. G. 2007. "A New R&D Order: The Rise of Big Engineering in the Second World War." In Vining, Margaret and Barton C. Hacker, (eds.), *Science in Uniform, Uniforms in Science: Historical Studies of American Military and Scientific Interactions*, pp. 99–114. Lanham, MD: Scarecrow Press.

38   US Department of Defense. 2000. "Navy to Launch Oceanographic Survey Ship Mary Sears." Press Release No. 640-00 (October 18). Accessed on April 9, 2014 at www.defense.gov/releases/release.aspx?releaseid=2714; Howes, Ruth H., and Caroline L. Herzenber. 2003. *Their Day in the Sun: Women of the Manhattan Project*. Philadelphia, PA: Temple University; Felt, Hali. 2012. *Soundings: The Story of the Remarkable Woman Who Mapped the Ocean Floor*. New York: Henry Holt and Co.; Chiang, Tsai-chien. 2013. *Madame Chien-Shiung Wu: The First Lady of Physics Research*. New York: World Scientific Publishing Company.

39   Russell, op. cit.

40   *Under the Sea-Wind*. New York: Oxford University Press, 1941; *The Sea Around Us*. New York: Oxford University Press, 1951 (winner of the 1952 National Book Award); *The Edge of the Sea*. New York: Houghton-Mifflin, 1955.

41   Carson, Rachel. 1962. *Silent Spring*. New York: Houghton-Mifflin, pp. 7–8.

42   Ibid., p. 9.

43   McLaughlin, Dorothy. 1998. "Silent Spring Revisited." National Public Television, Frontline: *Fooling with Nature*. Accessed on March 4, 2014 at www.pbs.org/wgbh/pages/frontline/shows/nature/disrupt/sspring.html; Lear, Linda J. 1993. "Rachel Carson's 'Silent Spring'." *Environmental History Review*, Vol. 17, No. 2:23–48, p. 38.

44   Lear, op. cit., p. 37.

45   Vosburgh, John. 1962. "The Editorial Trail." *Audubon Magazine*, Vol. 64, No. 6:306.

46   Darby, William J. 1962. "Silence, Miss Carson." *Chemical & Engineering News* (October 1): 62–63, p. 62; my thanks to Edmund Russell for bringing this review to my attention.

[47] This image first came to my attention in an excellent discussion of the gendered reaction to *Silent Spring*: Hazlett, Maril. 2004. "'Woman vs. Man vs. Bugs': Gender and Popular Ecology in Early Reactions to Silent Spring." *Environmental History*, Vol. 9, No. 4:701–729; *Farm Chemicals*. 1963. Vol. 126, October. Courtesy of the Linda Hall Library of Science, Engineering and Technology, Kansas City, Missouri.

[48] Baldwin, Ira L. "Chemicals and Pests." *Science*, Vol. 137, No. 3535:1042–1043, p. 1043; for Baldwin's comments on his participation in biological weapons development, see "Ira Baldwin's Oral History," PBS, *American Experience*. Accessed on March 4, 2014 at www.pbs.org/wgbh/americanexperience/features/primary-resources/weapon-baldwin-oral-history/.

[49] President's Science Advisory Committee. 1963. *Use of Pesticides*. May 15. Accessed on March 4, 2014 at www.jfklibrary.org/Asset-Viewer/Archives/JFKPOF-087-003.aspx.

[50] Greenberg, Daniel S. 1963. "Pesticides: White House Advisory Body Issues Report Recommending Steps to Reduce Hazard to Public." Science, Vol. 140, No. 3569:878-879, p. 878.

[51] Hume, C.W. 1963. "An American Prophetess." *Nature*, Vol. 198, No. 4976:117.

[52] Weart, Spencer R. 2012. *The Rise of Nuclear Fear*. Cambridge, MA: Harvard University Press.

[53] Heberlein, Thomas A. 2012. *Navigating Environmental Attitudes*. New York: Oxford University Press.

[54] US Census Bureau. *Statistical Abstract of the United States*. 1963. Washington, DC: US Government Printing Office, Table 305, "Detailed Occupation of Employed Persons, by Sex: 1960," p. 232. Accessed on March 6, 2014 at www.census.gov/prod/www/statistical_abstract.html.

[55] Landivar, Liana Christin. 2013. "Disparities in STEM Employment by Race, Sex, and Hispanic origin." US Census Bureau, American Community Survey Reports, Table 3: Employment in STEM Disciplines, 2011. Accessed on March 6, 2014 at www.census.gov/prod/2013pubs/acs-24.pdf. For a breakdown by terminal degree (bachelor's, master's, and doctorate), see National Center for Science and Engineering Statistics. 2013. "Women, Minorities, and Persons with Disabilities in Science and Engineering." Table 9-5: Employed Scientists and Engineers, by Occupation, Highest Degree Level, and Sex: 2010. Accessed on March 25, 2014 at www.nsf.gov/statistics/wmpd/2013/sex.cfm. My thanks to Natalie Parker for helping me locate these data on women's participation in science, technology, engineering and mathematics (STEM) disciplines.

[56] Holmes, Mary Anne, Suzanne O'Connell, Connie Frey, and Lois Ongley. 2008. "Gender Imbalance in US Geoscience Academia." *Nature Geoscience*, Vol. 1, No. 2:79–82.

[57] American Geological Institute. 2009. *Status of the Geoscience Workforce*. "Report Summary," p. 12 and "Chapter 2: Four-Year Colleges and Universities," p. 2. Accessed on April 25, 2014 at www.americangeosciences.org/sites/default/files/2009-StatusReportSummary.pdf and www.americangeosciences.org/sites/default/files/2009-FourYrInstitutions_rev082509.pdf.

58 For an interesting and insightful discussion of the many factors produ-
    cing the underrepresentation of women in science, engineering, and tech-
    nology, see Hewlett, Sylvia Ann, Carolyn Buck Luce, Lisa J. Servon, Laura
    Sherbin, Peggy Shiller, Eytan Sosnovich, and Karen Sumberg. 2008. *The
    Athena Factor: Reversing the Brain Drain in Science, Engineering, and Technology.*
    Harvard Business Review Research Report. Accessed on April 25, 2014 at
    http://documents.library.nsf.gov/edocs/HD6060-.A84-2008-PDF-Athena
    -factor-Reversing-the-brain-drain-in-science,-engineering,-and-technology.
    pdf; see also "a timeline of sexist incidents in geek communities" from
    1973–2014 on the Geek Feminism Wiki. Accessed on April 25, 2014 at http://
    geekfeminism.wikia.com/wiki/Timeline_of_incidents.

59 Moss-Racusin, Corinne A., John F. Dovidio, Victoria L. Brescoll, Mark
    J. Graham, and Jo Handelsman. 2014. "Science Faculty's Subtle Gender
    Biases Favor Male Students." *Proceedings of the National Academy of
    Sciences* (early edition online). Accessed on March 7, 2014 at www.pnas.
    org/content/early/2012/09/14/1211286109.full.pdf; Correll, S.J. 2004.
    "Constraints into Preferences: Gender, Status, and Emerging Career
    Aspirations." *American Sociological Review*, Vol. 69, No. 1: 93–113; Hill,
    C., C. Corbett, and A. St. Rose. 2010. *Why So Few? Women in Science,
    Technology, Engineering, and Mathematics.* Washington, DC: AAUW.
    Accessed on March 7, 2014 at www.aauw.org/research/why-so-few/;
    National Academy of Sciences. 2007. *Beyond Bias and Barriers: Fulfilling
    the Potential of Women in Academic Science and Engineering.* Washington,
    DC: National Academies Press; Huang, G., N. Taddese, and E. Walter.
    2000. *Entry and Persistence of Women and Minorities in College Science and
    Engineering Education.* Washington, DC: US Department of Education,
    National Center for Education Statistics. Accessed on March 7, 2014 at
    https://nces.ed.gov/Pubsearch/pubsinfo.asp?pubid=2000601; Ecklund,
    Elaine Howard, Anne E. Lincoln, and Cassandra Tansey. 2012. "Gender
    Segregation in Elite Academic Science." *Gender and Society*, Vol. 26,
    No. 5:693–717.

60 Kilmartin, Christopher. 2005. "Depression in Men: Communication, Diagnosis
    and Therapy." *Journal of Men's Health and Gender*, Vol. 2, No. 1:95–99;
    Moller-Liemkuhler, Anne Maria. 2002. "Barriers to Help Seeking by Men: A
    Review of Sociocultural and Clinical Literature with Particular Reference to
    Depression." *Journal of Affective Disorders*, Vol. 71, No. 1:1–9.

61 Risberg, Gunilla, Eva E. Johansson, and Katarina Hamberg. 2009. "A
    Theoretical Model for Analyzing Gender Bias in Medicine." *International
    Journal for Equity in Health*, Vol. 8 (August). Accessed on March 6, 2014 at
    www.ncbi.nlm.nih.gov/pubmed/19646289?dopt=Abstract&holding=f1000,f10
    00m,isrctn.

62 Beery, Theresa. 1995. "Gender Bias in the Diagnosis and Treatment of
    Coronary Artery Disease." *Heart and Lung*, Vol. 24, No. 6:427–435, p. 427.

63 Ibid.; Ruiz, M. Teresa, and Lois M. Verbrugge. 1997. "A Two-Way View of
    Gender Bias in Medicine." *Journal of Epidemiology and Community Health*,
    Vol. 51, No. 2:106–109.

64   Vaccarino, Viola. 2006. "Angina and Cardiac Care: Are There Gender Differences, and If So, Why?" *Circulation*, Vol. 113, No. 4:467–469, p. 467; see also Holdcroft, Anita. 2007. "Gender Bias in Research: How Does It Affect Evidence-based Medicine?" *Journal of the Royal Society of Medicine*, Vol. 100, No. 1:2–3.

65   National Institutes of Health. 1994. "NIH guidelines on the inclusion of women and minorities as subjects in clinical research." Accessed on March 6, 2014 at http://grants2.nih.gov/grants/guide/notice-files/not94-100.html.

66   H.R. 1531: Breast Cancer Patient Protection Act of 2013. Accessed on March 6, 2014 at www.govtrack.us/congress/bills/113/hr1531.

67   Pinn, Vivian W. 2005. "Research on Women's Health: Progress and Opportunities." *Journal of the American Medical Association*, Vol. 294, No. 11:1407–1410.

68   Kent, Jennifer A., Vanisha Patel, and Natalie A. Varela. 2012. "Gender Disparities in Health Care." *Mount Sinai Journal of Medicine*, Vol. 79:555–559. Foulkes, Mary A. 2011. "After Inclusion, Information and Inference: Reporting on Clinical Trials Results After 15 Years of Monitoring Inclusion of Women." *Journal of Women's Health*, Vol. 20, No. 3: 829–836; Geller, Stacie E., Abby Koch, Beth Pellettieri, and Molly Carnes. 2011. "Inclusion, Analysis, and Reporting of Sex and Race/Ethnicity in Clinical Trials: Have We Made Progress?" *Journal of Women's Health*, Vol. 20, No. 3:315–320; Bird, Chloe E., Allen Fremont, Mark Hanson. 2014. *Mapping Gender Differences in Cardiovascular Disease and Diabetes Care*. Rand Corporation. Accessed on March 17, 2014 at www.rand.org/pubs/research_reports/RR539.html; Cahill, Larry. 2014. "Fundamental Sex Difference in Human Brain Architecture." *Proceedings of the National Academy of Sciences*, Vol. 111, No. 2:577–578.

69   O'Lear, Shannon. 2015. "Climate Silence and Slow Violence: A View from Political Geography and STS on Mobilizing Technoscientific Ontologies of Climate Change." *Political Geography*, Vol. 48 (October):1–10.

70   Tuana, Nancy. 2013. "Gendering Climate Knowledge for Justice: Catalyzing a New Research Agenda." In Alston and Whittenbury, op. cit., pp. 17–31; Harding, Sandra. 1991. *Whose Science? Whose Knowledge? Thinking from Women's Lives*, Ithaca, NY: Cornell University Press; Haraway, Donna J. 1991. *Simians, Cyborgs and Women: The Reinvention of Nature*. New York: Routledge.

71   Singer, Fred. 1992. "Warming Theories Need a Warning Label." *Bulletin of the Atomic Scientists* (June):34–39'; Taylor, James. 2013. "Peer-Reviewed Survey Finds Majority of Scientists Skeptical of Global Warming Crisis." *Forbes* (February 13). Accessed on April 9, 2014 at www.forbes.com/sites/jamestaylor/2013/02/13/peer-reviewed-survey-finds-majority-of-scientists-skeptical-of-global-warming-crisis/.

72   Demeritt, David. 1998. "Science, Social Constructivism and Nature." In Braun, B., and N. Castree (eds.), *Rethinking Reality: Nature and the Millennium*. New York: Routledge, pp. 173–193, p. 175.

73   Intergovernmental Panel on Climate Change (IPCC). 2007. "Frequently Asked Question 8.1: How Reliable Are the Models Used to Make Projections of Future Climate Change?" In Solomon, S., D. Qin, M. Manning, Z. Chen, M. Marquis, K.B. Averyt, M.Tignor, and H.L. Miller (eds.), *Climate Change 2007: The Physical Science Basis. Contribution of*

Working Group I to the Fourth Assessment Report of the Intergovernmental Panel on Climate Change. Cambridge: Cambridge University Press, pp.117–118.

74 IPCC. 2014. "Summary for Policymakers." *Climate Change 2014: Impacts, Adaptation, and Vulnerability.* Accessed on April 1, 2014 at http://ipcc-wg2. gov/AR5/report/final-drafts/; AR5 Working Group II's "Technical Summary" also references "women" and "gender," but the terms appear fewer than a dozen times in the 70-page document; again the emphasis is on "human" impacts, adaptation, and vulnerability.

75 European Molecular Biology Organization, op. cit.

76 MacGregor, Sherilyn. 2010. "A Stranger Silence Still: The Need for Feminist Social Research on Climate Change." *Sociological Review,* Vol. 57, No. s2:124–140.

77 Cudworth, Erika, and Stephen Hobden. 2011. "Beyond Environmental Security: Complex Systems, Multiple Inequalities and Environmental Risks." *Environmental Politics,* Vol. 20, No. 142–159, p. 46; see also Salleh, Ariel. 2009. "Ecological Debt: Embodied Debt." In Salleh, A. (ed.), *Eco-sufficiency and Global Justice: Women Write Political Ecology.* London: Pluto Press, Chapter 1. Accessed on May 21, 2014 at www.womin.org.za/images/the-alternatives/ ecofeminism-social-reproduction-theory/A%20Salleh%20-%20Ecological%20 Debt%20is%20Embodied%20Debt.pdf.

78 Cohen, Marjorie Griffin. 2014. "Gendered Emissions: Counting Greenhouse Gas Emissions by Gender and Why It Matters." *Alternate Routes: A Journal of Critical Social Research,* Vol. 25, No. 1:55–80; see also Spitzner, Mieke. 2009. "How Global Warming Is Gendered: A View from the EU." In Salleh, op. cit., pp. 218–229.

79 Johnsson-Latham, Gerd. 2007. *A Study in Gender Equality as a Prerequisite for Sustainable Development: What We Know about the Extent to Which Women Globally Live in a More Sustainable Way Than Men, Leave a Smaller Ecological Footprint and Cause Less Climate Change.* Report to the Environment Advisory Council, Ministry of the Environment. Sweden. Accessed on April 9, 2014 at www.gendercc.net/fileadmin/inhalte/Dokumente/Actions/ ecological_footprint__johnsson-latham.pdf.

80 Ibid., pp. 68–72.

81 MacGregor, op. cit., p. 135; the EcoMom Alliance (accessed on April 10, 2014 at https://www.facebook.com/EcoMomAlliance) is not to be confused with the commercial EcoMom.com (accessed on April 10, 2014 at www.ecomom. com/).

82 Polakovic, Gary. 2012. "Are Women Greener than Men?" *Los Angeles Times* (June 13). Accessed on April 9, 2014 at http://articles.latimes.com/2012/ jun/13/opinion/la-oe-polakovic-gender-and-the-environment-20120613; see also Alber, Gtelind. 2009. "Gender and Climate Change Policy." In Guzmán, José Miguel, George Martine, Gordon McGranahan, Daniel Schensul, and Cecilia Tacoli (eds.), *Population Dynamics and Climate Change.* New York: United Nations Population Fund and International Institute for Environment and Development, pp. 149–163, p. 159.

83 *New Scientist.* 2007. "Are Men to Blame for Global Warming?" Vol. 196, No. 2629:4.

[84] Banerjee, Damayanti, and Michael Mayerfeld Bell. 2007. "Ecogender: Locating Gender in Environmental Social Science." *Society and Natural Resources: An International Journal*, Vol. 20, No. 1:3–19.

[85] Giddens, Anthony. 2009. *The Politics of Climate Change*. London: Polity Press; MacGregor, op. cit., p. 125.

[86] Wildcat, Daniel R. 2009. *Red Alert: Saving the Planet with Indigenous Knowledge*. Golden, CO: Fulcrum Publishing.

[87] Litfin, Karen T. 1997. "The Gendered Eye in the Sky: A Feminist Perspective on Earth Observation Satellites." *Frontiers: A Journal of Women's Studies*, Vol. 18, No. 2:26–47, p. 30.

[88] Litfin, op. cit., p. 39.

[89] Mies, Maria, and Vandana Shiva. 1993. *Ecofeminism*. London: Zed Books, p. 47; for a discussion of ecofeminist approaches and an admonition against essentialist assumptions about women as universal environmentalists, see MacGregor, Sherilyn. 2006. *Beyond Mothering Earth: Ecological Citizenship and the Politics of Care*. Vancouver: University of British Columbia Press.

[90] Bachram, Heidi. 2004. "Climate Fraud and Carbon Colonialism: The New Trade in Greenhouse Gases." *Capitalism, Nature, Socialism*, Vol. 15, No. 4: 1–16; Agarwal, Anil and Sunita Narain. 1991. *Global Warming in an Unequal World: A Case of Environmental Colonialism*. New Delhi: Center for Science and Environment.

[91] United Nations. 2014. *UN-REDD Programme*. Accessed on April 10, 2014 at www.un-redd.org/.

[92] Durban Group for Climate Justice. 2010. *Durban Statement on REDD*. Accessed on April 10, 2014 at www.durbanclimatejustice.org/press-releases/durban-statement-on-redd.html.

[93] International Union for Conservation of Nature. 2014. "Gender Equality within the REDD and REDD-plus Framework." Accessed on April 10, 2014 at www.tnrf.org/genderreport.pdf, p. 1.

[94] UN-REDD Programme. 2011. "Designing and Implementing Gender-Responsive REDD+ Strategies." *UN-REDD Programme Newsletter*, No. 21 (August). Accessed on April 10, 2014 at www.un-redd.org/Newsletter21/Gender_Responsive_REDD_Strategies/tabid/54807/Default.aspx.

[95] Nixon, Rob. 2011. *Slow Violence and the Environmentalism of the Poor*. Cambridge, MA: Harvard University Press.

[96] Cochran, Patricia, Orville H. Huntington, Caleb Pungowiyi, Stanley Tom, F. Stuart Chapin III, Henry P. Huntington, Nancy G. Maynard, and Sarah F. Trainor. 2013. "Indigenous Frameworks for Observing and Responding to Climate Change in Alaska." *Climatic Change*, Vol. 120, No. 3:557–567; Whyte, Kyle Powys. 2014. "Indigenous Women, Climate Change Impacts, and Collective Action." *Hypatia*, Vol. 29, No. 3; see also US National Climate Assessment. 2014. "Indigenous Peoples." Accessed on June 16, 2014 at http://nca2014.globalchange.gov/highlights/report-findings/indigenous-peoples.

[97] Israel, Andrei L., and Carolyn Sachs. 2013. "A Climate for Feminist Intervention: Feminist Science Studies and Climate Change." In Alston, M. and

K. Whittenbury (eds.), *Research Action and Policy: Assessing Impacts of Climate Change*. London: Springer, p. 43.

[98]   MacGregor, op. cit., p. 124.

[99]   Wheeler, Tim, and Joachim von Braun. 2013. "Climate Change Impacts on Global Food Security." *Science*, Vol. 341, No. 6145:508–513.

[100]   Ibid., p. 510.

5
GENDER AND THE MILITARY-SCIENCE COMPLEX

In this chapter, we will focus on the longstanding relationship between two historically gendered institutions: science and the military. As we saw in Chapter 4, until very recently science has been the almost exclusive domain of men, and thus has been shaped by men's interests and agendas. No institution is more masculine than the military, with its historically male-dominated personnel, strict codes of honor, rigid hierarchical authority structure, and manly values of strength, bravery, toughness, patriotism, and heterosexual virility. As the last chapter briefly noted, military funding and collaboration have been critical to the historical development of many scientific and engineering fields, such as chemistry, biology, physics, aerospace engineering, and electrical engineering. This chapter focuses on the ongoing intimate liaison between US science and the US Department of Defense. Our goals are to understand the extent of the military funding of scientific research and the implications of this support for shaping climate change research. Of special interest is the connection between military men and men of science. We ask how military funding interacts with the male overrepresentation in climate-related sciences to shape particular aspects of climate change science. Some of the consequences of militarized climate science include a disinterest in the gendered dimensions of climate change, a fascination with large-scale interventions into the global climate system, and the increasing characterization of climate change as a "national security" problem. The first half of this chapter will map several past and present features of the US military-science complex, and will show how the United States compares to other countries in the extent of the military funding of science. The second half of the chapter focuses specifically on the influence of the militarization of US science on US climate change research.

Masculinity and the Military Support of Science[1]

Gender cultures are deeply ingrained. When I teach undergraduate sociology classes, I often ask students to name the most offensive non-racial name they can be called. Male students typically report names that imply weakness, girlishness, or homosexuality; female students typically report names that imply bossiness or sexual promiscuity. When I ask students if they'd mind being called the other gender's insulting name, they laugh: males think it's funny to be called sluts, and females don't blink at being called cowards. I've conducted this informal natural experiment for over 30 years, and the results haven't changed. These consistently gendered responses explain to me why it is mostly men who line up for combat service in most wars, and why those who don't answer the "call of duty" can be ostracized as traitors and weaklings. There is nothing comparable for women in political culture. Women may be citizens, but they are seldom considered patriots. Both women and men are brought up according to a gender "aesthetic" that determines what "feels" feminine or masculine.[2] Gender aesthetics can vary by time, place, race, or class, but dominant or "hegemonic" femininity and masculinity have a persistent, powerful moral gravitational pull on women and men.[3] The contemporary US "national style of manhood" reflects the combined allure of patriotism, manliness, and duty.[4] This is a powerful mix that extends beyond those in uniform and is recognized by both women and men. As a result, when men in science are called upon to serve men in war, they quite often do so willingly and enthusiastically. To do less would be treason.[5]

The gender socialization of many male climate scientists and engineers articulates very well with the prestige and power of the US Department of Defense (DOD), and they have a blind spot when it comes to the military funding of science.[6] Researchers who consider themselves progressive, non-militaristic, or even critical of US military undertakings (such as the Vietnam War or the invasion of Iraq), seldom think twice when it comes to accepting DOD funding – as long as it does not violate their personal ethics. They fail to recognize their role in supporting and legitimating the overall US military mission by participating in it; they are simply funding their research.

Even social scientists, the least likely to be funded by military agencies, can set aside misgivings when defense funding is available. In 2013, I interviewed a social scientist about the decision to accept funding from the US Department of Defense Minerva Initiative for a project on a nonmilitary topic of long-standing interest to the researcher.[7] I asked, "Why did you include a section of the proposal on political instability, civil war, and violence?" The researcher's response was, "Well, I'm not really interested in that, but I thought they would be." The proposal's section on violent political conflicts was only a part of the larger research project, but the project's design, data collection, data analysis, and the research team's time and effort would have to be adjusted to appeal to its military sponsors.[8] The addition of the political violence section was not obsequious servility on the part of the researcher; the Minerva funding program required researchers to indicate their project's "impact on DoD capabilities and broader implications for national defense."[9]

In my interviews with natural scientists and engineers, many had received DOD funding, and most said they would accept it. I was told of only three conditions under which DOD funding would be declined: if the research was weapons-related, if the results could not be published, or if the project involved tracking individuals. There is another condition under which many scientists and engineers seem willing to take the DOD's funding: plausible deniability. The author of *Wired for War: The Robotics Revolution and Conflict in the 21st Century* commented about the disingenuousness of some academic researchers regarding the war-making relevance of their "basic" research:

> At the end of the day people need to remember what the D in DARPA [a DOD R&D funding program] stands for. It stands for Defense … Too often scientists try and kid themselves … [They] act like just because I work on this system that is not directly a weapon system I have nothing to do with war … [A researcher who was] working on a Navy contract on a robot that would play baseball [said] "I don't have anything to do with war." Come on. You think the Navy is funding this because they want a better Naval Academy baseball team?" … tracking and intercepting a fly ball could be analogous to tracking and intercepting a missile.[10]

DOD funding matters for another reason that was not on the exclusion list of any of the researchers I interviewed, nor does it appear in the literature on the ethics of military funding: the consistently-reported inefficiency and corruption of the DOD in many or most of its missions. Study after study has shown that the US Department of Defense mismanages its budget, misplaces billions of dollars, and misuses the public trust.[11] Disclosures of DOD's fiscal fecklessness raise serious questions about the wisdom of putting the country's scientific fortunes in the hands of an organization with a militaristic agenda and a dismal track record of spending wisely.

Data are not available for much DOD-funded scientific research, and even when research is unclassified, it is difficult to gather systematic information on what and who are being funded by the dozens of DOD initiatives. Classified research is even more impenetrable and creates a career dilemma for researchers whose work is shrouded from their peers. Publishing research findings is important for the open flow of scientific information, replicability of results, and the advancement of knowledge. It is also critical to building the reputations of scientists, and thus creates a conundrum for those who choose to conduct classified research: where to publish? The answer: classified or "dark" journals such as the *Journal of Sensitive Cyber Research and Engineering*, which asks its authors "to provide titles and abstracts that don't have to be kept secret, so the journal can appear in public indexes."[12]

Two of the more accessible DOD funding programs for university faculty are the Defense Advanced Research Projects Agency (DARPA) and the Minerva Initiative.[13] The goal of the Minerva Initiative, established in 2008, is "to improve DoD's basic understanding of the social, cultural, behavioral, and political forces that shape regions of the world of strategic importance to the US."[14] During the period 2009–2015, the Minerva Initiative funded 72 social science research projects, and all of the projects focused on military concerns. For instance, 56 (78 percent) of the project titles contained words such as "military," "stability," "threat," "conflict," "terrorism," "violence," "crisis," "extremism," "defense," "disruption," "destruction," "security," "war," and "weapons," and all project abstracts indicated that some aspect of the project had to do with political conflict, instability, or threat.[15] Although women constitute more than 60 percent of social scientists, only 19 (26 percent) of the 61 Minerva lead Principal Investigators (PIs) were women. This gender imbalance reflects the broader appeal of security-related, military-funded projects to male investigators, even in the social sciences.

Unlike Minerva, which targets social scientists, DARPA, established in 1958, has a more natural science and engineering agenda. The goal of DARPA is "to prevent strategic surprise from negatively impacting US national security and create strategic surprise for US adversaries by maintaining the technological superiority of the US military."[16] DARPA's Young Faculty Award (YFA) program's goal is "to identify and engage rising stars in junior faculty positions at US academic institutions … [e]arly in their careers so they may develop their research ideas in the context of DoD needs."[17] During the period 2010–2014, DARPA granted 175 Young Faculty Awards. Awardee projects reflected the technical nature of their research and are less easily identifiable as defense-related ("applied algebraic topology," "a planar thermal diode," "photons in gauge fields"), although some topics offer clues to their defense-related utility ("looking around corners using transient imaging," "autonomous robots," "jet fuel production from biomass-derived lignin remote locations").[18] Women constitute a minority of scientists and engineers working in the fields funded by the DARPA YFA program, and 31 women constitute 18 percent of YFA recipients. The small number of women in DARPA's "rising star" program provides further evidence of the special appeal of DOD research priorities and funding to male researchers (and perhaps the special appeal of male researchers to the DOD).

If a researcher, male or female, simply adds a section or frames a proposal to satisfy a funding agency, military or not, does it matter much to the outcome of the research? This question suggests one of Thomas Pynchon's famous proverbs for paranoids: "If they can get you asking the wrong questions, they don't have to worry about answers."[19] In the case of DARPA's YFA program, the goal is to mold the career of new scientists and engineers to fit DOD's agenda and needs. But not all DOD funding programs are dedicated to recalibrating the trajectory of a researcher's entire career or even to reshaping an entire research project. So what does it matter if a researcher accepts military funding? Studies of gift giving and indebtedness suggest that it matters quite a bit. Researchers have found that recipients of even a single grant are quite likely to feel an obligation to the funding source.[20] Funders' influence on research was documented in a 2002 survey of 3247 early and midcareer scientists who had received funding from the US National Institutes of Health (NIH): 15.5 percent reported that they changed the research design, methodology, or results of a study in response to pressure from a funding source (not necessarily NIH).[21]

The majority of published studies of funders' influence on scientific research have focused on various aspects of medicine. In a 2005 study of bias in research funded by private companies, researchers compared the results of studies of the effectiveness of treatments and drugs funded by for-profit organizations with the results of studies funded by nonprofit foundations or government agencies. They found that two-thirds of for-profit funded studies favored newer treatments or drugs, whereas fewer than half of nonprofit or government-funded studies favored newer treatment or drugs.[22] A 2007 review of research on the health effects of commonly-consumed beverages found that no study receiving industry funding reported unfavorable conclusions compared to 37 percent of non-industry funded studies.[23] Researchers summarized their findings: "Industry funding of nutrition related scientific articles may bias conclusions in favor of sponsors' products, with potentially significant implications for public health."[24] Both researchers and practitioners are vulnerable to bias stemming from the "gift effect." Physicians' treatment and prescribing behavior has been shown to be influenced by pharmaceutical industry gifts, samples, meals, conference travel, honoraria, and research funding, leading researchers to conclude that "The present extent of physician-industry interactions appears to affect prescribing and professional behavior and should be further addressed at the level of policy and education."[25]

These and other concerns about the influence of the pharmaceutical industry on research and medical practice were heightened in 2004 when Merck & Co.'s prescription arthritis pain drug Vioxx (rofecoxib) was linked to heart attack and stroke and withdrawn from the market. Merck had funded the VIGOR (Vioxx Gastrointestinal Outcomes Research) study of Vioxx's safety and efficacy, which was published in the prestigious *New England Journal of Medicine.* The withdrawal of the drug generated apologies and recriminations about the review process, misrepresentation and omission of data, and editorial lapses at the journal.[26] In 2008, the pharmaceutical industry organization, PhRMA, issued a code of ethics designed to reassure doctors, patients, and regulators; this was followed by several pharmaceutical companies who began publishing information on their payments to doctors and other health professionals for promotional talks, research, and consulting.[27] The Physician Payments Sunshine Act, part of the 2010 federal Affordable Care Act, requires some reporting of drug company payments to physicians working with federal health insurance programs, but the funding of research and payments to doctors by pharmaceutical companies remains largely voluntarily disclosed and unregulated.[28]

Like medical industry funding, DOD funding has the capacity to set research priorities and shape scientific inquiry, influencing the research questions, data collected, conclusions reached, and/or findings reported. Unlike the aura associated with most industries, DOD funding reflects the luster of militarized masculinity, with its appeal to the disproportionately male membership in most natural sciences and all engineering fields. Research for the national defense invokes a patriotic and gendered ethos which encourages scientists, especially male scientists, to defer to or embrace DOD goals, allowing defense agencies to influence their research agendas.

Studies of organizational culture, including the culture of science, show that both men and women are influenced by the norms and expectations of organizations in which they work.[29] Both female and male natural scientists and engineers are trained and work in a scientific and professional culture that accepts, even embraces, military funding of research. Because of their upbringing and their socialization to norms of masculinity, however, men tend to be more easily influenced by the prestige and power of the military and the authority of men in uniform than, say, women.[30] As a result, in scientific fields dominated by men, such as climate change science, we should expect to see reflections of masculine, military organizational culture and interests, especially when DOD missions and funding are involved.

The Military Funding of US Science and Engineering

If DOD funding matters for managing and mismanaging limited research resources and potentially distorting or even militarizing funded researchers' scientific agenda, then how much of the US scientific research budget actually comes from the DOD? Table 5.1 shows federal funding of Research and Development (R&D) by agency for the 2012 (actual), 2013 (estimated), and 2014 (Conference Committee recommended) fiscal years (FY).[31] Only agencies with R&D budgets over $2.5 million are included in the table.

We can see from this table that defense R&D exceeded nondefense R&D in all three years, and the DOD received far more federal basic research funding than any other agency. During the 2012–2014 period, half of federal research funding went to the DOD. Other defense-related R&D funding, such as the Department of Energy's Atomic Energy Defense program, completed the US defense R&D total listed at the bottom of the table. The table divides DOD basic research funding

Table 5.1 Federal Research and Development Funding by Agency, 2012–2014[32] (in Millions of Dollars)

	FY2012	FY2013	FY2014
Department of Defense	**74,460**	**68,063**	**66,095**
Science & Technology*	*13,330*	*12,712*	*13,737*
All other DOD R&D	*61,130*	*55,325*	*52,357*
Department of Energy	**10,811**	**10,027**	**11,820**
Atomic Energy Defense	*4257*	*3914*	*4713*
Office of Science	*4463*	*4231*	*4662*
Energy Programs	*2091*	*1882*	*2445*
NASA	**11,315**	**10,566**	**11,708**
National Science Foundation	**5705**	**5510**	**5844**
Health & Human Services	**31,375**	**29,667**	**30,734**
Defense R&D	78,717	71,950	70,808
Nondefense R&D	63,804	60,794	65,395

* DOD Science & Technology includes 6.1 (basic research), 6.2 (applied research), and 6.3 (advanced technology programs)[33]

into two categories: "Science & Technology" (6.1, 6.2, and 6.3) and "All other R&D."[34] The "All other R&D" category represented 79 percent of DOD research funds in FY2014 and mainly supports military mission-related research activities (developing software and hardware for weapon systems, war-related technologies, and the like).[35] As Table 5.1 shows, Health and Human Services (HHS) had the largest nondefense R&D budget in all years; HHS spends 95.6 percent of its R&D funding to support the NIH and their mainly medical research. NASA and the Department of Energy (DOE) ranked 3rd and 4th respectively in federally funded R&D and both fund defense-related projects.

Military Funding and the National Science Foundation

The smallest amount of major federal R&D funding in Table 5.1 is allocated to the National Science Foundation (NSF), whose mission is the widest-ranging of the agencies – to support basic research in all of the sciences, mathematics, and engineering. Despite this broad portfolio, in 2014 the NSF received only 4.3 percent of all federal R&D funding, and only 8.9 percent of nondefense R&D funding. This low level of funding compared to other agencies is notable and odd, since NSF is considered the gold standard of peer-reviewed excellence in US science and engineering. The NSF's highly-respected peer review system's main criteria for funding are scientific merit and broader impacts, and its emphasis is on supporting pathbreaking research that is considered to be "transformative."[36] The NSF funds only one in five of the proposals it receives. In 2013, the NSF received 49,013 research proposals and made 10,844 awards (a funding rate of 22 percent). The median annual award amount was $116,554.[37] These figures add up to a small and very competitive amount of support for nondefense research awarded by the most prestigious science funding agency in the United States.

As Table 5.1 shows, in 2014, the DOD's Science and Technology basic research budget ($13.737 billion) was 2.4 times greater than the NSF's basic research budget ($5.844 billion). The NSF's comparatively modest funding must be available to researchers investigating a broad array of topics in science and engineering, whereas DOD has a specific mission to fund only projects related to defense and national security. NSF's motto, "Where Discoveries Begin," celebrates its emphasis on research conducted for the sake of advancing knowledge.[38] Despite its broad research portfolio, motto embracing basic scientific discovery, and the relatively limited amount of research funding it can award for nondefense basic science, the NSF is also involved in defense-related research activities. As it turns out, that involvement was decreed in the legislation that established the NSF at the height of the Cold War. The US 81st Congress enacted the National Science Foundation Act of 1950, "To promote the progress of science; to advance the national health, prosperity, and welfare; *to secure the national defense*; and for other purposes" [italics added].[39] The NSF was directed by the act to initiate and support basic research and educate students in the sciences and engineering, foster the international interchange of scientific information, and initiate and support national defense scientific research activities at the request of the Secretary of Defense.[40]

Although the majority of its awards are for non-defense-related research, the NSF remains part of the US military-science complex. For instance, the NSF works with the US Departments of Defense and Homeland Security on jointly-funded initiatives and logistical support, especially in polar research.[41] Beginning in 2003, the DOD co-funded the NSF's ASSURE (Awards to Stimulate and Support Undergraduate Research Experiences) program "To support particular REU [Research Experiences for Undergraduates] sites that focus on research relevant to DOD's interests."[42] All of the nearly 60 REU projects listed on the ASSURE website are in the natural sciences and engineering, but the DOD-NSF collaboration also extends to funding social science research. In 2008 the NSF signed a Memorandum of Understanding (MOU) with the DOD to:

> allow researchers to apply for grants to study subjects that may be of interest to US national security. Officials anticipate the MOU will fund work leading to new knowledge about topics such as religious fundamentalism, terrorism and cultural change. The results may have uses for US armed forces and other DoD agencies.[43]

These agreements are consistent with the NSF's founding charter, and despite its apolitical focus on advancing knowledge by funding high-quality basic science, the NSF's budget frequently is held hostage by politicians with a partisan agenda. For instance, in 2014, Senator Tom Coburn (R-Oklahoma) introduced an amendment to federal funding legislation that prohibited NSF funding for political science projects unless the NSF director certified "projects as vital to national security or the economic interests of the United States."[44] In 2015 another assault on NSF research unpopular among conservatives, the America COMPETES Act, proposed a 45 percent cut in NSF Social, Behavioral, and Economic Sciences, and an 8 percent cut in NSF's Geosciences; the latter funds a good deal of climate change research. Both legislative proposals were revised, but like all political bargains, everyone stands to gain something in the process. The NSF-DOD collaboration benefits both the DOD and the NSF. It allows US defense and security agencies to gain the legitimacy of the NSF's prestige as a discerning judge of world-class science (most DOD awards are not peer reviewed), and the NSF gains cover from the critical eyes of some in Congress bent on reducing its funding. In order to protect themselves from the NSF's sometimes too-high standards, defense and security agencies reserve the right to in-house review and fund some projects even when collaborating with NSF. The NSF turns a blind eye and expands its budget while doing the bidding of the DOD and Department of Homeland Security (DHS) and affirming the goal of science in the service of national security.

The sanguinity of Science about military funding of research projects was evident when the leading science journal, *Nature*, referred to one major NSF-DOD collaboration as a "win-win" for the funding of science.[45] This mainly natural science journal lectured in its pages to social scientists who showed less than full-throated enthusiasm about the offer of military collaboration:

> Social scientists ... should embrace the opportunities that the AAA [American Anthropological Association] pointed out last November in a report on engagement with the military. These include studying military and intelligence organizations from the inside and educating the military about other cultures and societies.[46]

The AAA was restrained in its response to military funding "opportunities," stressing instead both "the opportunities and risks to those anthropologists choosing to engage with the work of the military, security, and intelligence arenas ... We advise careful analysis of specific roles, activities, and institutional contexts of engagement."[47]

Controversies Surrounding the Military Funding of Science

DOD funding does not appear to be a source of much debate in the natural sciences and engineering, but this complacency is not typical of the social sciences. Even though there are some social scientists funded by the DOD, military funding is a much more contentious issue in their disciplines. Most social scientists I spoke with said they would not seek or accept DOD funding for their research. This reticence about DOD funding is, if my arguments here about men and militarization hold, in part a reflection of the greater proportion of women in the social sciences. That said, misgivings about DOD funding of research among social scientists pale when it comes to the issue of social and behavioral scientists' direct participation in the military's own research and activities. In 2005 the American Psychological Association's (APA) Report of the Presidential Task Force on Psychological Ethics and National Security (PENS Report) endorsed psychologists' participation in detainee interrogations (a practice which was opposed by the American Medical Association and the American Psychiatric Association).[48] A coalition of professional and public interest organizations and 2400 individuals signed a petition calling for the report's annulment.[49] The APA spoke strongly against its previous position in December, 2014, when the US Senate's Select Committee on Intelligence issued critical and discrediting findings in a report about the Central Intelligence Agency's (CIA) detention and interrogation program during the George W. Bush administration: "The new details provided by the report regarding the extent and barbarity of torture techniques used by the CIA are sickening and morally reprehensible."[50]

At least as much disciplinary disagreement surrounds the US Army's Human Terrain System (HTS) program, which "develops, trains, and integrates a social science based research and analysis capability to support operationally relevant decision-making, to develop a knowledge base, and to enable sociocultural understanding across the operational environment."[51] The HTS practice of embedding anthropologists in military units generated accusations of "weaponizing anthropology," and motivated the AAA to issue a statement expressing its official disapproval of the HTS program:

> The Executive Board of the American Anthropological Association concludes (i) that the HTS program creates conditions which are likely to place anthropologists in positions in which their work will be in violation of the AAA Code of Ethics and (ii) that its use of anthropologists poses a danger to both other anthropologists and persons other anthropologists study.[52]

Reports of sexual abuse directed against female HTS anthropologists by their male HTS and armed forces colleagues generated an official

Army "climate survey" of the program to investigate race and gender discrimination as well as complaints involving national origin discrimination. As one female HTS member reported:

> Sexual harassment is prevalent and sexist behavior is an everyday occurrence; I was sexually harassed in the field repeatedly; sexual comments and jokes are rampant; nearly every female in the program faces some form of sexual harassment.[53]

Sexual harassment of women HTS members by US Army personnel is part of a well-documented and extensive pattern of sexual harassment of women service personnel in the US armed services.[54] The semi-civilian status of HTS women anthropologists apparently did not insulate them from the masculinist military culture of sexual abuse.

The African Studies Association also has been the site of a flare-up over DOD funding of academic programs and research. African Studies is part of a network of international area studies and language programs initiated during the Cold War and originally funded under the US National Defense Education Act of 1958. Title VI language and area studies programs and National Resource Centers are now managed by the Department of Education (DOE).[55] Since DOE funding has declined for these programs in the last few decades, and as the African continent has become more strategically important in the post-9/11 global milieu, some Africanists are questioning the wisdom of accepting expanded funding from the DOD's National Security Education Program (NSEP) to support language and area studies.[56] Part of the debate centers on the implications of NSEP funding for "militarizing African studies."[57]

Even in disciplines, such as geography, with long-standing involvement in military planning and campaigns, researchers and their work can become targets of criticism over military funding. A geography research project that recently came under fire involved a DOD-funded Indigenous communities mapping project in Mexico, one of a set of so-called Bowman Expeditions projects.[58] The issue in this case centered on the extent to which the communities being mapped were aware of the researchers' DOD funding and the US and Mexican military's potential interest in the use of Indigenous spatial knowledge.[59]

These and other disputes in the social sciences over the military funding of research and education, use of social science knowledge in military campaigns, and recruitment of social scientists for military operations are rooted, in part, in historical controversies about the extent to which social science researchers historically have been willing or unwitting servants of military power. For instance, Project Camelot was a social science research program established in 1964 to study the conditions fostering civil conflict and insurgencies. Project Camelot's focus dovetailed with the US military's interest in counterinsurgency, history of clandestine involvement in Latin American politics, and escalation of the Vietnam War. When concerns about the program intensified, a National Academy of Sciences (NAS) committee was convened to investigate the accusations that social scientists appeared to be involved in US intelligence gathering to the detriment of legitimate scientific inquiry. The NAS committee reported that it had "frank reservations" about the project, and Project Camelot was ended in 1965.[60]

These historical and contemporary controversies illustrate the potential of DOD funding to raise questions about the validity of research and objectivity of researchers. Debates about the motives underlying DOD-funded research recognize that a funding agency as powerful and culturally significant as the DOD can accomplish its own goals whether or not they are the same as those of an individual researcher. This is not only true for social science research, but for natural science and engineering research as well. Despite their more accepting view of receiving military funding and working on defense projects, there are some disagreements among natural scientists over classified research restrictions on the free flow of scientific information.

An example is the MEDEA program, revived in 2009 by the CIA to release spy satellite and other classified data on Earth's environment, including climate-change-related phenomena, only to selected scientists with security clearances. This restriction clashed with the scientific culture of open access to data for purposes of research and verification of results. One atmospheric scientist with access to the restricted data described them as "very important economically and logistically" for resource detection and development when the Arctic thaws.[61] The

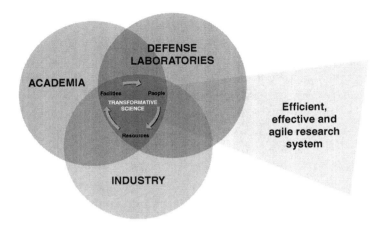

Figure 5.1 United States Army Research Laboratory Strategic Mission[64]

program was attacked on all sides – by Congressional Republicans who opposed funding environmental or climate research and by some scientists who objected to the program's secrecy and restrictions. The President of the NAS, who had a longstanding association with the MEDEA program, defended the secret program, commenting, without any apparent irony, "People who don't know details are the ones who are complaining."[62]

Expanding on and updating former President Eisenhower's admonition, the military-industrial-*science* complex is the new American scientific normal. It can be heard in the US Army Research Laboratory's mission statement: "provide innovative science, technology, and analysis to enable full spectrum Army operations ... [It] leverages America's most substantial intellectual resource – its academic scientific research community,"[63] and it can be seen in Figure 5.1.

American "Exceptionalism" in the Military Funding of Science

In order to assess the implications of the ratio of military to non-military funding for US basic science, including climate science, it is useful to place the structure of scientific funding in the United

States in an international context. In most respects, the US is an out-lier. It spends a far greater percentage of its gross domestic prod-uct (GDP) on its military,[65] with 2012 military expenditures totaling $682 billion.[66] This figure was many times greater than the next two highest military spenders: four times greater than China's military expenditures ($166 billion) and 7.5 times greater than the military expenditures of the Russian Federation ($90 billion).[67] The US mili-tary R&D budget is even more out of line when viewed from an international R&D spending perspective. Table 5.2 compares the US with eight other major world powers on total R&D expenditures, military R&D expenditures, percentage of R&D that is financed by the public sector, percentage of public-financed R&D that goes to the military, percentage of GDP spent on military R&D, and per-centage of GDP spent on civilian R&D.

Table 5.2 shows that the extent of the militarization of R&D in the US is far greater than that of other major economies, spending nearly three times as much on R&D as its two closest spenders – China and Japan (column 1). US military R&D expenditures are 10 times higher than any other country (column 2). Despite our greater wealth, the US is equal to or lags behind most other wealthy countries in its percent-age of public-financed R&D (column 3). US military R&D consumes a much greater percentage of publicly financed R&D compared to other major powers (column 4), and the US military R&D budget as a per-centage of GDP is twice as great as that of the Russian Federation, three times greater than that of the United Kingdom (the two closest cases), and vastly exceeds the expenditures of other wealthy countries (column 5). Despite the importance of R&D to economic development, of the nine countries compared in Table 5.2, US public sector investment in civil-ian R&D as a percentage of GDP (0.43 percent) is the second lowest (only the Russian Federation was lower, at 0.34 percent) (column 6). US investments in military R&D outpace its investments in civilian R&D (0.60 percent of GDP in military R&D compared to the 0.43 percent of GDP in civilian R&D) (columns 5 and 6). We can only conclude from these data that military R&D is a US government priority – one that is not shared by other major world economies.

Table 5.2 International Military and Civilian R&D Expenditures[68]

	(1) TOTAL R&D EXPENDITURES IN US $ BILLIONS (2004)	(2) MILITARY R&D EXPENDITURES IN US $ BILLIONS (2004)	(3) % PUBLIC FINANCED R&D (2004)	(4) MILITARY R&D AS % PUBLIC FINANCED R&D (2004)	(5) MILITARY R&D AS % OF GDP (2003–2006)	(6) CIVILIAN R&D AS % OF GDP (2003–2006)
China	102.6	5.0	30	16	n.a.	n.a.
France	39.7	3.5	39	23	0.21	0.72
Germany	58.7	1.0	30	6	0.05	0.72
Italy	17.7	0.4	51	4	0.01	0.61
Japan	112.7	1.0	18	5	0.04	0.66
Korea	24.3	0.8	24	13	0.14	0.72
Russian Fed.	16.5	4.0	61	40	0.37	0.34
United Kingdom	33.7	3.4	31	32	0.22	0.50
United States	312.5	54.1	31	56	0.60	0.43

In light of what we've seen above about the capacity of funding agencies to influence the research agenda of the scientists working for them, we should expect to see the imprimatur of the US defense sector on the science it funds. While much of this chapter has focused on the military funding of science, it is important to restate the place of gender in this discussion. The military's personnel, culture, structure, and mission represent an institutionalization of masculinity that is unparalleled in US society.[68] The next sections explore the implications of the militarization of science for two trends in climate change science: "securitization" and geoengineering.

Defending Against the Threat of Climate Change

The DOD not only funds research, it directly supports a network of dozens of national laboratories, centers, and research facilities that conduct classified and unclassified research and support the scientific activities of DOD-funded and other civilian researchers.[69] Many of these facilities historically and currently are used for mainly military research, development, and testing missions. For instance, three of the major DOD labs (Los Alamos National Laboratory, Lawrence Livermore National Laboratory, and Sandia National Laboratories) were involved in nuclear, chemical, and biological weapons programs during and after the Second World War. When the US signed and ratified the international Biological Weapons Convention in 1975 and the Chemical Weapons Convention in 1997, these labs officially shifted their mission to chemical and biological weapons detection and disposal. When the Soviet Union collapsed in 1989, the US and Russia implemented two nuclear strategic arms reduction treaties (START1 and New START) in 1991 and 2011 the nuclear weapons development mission of these labs was officially shifted to nuclear weapons maintenance.[70] These developments meant that. Many national labs had to refocus their missions in order to justify continued funding. Since military readiness and security had been their raison d'être, it was a logical shift to identify other security needs, in particular energy security and, more recently, environmental security.[71]

The September 11, 2001 terrorist attacks on the US provided a political and cultural atmosphere of crisis that led to a proliferation of so-called security threats that extended well beyond airports and borders into everyday life: "energy security," "food security," "water security," "health security," "bio-security," "environmental security," "climate security," "human security," "economic security," "homeland security," even "military security."[72] What formerly were defined as "shortages," "famines," "droughts," "epidemics," "recessions," or "attacks," were "securitized," i.e. reframed in the language of security threats. Books, articles, websites, organizations, academic programs, and experts on various insecurities multiplied.[73] An example can be seen in the references to "stability," "disputes," "threats" to "peace," and "climate wars" in the International Institute for Strategic Studies (IISS) statement on Climate Change and Security:

> The IISS believes climate change could have a serious effect on regional and global *stability*, and researches how global warming may affect *disputes* over territory, water, and other resources or could otherwise *threaten peace*. It also studies the mechanisms for averting "*climate wars*" [italics added].[74]

Many US national labs have joined in the security-writ-large enterprise, since who are better than military and weapons labs to deal with security threats? At a 2012 groundbreaking ceremony for a biological research facility in New Mexico, two officials from Los Alamos National Laboratory, home of the Manhattan Project which developed the atomic bomb, commented on the facility's dual security potential contributions – energy and food:

> Research into alternative forms of energy, of which biofuels is a key component, is one of the major national security imperatives of this century. Energy security is vital to our future national security and the efficient functioning of our market economy ... Just as exciting as our research in biofuels – and absolutely critical – is our work in global food security. Climate change is making it more difficult to grow enough

food for our earth's population. This is especially apparent in emerging economies; we've already seen that food security issues drive political unrest. The recent upheaval in Tunisia began when citizens protested food inflation, and a subsequent lack of food in the markets.[75]

In the same year, Sandia National Labs and Northrup Grumman, a private global security company, established the Center for Climate and Security, for "exploring the national security risks of climate change."[76] The slogan of Lawrence Livermore National Laboratory, where the hydrogen bomb was developed, is: "Science and Technology in the National Interest." Its scientists research "water security," "food security," "environmental security," and "energy security."[77] Lawrence Livermore, along with Los Alamos and Sandia National Labs, also provides computer and other resources for large-scale climate modeling and other climate change-related research projects.[78]

The DOD's interest in funding climate change science and the involvement of national defense laboratories in researching the various security threats associated with climate change are militarizing climate change and encouraging both the public and researchers to think about climate change as a national security risk.[79] Among the more common climate change-related security threats is the specter of hordes of hungry, thirsty climate refugees clambering over our border fences, carrying diseases, consuming our resources, and coveting our land. For instance, much of the climate security literature focuses on environmental migrants and their threat to many of the very countries whose emissions and consumption created the climate change problem in the first place.[80]

This emphasis on security threats creates an atmosphere of danger and mobilization for defense when discussing climate change, when a more productive approach would be to view climate change as a problem to address directly by reducing its rate and impacts. As we grapple with the problems of climate change, it is important not to let a focus on security threats crowd out the need for progress on climate change mitigation (stopping the causes of climate change) and adaptation (developing strategies for coping with its effects). As it turns out, the US military itself actually is facing a major climate change-related security threat. Ironically, this threat is not in the contemporary lexicon of militarized climate security threats. The threat is, however, arguably the greatest hazard from climate change facing the US military: "coastal security."

The military's coastal security problem does not involve the need to plan for defense against invasions by climate refugees. It involves the need to plan for how to respond to the gradual, and inevitable, inundation and eventual submersion of trillions of dollars' worth of coastal military infrastructure, installations, and bases around the world as sea levels rise. For instance, not only civilian real estate has been affected by the downtown flooding of Norfolk, Virginia, described in Chapter 2. Norfolk also is home to US Naval Station Norfolk,

> the world's largest naval station, supporting 75 ships and 134 aircraft alongside 14 peers and 11 aircraft hangars. The base houses the largest concentration of US Navy forces. Their operations conduct an average of 275 flights per day or one every six minutes. It is the hub for Navy logistics going to the European and Central Command theaters of operations, and to the Caribbean.[81]

Naval Station Norfolk is only the largest of dozens of naval bases and military coastal installations in the US and abroad.[82] In 2014 the DOD released its *Climate Change Adaptation Roadmap*. The tone and contents of the report could have been lifted right out of an IPCC document:

> Among the future trends that will impact our national security is climate change. Rising global temperatures, changing precipitation patterns, climbing sea levels, and more extreme weather events will intensify the challenges of global instability, hunger, poverty, and conflict. By taking a proactive, flexible approach to assessment, analysis, and adaptation, the Defense Department will keep pace with a changing climate, minimize its impacts on our missions, and continue to protect our national security.[83]

Like so many assessments of the impacts of climate change, this report warns that the costs of dealing with the problems will only increase with time, and argues that now is the moment to act. The details of the report, however, reveal that very little actually is being done beyond managing the day-to-day challenges that bases already are experiencing.[84]

Geoengineering: "Playing God to Save the Planet"

So what should be done to mitigate and adapt to global climate change? No consideration of the militarization of climate change science would be complete without a discussion of geoengineering: "the deliberate large-scale manipulation of the planetary environment to counteract anthropogenic climate change."[85]

Analysts typically divide geoengineering approaches into two categories:

1) Carbon dioxide removal (CDR) techniques, which remove CO_2 from the atmosphere, attempting to address the root cause of climate change;
2) Solar radiation management (SRM) techniques that reflect a small percentage of the sun's light and heat back into space, attempting to offset effects of increased greenhouse gas concentrations by causing the Earth to absorb less solar radiation.[86]

A 2009 British Royal Society (of Science and Engineering) report on geoengineering summarized the potential and pitfalls of large-scale planetary engineering efforts:

> Most nations now recognise the need to shift to a low-carbon economy, and nothing should divert us from the main priority of reducing global greenhouse gas emissions. But if such reductions achieve too little, too late, there will surely be pressure to consider a "plan B" – to seek ways to counteract the climatic effects of greenhouse gas emissions by "geoengineering". Many proposals for geoengineering have already been made – but the subject is bedevilled by much doubt and confusion. Some schemes are manifestly far-fetched; others are more credible, and are being

investigated by reputable scientists; some are being promoted over-optimistically.[87]

Geoengineering is not unique to the current era of climate change science. It is described by one historian of science and technology as an approach in which climate geoengineers "play God" in order to "save the planet."[88] Geoengineering responses to climate change were included in the 1992 publication of the NAS report, "Policy Implications of Greenhouse Warming: Mitigation and Adaptation and the Science Base."[89] Many of the report's recommendations plowed familiar ground: reduce or offset current carbon emissions, change energy policy to reduce consumption and increase efficiency, use forest offsets by reducing global deforestation and increasing forest cover. The report's consideration of geoengineering options led readers into more exotic realms, in which mirrors are launched into space orbit to reflect the sun's rays; solar reflective balloons are lifted into the stratosphere; lasers are used to remove chlorofluorocarbons; the oceans are fertilized with iron to cause massive phytoplankton blooms to increase ocean absorption of carbon dioxide (CO_2); rail guns and rockets are used to shoot and maintain a high-altitude cloud of dust, sulfuric acid aerosols, or nanoparticles reminiscent of a volcanic eruption, to shade the planet and build up Arctic ice.[90]

The NAS report goes into some detail about delivery scenarios, costs, feasibility, and unintended consequences. The assessments are far from conclusive, and the report warns that scientists are nowhere near ready to deploy these techniques. But there's an optimistic, almost fanciful tone to the geoengineering section of the report that seemed to minimize disaster and inject a bit of gaiety into its consideration of geoengineering efforts to increase stratospheric dust:

> It appears that destruction of stratospheric ozone due to chemical reactions on the surface of added dust or aerosol in the stratosphere is a possible side effect that must be considered and understood before this possible mitigation option can be considered for use ... Note that the dust can be expected to produce

visible optical effects, such as spectacular sunsets, as in the case of volcanic dust.[91]

Some geoengineering plans developed in the years since the NAS report are fairly straightforward, though not without critics. An example of a CDR geoengineering plan is underground carbon sequestration – removing carbon from the atmosphere by pumping CO_2 into subterranean spaces such as those created by gas or oil extraction or in saline aquifers.[92] This approach would be local, rather than planetary, and would not call for adapting the entire global substructure. One carbon sequestration strategy was considered promising enough for the US Department of Energy to fund two demonstration projects, involving collaboration among national labs and university researchers, to combine CO_2 sequestration and enhanced geothermal system (EGS) techniques:[93]

> The idea for the use of supercritical CO_2 was first proposed in 2000 by Los Alamos national laboratory physicist Donald Brown. Supercritical CO_2, a pressurized form that is part gas and part liquid, is less viscous than water and so should flow more easily through rock ... In 2006, Karsten Pruess, a hydrologist at Lawrence Berkeley, performed the first detailed modeling of the technology. Pruess projected that an EGS project could produce approximately 50 percent more heat with carbon dioxide than with water.[94]

The safety and efficacy of sequestering large amounts of carbon on the scale needed to reduce CO_2 emissions have not been demonstrated, so the approach is considered experimental.[95]

"Albedo yachts" are an SRM geoengineering plan being developed by staff at another national lab, the National Center for Atmospheric Research. One conception of the plan would involve launching up to 1500 ships with wind-powered propulsion and pumps designed to suck up ocean water to generate a mist of sea water that would rise into the atmosphere to help reflect the sun's rays and reduce ocean heat absorption.[96]

Figure 5.2 Albedo Yachts[98]

> Wind-driven spray vessels will sail back and forth perpendicu-
> lar to the local prevailing wind and release micron-sized drops
> of seawater into the turbulent boundary layer beneath mar-
> ine stratocumulus clouds. The combination of wind and vessel
> movements will treat a large area of sky. When residues left after
> drop evaporation reach cloud level they will provide many new
> cloud condensation nuclei giving more but smaller drops and so
> will increase the cloud albedo to reflect solar energy back out to
> space ... The method is *not* intended to make new clouds. It will
> just make existing clouds whiter.[97]

The albedo yacht proposal has not been tested, but its designers share a
common characteristic with most other geoengineers. Geoengineering
is a largely male enterprise. This should not be surprising since the
majority of engineers are men. There is also a military dimension to
geoengineering. Some of its most prominent advocates are men who
have worked on military projects.

Several prominent advocates of geoengineering approaches outlined above met at a 2006 National Aeronautics and Space Administration (NASA) workshop on "managing solar radiation."[99] Of the 36 participants, only four were women, one of whom was an administrative consultant. The military backgrounds and defense-related work of a number of the participants contributed to the nearly for-men-only character of the workshop. One of the most voluble workshop participants was physicist Lowell Wood (protégé of Edward Teller, father of the hydrogen bomb),[100] who had spent his career at Lawrence Livermore National Labs, "where he served as one of the Pentagon's chief weapon designers and threat analysts."[101] Wood advocated shooting sulfate or nanoparticles into the Arctic atmosphere either with aircraft continuously circumnavigating the Arctic, or a 25-kilometer sky hose hooked up to a military super blimp, or large artillery pieces. The military-style (shooting), large-scale, and "all-out" tenor of these assaults on solar radiation led one observer to comment that the approach was "basically declaring war on the stratosphere."[102] Wood and other participants offered up many imaginative, and some far-fetched, approaches to reducing the sun's light. The only historian of science and technology attending the workshop commented on the potential consequences of the historical ignorance of the scientists and engineers participating in the far-ranging discussions about how to "manage" solar radiation:

> Largely unaware of the long and checkered history of weather and climate control and the political and ethical challenges it poses, or somehow considering themselves exempt, the new Titans [of geoengineering] see themselves as heroic pioneers, the first generation capable of alleviating or averting natural disasters. They are largely oblivious to the history of the charlatans and sincere but deluded scientists and engineers who preceded them. If we fail to heed the lessons of that history ... We risk repeating the mistakes of the past, in a game with much higher stakes.[103]

The arrogance and recklessness of these schemes is not characteristic of all geoengineering proposals. Many of the papers included in a Royal Society's special issue on "Geoscale Engineering to Avert Dangerous Climate Change" were careful attempts to assess a range of strategies.[104]

In 2015 the US National Academy of Sciences investigated the costs and benefits of geoengineering, but did not arrive at consensus about the wisdom of "albedo modification" and "climate intervention."[105] Whatever the merits of reviewing and renaming, many geoengineering approaches share in common a certain nationalistic, even militaristic arrogance about the right of US or UK (or Chinese? or Indian?) scientists and engineers to attempt to alter fundamental and far-reaching planetary processes. By its very nature, much geoengineering would be on a military scale, and would of necessity require political approval.[106] Whether it is called albedo modification or climate intervention, geoengineering conjures up a vision of national mobilization and declaration of war on climate change – a last-ditch effort, no matter the consequences.[107]

Geoengineering solutions and their mostly male designers and advocates offer no suggestions for seeking global consensus about their proposals. Nor do their plans contain any direction for addressing the justice and equity implications for those who might be affected by geoengineering efforts. The problem of global consensus would be a serious obstacle to implementing most large-scale geoengineering projects. It might be easier to reengineer the planet than to engineer global consensus for a coherent and inclusive climate change policy. That certainly is the case in the US, where we have not been able to build a national consensus about the contours of climate change policy. In fact, we can't even agree about whether or not climate change is real. In the next chapter we will shine a gender spotlight on climate change skepticism.

Notes

[1] By "military" I refer to all of the armed forces of the US and their various interests and agendas associated with defense. This is not to overlook differences among the different services, including disagreements about funding priorities and goals; it is to emphasize that the military funding is not without an agenda, and that it is not simply a "pure science" enterprise.

[2] Mann, Bonnie. 2008. "Manhood, Sexuality, and Nation in Post-9/11 United States." In Sutton, B., S. Morgen, and J. Novkov, (eds.), *Security Disarmed: Critical Perspectives on Gender, Race, and Militarization*. New Brunswick, NJ: Rutgers University Press, pp. 179–197, p. 180.

3 Connell, R.W., and James W. Messerschmidt. 2005. "Hegemonic Masculinity: Rethinking the Concept." *Gender and Society*, Vol. 19, No. 6:829–859.

4 Mann, op. cit.

5 For a discussion of masculinity and nationalism, see Nagel, Joane. 1998. "Masculinity and Nationalism: Gender and Sexuality in the Making of Nations." *Ethnic and Racial Studies*, Vol. 21, No. 2:242–269.

6 Not all men are mindlessly militarized; I rely on the creative skepticism and intellectual honesty of many male scholars, especially the historians of science and technology whose work is cited in this chapter.

7 US Department of Defense. 2015. The Minerva Initiative. Accessed on May 26, 2015 at http://minerva.dtic.mil/.

8 Interview on November 6, 2013.

9 US Department of Defense. 2015. The Minerva Initiative. "Priority Research Topics for FY 2015." Accessed on May 26, 2015 at http://minerva.dtic.mil/ topics.html. Accessed on March 19, 2014 at http://minerva.dtic.mil/funded. html.

10 Henn, Steve. 2014. "When Robots Can Kill, It's Unclear Who Will Be to Blame." National Public Radio, March 21. Accessed on March 21, 2014 at www. npr.org/blogs/alltechconsidered/2014/03/21/291887341/when-robots-can-kill-its-unclear-who-will-be-to-blame.

11 US General Accounting Office. 2004. *DOD Business Systems Modernization: Billions Continued to be Invested with Inadequate Management Oversight and Accountability.* Accessed on March 21, 2014 at www.gao.gov/new.items/ d04615.pdf; Francis, David. 2014. "The $37 Billion Lesson DOD Could Learn from IBM." *The Fiscal Times* (January 20). Accessed on March 22, 2014 at www.thefiscaltimes.com/Articles/2014/01/30/37-Billion-Lesson-DOD-Could-Learn-IBM; Lubold, Gordon. 2014. "A Major Fraud Scandal Rocks the Army's Ranks." *Foreign Policy*, February 4. Accessed on March 22, 2014 at www.foreignpolicy.com/articles/2014/02/04/fps_situation_report_a_ major_fraud_scandal_rocks_the_armys_ranks; Paltrow, Scot J., and Kelly Carr. 2013. "How the Pentagon's Payroll Quagmire Traps American Soldiers." *Reuters Investigates*, July 2. Accessed on May 22, 2014 at www.reuters.com/investigates/ pentagon/#article/part1, www.reuters.com/investigates/pentagon/#article/part2, and www.reuters.com/investigates/pentagon/#article/part3.

12 Malakoff, David. 2013. "Cloak-and-Dagger Publishing." *Science*, Vol. 4, No. 6154:71; see also, *Journal of Sensitive Cyber Research and Engineering.* Accessed on April 2, 2014 at http://cybersecurity.nitrd.gov/jscore.

13 Defense Advanced Research Projects Agency (DARPA) at www.darpa.mil/ About.aspx and Minerva Initiative at http://minerva.dtic.mil/ (both accessed on March 30, 2014).

14 Minerva Initiative. 2015. *Program History and Overview.* Accessed on May 26, 2015 at http://minerva.dtic.mil/overview.html.

15 Minerva Initiative. 2014. *University-Led Research.* Accessed on December 10, 2014 at http://minerva.dtic.mil/funded.html.

16 Defense Advanced Research Projects Agency. 2014. *Our Work*. Accessed on December 10, 2014 at www.darpa.mil/our_work/.

17 US Department of Defense. 2015. *Opportunities at DARPA: Young Faculty Award*. Accessed on May 26, 2015 at www.darpa.mil/Opportunities/Universities/Young_Faculty.aspx.

18 Ibid.

19 Pynchon, Thomas. 1973. *Gravity's Rainbow*. New York: Penguin Books, p. 251; my thanks to Edmund Russell for bringing this quote to my attention.

20 Schwartz, B. 1967. "The Social Psychology of the Gift." *American Journal of Sociology*, Vol. 73, No. 1:1–11; Berking, Helmuth. 1999. *The Sociology of Giving*. Thousand Oaks, CA: Sage Publications.

21 Martinson, Brian C., Melissa S. Anderson, and Raymond de Vries. 2005. "Scientists Behaving Badly." *Nature*, Vol. 435, No. 9:737–738.

22 Ridker, Paul M., and Jose Torres. 2006. "Reported Outcomes in Major Cardiovascular Clinical Trials Funded by For-Profit and Not-For-Profit Organizations: 2000–2005." *Journal of the American Medical Association*, Vol. 295, No. 19:2270–2274; see also, Als-Nielsen, B., W. Chan, C. Gluud, and L.L. Kjaergard. 2003. "Association of Funding and Conclusions in Randomized Drug Trials: a Reflection of Treatment Effect or Adverse Events?" *Journal of the American Medical Association*, Vol. 290, No. 7:921–928; for an overview of the impact of funding on medical research, see Rehman, Jalees. 2012. "Can the Source of Funding for Medical Research Affect the Results?" *Scientific American* (September 23). Accessed on March 17, 2014 at http://blogs. scientificamerican.com/guest-blog/2012/09/23/can-the-source-of-funding-for-medical-research-affect-the-results/.

23 Lesser, Lenard I., Cara B. Ebbeling, Merrill Goozner, David Wypij, and David S. Ludwig. 2007. "Relationship between Funding Source and Conclusion among Nutrition-related Scientific Articles." *PLoS Medicine*, Vol. 4, No. 1:41–46.

24 Ibid., p. 41.

25 Wazana, Ashley. 2000. "Physicians and the Pharmaceutical Industry: Is a Gift Ever Just a Gift?" *Journal of the American Medical Association*, Vol. 283, No. 3:373–380, p. 373; my thanks to Edmund Russell for pointing out this example of funding influence on research outcomes and professional behavior.

26 Waxman, Henry A. 2005. "The Lessons of Vioxx – Drug Safety and Sales." *New England Journal of Medicine*, Vol. 352, No. 25:2476–2578; Smith, Richard. 2006. "Lapses at the *New England Journal of Medicine*." *Journal of the Royal Society of Medicine*, Vol. 99, No. 8:380–382.

27 Pharmaceutical Research and Manufacturers of America. 2008. *Code on Interaction with Healthcare. Professionals*. Accessed on March 17, 2014 at www.acpe-accredit.org/pdf/CodeonInteractionsHCProfessionals.pdf; see also ProPublica. 2014. "Dollars for Docs: How Industry Dollars Reach Your Doctors." Accessed on March 17, 2014 at http://projects.propublica.org/docdollars/.

28 Federal Register. 2013. *Medicare, Medicaid, Children's Health Insurance Programs: Transparency Reports and Reporting of Physician Ownership or*

Investment Interests. Accessed on March 17, 2014 at www.federalregister. gov/articles/2013/02/08/2013–02572/medicare-medicaid-childrens-health-insurance-programs-transparency-reports-and-reporting-of.

29 Kanter, Rosabeth Moss. 1993. *Men and Women of the Corporation.* New York: Basic Books, second edition; Guiso, Luigi, Ferinando Monte, Paola Sapienza, Luigi Zingales. 2008. "Culture, Gender, and Math." *Science,* Vol. 320, No. 5880:1164–1165; Maddox, Brenda. 2002. *Dark Lady of DNA.* New York: HarperCollins; Miller, G.E. 2004. "Frontier Masculinity in the Oil Industry: The Experience of Women Engineers." *Gender, Work & Organization,* Vol. 11, No. 1:47–73; Keller, Evelyn Fox. 1995. *Reflections on Gender and Science.* New Haven, CT: Yale University Press; Nye, Robert A. 1997. "Medicine and Science as Masculine 'Fields of Honor'." *Osiris.* Vol. 12:60–79; Zakaib, Gwyneth Dickey. 2011. "Science Gender Gap Probed." *Nature,* Vol. 470, No. 7333:153; Barinaga, Marcia. 1993. "Feminists Find Gender Everywhere in Science." *Science,* Vol. 260, No. 5:392–393. Kmec, Julie A. 2013. "Why Academic Stem Mothers Feel They Have to Work Harder Than Others on the Job." *International Journal of Gender, Science and Technology,* Vol. 5, No. 2:79–101.

30 Connell, R.W. 1995. *Masculinities.* Cambridge: Polity Press; Kimmel, Michael. 1996. *Manhood in America.* New York: Oxford University Press.

31 The US Office of Management and Budget defines "research and development" as "activities [that] comprise creative work undertaken on a systematic basis in order to increase the stock of knowledge, including knowledge of man, culture and society, and the use of the stock of knowledge to devise new applications." Accessed on March 19, 2014 at www.nsf.gov/statistics/randdef/fedgov.cfm.

32 Federal agencies not listed in Table 5.2 received less than $2.5 million in R&D funding. American Association for the Advancement of Science. 2014. *R&D in the FY2014 Omnibus: The Big Picture.* Accessed on March 18, 2014 at www. aaas.org/news/rd-fy-2014-omnibus-big-picture; see also National Science Foundation. 2014. *Science and Engineering Indicators, 2014,* Chapter 4: *Research and Development: National Trends and International Comparisons.* Accessed on March 18, 2014 at www.nsf.gov/statistics/seind14/index.cfm/chapter-4/c4h. htm.

33 For descriptions of all DOD R&D funding, including S&T 6.1–6.3 and "All other DOD R&D," see Fossum, Donna, Lawrence S. Painter, Valerie L. Williams, Allison Yezril, and Elaine Newton. 2000. *Discovery and Innovation: Federal Research and Development Activities in the 50 States, District of Columbia, and Puerto Rico;* Appendix B: Government-wide and DoD Definitions of R&D. RAND Corporation. Accessed on March 21, 2014 at www.rand.org/pubs/monograph_reports/MR1194.html.

34 A small percent of DOD research funding goes to "University programs" (about $1.1 billion in 2012).

35 For a very useful breakdown of DOD basic research funding, including a number of programs specifically for University investigators, see Murday, James. 2013. "Guide to FY 2014 Basic Research Funding at the Department of Defense," especially Table 1, p. 8. Accessed on March 21, 2014 at https://research.usc. edu/files/2011/05/Guide-to-FY2014-DOD-Basic-Research-Funding-.pdf.

36 National Science Foundation. 2014. "Introduction to Transformative Research." Accessed on March 18, 2014 at www.nsf.gov/about/transformative_research/; see also National Science Foundation. 2013. "Merit review." Accessed on March 18, 2014 at www.nsf.gov/bfa/dias/policy/merit_review/.

37 National Science Foundation. 2014. *Budget Internet Information System: Funding Rate by State and Organization from FY 2012 to 2013 for NSF.* Accessed on March 19, 2014 at http://dellweb.bfa.nsf.gov/awdfr3/default.asp.

38 National Science Foundation. Accessed on March 17, 2014 at www.nsf.gov.

39 *Public Law 507–81st Congress. Chapter 171–2-D Session.* S. 247. National Science Foundation Act of 1950. Accessed on March 18, 2014 at www.nsf.gov/about/history/legislation.pdf.

40 Ibid.

41 National Science Foundation. 2007. *Memorandum of Agreement between the Department of Defense and the National Science Foundation for the National Science Foundation's Polar Programs.* Accessed on March 17, 2014 at www.nsf.gov/about/contracting/rfqs/support_ant/docs/gen_management/moa_msc_effective_050107.pdf.

42 National Science Foundation. 2014. *REU Sites.* Accessed on March 19, 2014 at www.nsf.gov/crssprgm/reu/list_result.jsp?unitid=10023.

43 Interestingly, the photo attached to the NSF press release announcing MOU was of two men shaking hands, but neither was wearing a uniform: National Science Foundation. 2008. "NSF Signs Memorandum of Understanding with Department of Defense for National Security Research." Accessed on March 17, 2014 at www.nsf.gov/news/news_summ.jsp?org=NSF&cntn_id=111829&preview=false.

44 US Senate. 2014. Coburn Amendment 65 as amended. Accessed on December 10, 2014 at www.coburn.senate.gov/public/index.cfm?a=Files.Serve&File_id=91498db1-70c4-4d92-8c6a-6d97a89b1f25. The amendment was not approved, but the legislation it stalled had to be "hashed out behind closed doors." Stratford, Michael. 2014. "Poli Sci Victory, For Now." *Inside Higher Education* (January 24). Accessed on December 10, 2014 at www.insidehighered.com/news/2014/01/24/wake-coburn-amendment-repeal-social-science-groups-plot-path-forward.

45 Despite the "win-win" verdict on the joint NSF-DOD Minerva project celebrated in the July 2008 issue of *Nature*, the actual review guidelines on the DOD project website do not list any role for NSF reviewers.

46 "A Social Contract." *Nature*, Vol. 454, No. 7201:138 and Department of Defense, Minerva Initiative, "Frequently Asked Questions," see especially "The Proposal Process." Accessed on March 26, 2014 at http://minerva.dtic.mil/faqs.html; see also Mervis, Jeffrey. 2014. "Hints of Détente between NSF and Republicans." *Science*, Vol. 343, No. 6177:1298–1299.

47 American Anthropological Association. 2007. *AAA Commission on the Engagement of Anthropology with the US Security and Intelligence Communities.* Accessed on March 27, 2014 at www.aaanet.org/pdf/Final_Report.pdf.

48 American Psychological Association. 2005. *Report of the American Psychological Association Presidential Task Force on Psychological Ethics and National Security.*

Accessed on March 19, 2014 at www.apa.org/pubs/info/reports/pens.pdf; American Psychiatric Association. 2006. *Position Statement on Psychiatric Participation in Interrogation of Detainees*. Accessed on March 20, 2014 at www.psych.org/advocacy–newsroom/position-statements; American Psychiatric Association. 2008. *Letter to Secretary of Defense Robert M. Gates*. Accessed on March 20, 2014 at http://media.npr.org/documents/2008/sep/gatesletter.pdf; American Medical Association. 2006. *Opinion 2.068 – Physician Participation in Interrogation*. Accessed on March 20, 2014 at www.ama-assn.org/ama/pub/physician-resources/medical-ethics/code-medical-ethics/opinion2068.page.

49   "A Call for Annulment of the APA's PENS Report." Accessed on March 19, 2014 at http://ethicalpsychology.org/pens/. An APA referendum was held in 2008 and members overwhelmingly voted against PENS, but the controversy was not resolved and continued to cause dissension and debate in the organization (see Eidelson, Roy (2012), "Protecting Psychologists Who Harm: The APA's Latest Wrong Turn," *Psychology Today* (March 13); accessed on December 10, 2014 at www.psychologytoday.com/blog/dangerous-ideas/201203/protecting-psychologists-who-harm-the-apa-s-latest-wrong-turn).

50   American Psychological Association. 2014. "APA Applauds Release of Senate Intelligence Committee Report Summary" (December 9). Accessed on December 10, 2014 at www.apa.org/news/press/releases/2014/12/senate-intelligence.aspx; US Senate. 2014. *Committee Study of the Central Intelligence Agency's Detention and Interrogation Program*. Senate Select Committee on Intelligence. Accessed on May 27, 2014 at www.intelligence.senate.gov/study2014/sscistudy2.pdf.

51   Joseph, Paul. 2014. "Soft Counterinsurgency: Human Terrain Teams and US Military Strategy in Iraq and Afghanistan. New York: Palgrave Macmillan, p. 56.

52   Price, David H. 2011. *Weaponizing Anthropology*. Oakland, CA: AK Press; American Anthropological Association. 2007. *American Anthropological Association's Executive Board Statement on the Human Terrain System Project*. Accessed on March 19, 2014 at www.aaanet.org/pdf/eb_resolution_110807.pdf.

53   Vanden Brook, Tom. 2013. "Army Leaders Warned about Issues with Social Scientists."*USAToday*(September23).AccessedonApril20,2014atwww.usatoday.com/story/news/politics/2013/09/23/human-terrain-teams-anthropologists-iraq-afghanistan/2804321/.

54   Carroll, Chris. 2014. "Reports of Sexual Assault in the Military Climbed in FY 2013." *Stars & Stripes* (February 26). Accessed on April 18, 2014 at www.stripes.com/news/us/reports-of-sexual-assault-in-the-military-climbed-in-fy-2013-1.270162; see also US Department of Defense. 2015. *Department of Defense Annual Report on Sexual Assault in the Military, Fiscal Year 2014*. Accessed on May 26, 2015 at http://sapr.mil/public/docs/reports/FY14_Annual/FY14_DoD_SAPRO_Annual_Report_on_Sexual_Assault.pdf.

55   US Department of Education. 2014. *National Resource Centers Program.* Accessed on March 19, 2014 at www2.ed.gov/programs/iegpsnrc/index.html; US Department of Education. *Office of Post Secondary Education. Title VI Programs: Building a US International Education Infrastructure.* Accessed on March 19 at https://www2.ed.gov/about/offices/list/ope/iegps/title-six.html.

56   *Public Law 102–183. David L. Boren National Security Education Act of 1991.* Accessed on March 19, 2014 at www.intelligence.Senate.gov/davidlboren nationalsecurityact.pdf.

57   Nsia-Pepra, Kofi. 2014. "Militarization of US Foreign Policy in Africa: Strategic Gain or Backlash?" *Military Review,* January-February:50–59. Accessed on March 19, 2014 at http://usacac.army.mil/CAC2/MilitaryReview/Archives/English/MilitaryReview_20140228_art010.pdf; Wiley, David. 2012. "Militarizing Africa and African Studies in the US Africanist Response." *African Studies Review,* Vol. 55, No. 2:147–161.

58   The "Bowman Expeditions" are named after Isaiah Bowman, an American geographer who served first as territorial advisor to Pres. Woodrow Wilson and later to the US Department of State during the Second World War; see Bowman, Isaiah. 1916. *The Andes of Southern Peru: Geographical Reconnaissance along the Seventy-Third Meridian.* New York: Henry Holt and Company reproduced at www.gutenberg.org/files/42860/42860-h/42860-h.htm (accessed on March 19, 2014 at www.gutenberg.org/files/42860/42860-h/42860-h.htm).

59   Herlihy, Peter H., Jerome E. Dobson, Miguel Aguilar Robledo, Derek A. Smith, John H. Kelly, Aida Ramos Viera, and Andrew H. Hilburn. 2008. *México Indígena. The AGS Bowman Expeditions Prototype: Digital Geography of Indigenous Mexico.* Accessed on March 19, 2014 at www.academia.edu/1028008/THE_AGS_BOWMAN_EXPEDITIONS_PROTOTYPE_DIGITAL_GEOGRAPHY_OF_INDIGENOUS_MEXICO. The controversy revealed disagreement between the American Association of Geographers' (AAG) Indigenous Peoples Specialty Group (who complained to the AAG Executive Board about the project) and the American Geographical Society (one of the project principal investigators is AGS president) which supported the project and the Bowman Expeditions concept; see Louis, Renee Pualani, and Zoltán Grossman. 2009. Letter to the AAG Executive Board. Accessed on March 19, 2014 at http://academic.evergreen.edu/g/grossmaz/IPSGletterAAGboard.pdf; Wainwright, Joel. 2013. *Geopiracy: Oaxaca, Militant Empiricism, and Geographical Thought.* New York: Palgrave-Macmillan; Herlihy, Peter H., Jerome E. Dobson, Miguel Aguilar Robledo, Derek A. Smith, John H. Kelly, and Aida Ramos Viera. "A Digital geography of indigenous Mexico: Prototype for the American Geographical Society's Bowman Expeditions." *Geographical Review,* Vol. 98, No. 3:395–415; see also editorial letters, statements, and responses about the project in *Political Geography,* Vol. 29, No. 8(2010):413–423 and Vol. 30, No. 1(2011):110.

60   Horowitz, Irving Louis. 1967. *The Rise and Fall of Project Camelot.* Cambridge, MA: MIT Press; Lowe, George E. 1966. "The Camelot Affair." *Bulletin of the Atomic Scientists,* May:44–48.

61 Broad, William J. 2010. "C.I.A. Is Sharing Data with Climate Scientists." *New York Times* (January 4). Accessed on March 31, 2014 at www. nytimes.com/2010/01/05/science/earth/05satellite.html?_r=1&; Brumfiel, Geoff. 2011. "Military Surveillance Data: Shared Intelligence." *Nature*, Vol. 477, No.7365:388–389; for background on the MEDEA program, see Richelson, Jeffrey T. "Scientists in Black." *Scientific American*, Vol. 278, No. 2:48–55.

62 Broad, op. cit.; see also Snider, Annie. 2011. "Our Man in the Greenhouse: Why the CIA Is Spying on a Changing Climate." *Global Warning: A Project of the National Security Journalism Initiative*. Accessed on March 31, 2014 at http:// global-warning.org/main/intelligence/3/.

63 US Army Research Laboratory. 2014. Accessed on March 31, 2014 at www.arl. army.mil/www/default.cfm?page=2357.

64 Ibid.; see also the DOD's "Armed with Science" website. Accessed on April 1, 2014 at http://science.dodlive.mil/; my thanks to Cornelis Kees van der Veen for bringing this to my attention.

65 "GDP measures the monetary value of final goods and services – that is, those that are bought by the final user – produced in a country in a given period of time (say a quarter or a year). It counts all of the output generated within the borders of a country." Callen, Tim. 2012. "Gross Domestic Product: An Economy's All." International Monetary Fund. Accessed on March 23, 2014 at www.imf.org/external/pubs/ft/fandd/basics/gdp.htm.

66 Stockholm International Peace Research Institute (SIPRI). 2014. *SIPRI Military Expenditure Database*. Accessed on March 20, 2014 at http://milex-data.sipri.org/files/?file=SIPRI+milex+data+1988–2012+v2.xlsx; most published data on military expenditures are gathered by nongovernmental organizations (NGOs) like this one or by governmental agencies such as the US Arms Control and Disarmament Agency; for a discussion of bias in estimates of military spending, see Lebovic, James H. 1998. "Consider the Source: Organizational Bias in Estimates of Foreign Military Spending." *International Studies Quarterly*, Vol. 42, No. 1:161–174; despite these criticisms, most researchers rely on data from NGOs like the SIPRI because it provides the most accurate and extensive data available.

67 Ibid.

68 Except perhaps some professional sports which are not major funders of scientific research. An interesting exception is the National Football League's embrace of its own research and dismissal of established medical findings about the impact of concussions on brain health. Fainaru-Wada, Mark, and Steve Fainaru. 2013. League of Denial: The NFL, Concussions and the Battle for Truth. New York: Crown Archetype.

69 Brzoska, Michael. 2005. "Trends in Global Military and Civilian Research and Development (R&D) and their Changing Interface." Institute for Peace Research and Security Policy, University of Hamburg. Accessed on March 20, 2014 at www.ifsh.de/pdf/aktuelles/india_brzoska.pdf; Dunne, J. Paul, and Derek Braddon. 2008. "Economic Impact of Military R&D." Flemish Peace Institute. University of the West of England. Accessed on August 3, 2014 at

www.flemishpeaceinstitute.eu/sites/vlaamsvredesinstituut.eu/files/files/reports/vvi_web_rapport_militairerend_en.pdf.

70 US Department of Homeland Security. 2014. *National and Federal Laboratories and Research Centers.* Accessed on March 21, 2014 at www.dhs.gov/national-federal-laboratories-research-centers.

71 US Department of State. 2014. New START. Accessed on March 21, 2014 at www.state.gov/t/avc/newstart/index.htm; Center for Nonproliferation Studies. 2013. "US Nuclear Weapons Budget: An Overview." *Nuclear Threat Initiative.* Accessed on March 21, 2014 at www.nti.org/analysis/articles/us-nuclear-weapons-budget-overview/; Medalia, Jonathan E. 2014. "In Brief: U.S. Nuclear Weapon 'Pit' Production: Background and Options." Congressional Research Office, March 20. Accessed on March 21, 2014 at www.fas.org/sgp/crs/nuke/R43428.pdf.

72 For instance, Los Alamos National Laboratory, Lawrence Livermore National Laboratory, Sandia National Laboratories. 2014. *Lab Directed Research and Development: Global Security: Understanding Climate Change.* Accessed on March 21, 2014 at http://tri-lab.lanl.gov/index.php/global-security; see also Wallace, Terry. "Emerging Threats to Global Security." Los Alamos National Laboratory, NM, Bradbury Science Museum. Accessed on March 21, 2014 at www.lanl.gov/newsroom/news-releases/2014/March/03.06-global-security-talk.php.

73 An Internet search on any of these terms will produce many examples.

74 Ibid.

75 International Institute for Strategic Studies. 2013. Accessed on March 21, 2014 at www.iiss.org/en/research/climate-s-change-s-and-s-security.

76 Roark, Kevin. 2012. "Facility Will Focus on Bioenergy, Global Food Security." Los Alamos National Laboratory, NM. Accessed on March 21, 2014 at www.lanl.gov/newsroom/news-releases/2012/May/05.22-bioenergy-facility.php.

77 The Center for Climate and Security. 2012. "New Sandia Labs and Northrup Grumman Partnership Includes Climate Change Research." Accessed on March 21, 2014 at http://climateandsecurity.org/tag/sandia-national-labs/.

78 Lawrence Livermore National Laboratory. 2006. "New Climate Research Reveals Growing Risk of Water Shortages and Flooding in California." Accessed on March 21, 2014 at www-pls.llnl.gov/?url=science_and_technology-earth_sciences-risk; "Climate and Agriculture: Change Begets Change." Accessed on March 21, 2014 at www-pls.llnl.gov/?url=science_and_technology-earth_sciences-agriculture.

79 National Nuclear Security Administration (NNSA). 2010. "NNSA Marks Earth Day by Highlighting Role in Climate Modeling, Commitment to Energy Efficiency." Press release accessed on March 21, 2014 at www.nnsa.energy.gov/mediaroom/pressreleases/04.22.10; see also NNSA. 2014. "NNSA's National Laboratories Engaged in Climate Modeling, Data Gathering." Accessed on March 21, 2014 at www.nnsa.energy.gov/mediaroom/features/climatemodeling; see also Los Alamos National Laboratory, the Climate, Ocean and Sea Ice Modeling Group. Accessed on March 23, 2014 at http://oceans11.lanl.gov/drupal/Home.

80 Nagel, Joane. 2015. "Gender, Conflict, and the Militarization of Climate Change." *Peace Review*, Vol. 27, No. 2:1–6.

[81] Lobell, David B., Marshall B. Burke, Claudia Tebaldi, Michael D. Mastrandrea, Walter P. Falcon, and Rosamond L. Naylor. 2008. "Prioritizing Climate Change Adaptation Needs for Food Security in 2030." *Science*, Vol. 319, No. 5863:607–610; Scheffran, Jurgen, P. Michael Link, and Janpeter Schilling. 2012. "Theories and Models of Climate Security Interaction: Framework and Application to a Climate Hotspot in North Africa." In Scheffran, J., M. Brzoska, H.G. Brauch, P.M. Link, and J. Schilling (eds.), *Climate Change, Human Security and Violent Conflict*. Berlin: Springer-Verlag, pp. 91–131; Reuveny, Rafael. 2007. "Climate Change Induced Migration and Violent Conflict." *Political Geography*, Vol. 26, No. 6:656–673; White, Gregory. 2011. *Climate Change and Migration: Security and Borders in a Warming World*. New York: Oxford University Press; for a less alarmist take, though one still framed in the language of security, see Dalby, Simon. 2009. *Security and Environmental Change*. Cambridge: Polity Press; see the series of articles in *Scientific American* magazine on Bangladesh and climate migration at www.scientificamerican.com/article/climate-change-refugees-bangladesh/ (accessed March 30, 2014).

[82] Military.com Base Guide. 2014. "Naval Station Norfolk: Welcome to the World's Largest Naval Station." Accessed on March 21, 2014 at www.military.com/base-guide/naval-station-norfolk.

[83] US Navy. 2014. "Navy Facilities within the US." Accessed on March 21, 2014 at www.navy.mil/navydata/bases/navbases.html; US Navy. 2014. "List of Homeports." Accessed on April 30, 2014 at www.navy.mil/navydata/ships/lists/homeport.asp.

[84] US Department of Defense. 2014. "DoD Releases 2014 Climate Change Adaptation Roadmap," (October 13). Accessed on December 10, 2014 at www.defense.gov/releases/release.aspx?releaseid=16976.

[85] Department of Defense. 2014. *Climate Change Adaptation Roadmap*. Accessed on December 10, 2014 at www.acq.osd.mil/ie/download/CCARprint.pdf.

[86] The Royal Society. 2009. *Geoengineering the Climate: Science, Governance and Uncertainty*. London: The Royal Society. Accessed on March 21, 2014 at http://royalsociety.org/uploadedFiles/Royal_Society_Content/policy/publications/2009/8693.pdf.

[87] Ibid., p. ix.

[88] Ibid., p. v.

[89] Fleming, James Rodger. 2007. "The Climate Engineers: Playing God to Save the Planet." *Wilson Quarterly*, Vol. 31, No. 2:46–60; see also Hamblin, Jacob Darwin. 2013. *Arming Mother Nature: The Birth of Catastrophic Environmentalism*. New York: Oxford University Press, pp. 160–163.

[90] National Research Council. 1992. *Policy Implications of Greenhouse Warming: Mitigation, Adaptation, and the Science Base*. Washington, DC: The National Academies Press.

[91] Ibid., pp. 433–464.

[92] Ibid., p. 451.

[93] US Department of Energy. 2008. *Carbon Sequestration through Enhanced Oil Recovery*. Accessed on March 22, 2014 at www.netl.doe.gov/publications/factsheets/program/Prog053.pdf; Glammar, Daniel E., Robert G. Bruant, Jr., and Catherine A. Peters. 2005. "Forsterite Dissolution and Magnesite Precipitation

at Conditions Relevant for Deep Saline Aquifer Storage and Sequestration of Carbon Dioxide." *Chemical Geology*, Vol. 217, Nos. 3–4:257–276.

[94]   According to the US Department of Energy, "An Enhanced Geothermal System (EGS) is a man-made reservoir, created where there is hot rock but insufficient or little natural permeability or fluid saturation. In an EGS, fluid is injected into the subsurface under carefully controlled conditions, which cause pre-existing fractures to re-open, creating permeability. Increased permeability allows fluid to circulate throughout the now-fractured rock and to transport heat to the surface where electricity can be generated"; see US Department of Energy. 2014. "What is an Enhanced Geothermal System (EGS)?" Accessed on March 22, 2014 at www1.eere.energy.gov/geothermal/pdfs/egs_factsheet. pdf.

[95]   *Geothermal Digest*. 2009. "Marrying CO_2 and EGS: the Waste Gas Presents Many Advantages in Some Unknowns." Accessed on March 22, 2014 at http:// geothermaldigest.net/blog/2009/12/08/more-on-co2-and-egs-the-waste-gas-presents-many-advantages-and-some-unknowns/; see also Brown, Donald. 2000. "Geothermal Power Production Utilizing Supercritical CO_2 Combined with Deep Earth Carbon Sequestration." Los Alamos National Laboratory, NM. Accessed on March 22, 2014 at https://web.anl.gov/PCS/acsfuel/ preprint%20archive/Files/45_4_WASHINGTON%20DC_08-00_0766.pdf.

[96]   Little, Mark G., and Robert B. Jackson. 2010. "Potential Impacts of Leakage from Deep CO_2 Geosequestration on Overlying Freshwater Aquifers." *Environmental Science and Technology*, Vol. 44, No. 23:9225–9232; Zoback, Mark D., and Steven M. Gorelick. 2010. "Earthquake Triggering and Large-Scale Geologic Storage of Carbon Dioxide." *Proceedings of the National Academy of Sciences*, Vol. 109, No. 26:10164–10168; see response to Zoback and Gorelick, op. cit.: Juanez, Ruben, Howard Herzog, and Brad Hagar. 2012. "No Geologic Evidence That Seismicity Causes Fault Leakage That Would Render Large-Scale Carbon Capture and Storage Unsuccessful." *Proceedings of the National Academy of Sciences*, Vol. 109, No. 52; and see Zoback, Mark D., and Steven M. Gorelick. 2012. "Reply to Juanes *et al.*: "Evidence That Earthquake Triggering Could Render Long-Term Carbon Storage Unsuccessful in Many Regions." *Proceedings of the National Academy of Sciences*, Vol. 109, No. 52.

[97]   Mims, Christopher. 2009. "'Albedo Yachts' and Marine Clouds: A Cure for Climate Change?" *Scientific American* (October 21). Accessed on March 22, 2014 at www.scientificamerican.com/article/albedo-yachts-and-marine-clouds/.

[98]   Salter, Stephen, Graham Sortino, and John Latham. 2008. "Seagoing Hardware for the Cloud Albedo Method of Reversing Global Warming." *Philosophical Transactions of the Royal Society*, Vol. 366, No. 1882:3389–4006, p. 3389.

[99]   Ibid.

[100] Lane, Lee, Ken Caldiera, Robert Chatfield, and Stephanie Langhoff. 2007. "Workshop Report on Managing Solar Radiation." NASA Ames Research Center, California. Accessed on March 24, 2014 at http://ntrs.nasa.gov/archive/ nasa/casi.ntrs.nasa.gov/20070031204.pdf.

[101] Heppenheimer, T. 1989. "New Director Shifts Balance of Power at Livermore Lab." *The Scientist*, (August 7). Accessed on March 24, 2014 at www.the-scientist.com/?articles.view/articleNo/10529/title/New-Director-Shifts-Balance-Of-Power-At-Livermore-Lab/.

[102] Fleming, 2007, op. cit., p. 48.

[103] Ibid.

[104] Ibid., p. 50.

[105] Royal Society. 2008. *Geoscale Engineering to Avert Dangerous Climate Change.* Philosophical Transactions of the Royal Society, Vol. 366. Accessed on March 24, 2014 at http://rsta.royalsocietypublishing.org/content/366/1882.toc.pdf.

[106] Committee on Geoengineering Climate. 2015. *Climate Intervention: Carbon Dioxide Removal and Reliable Sequestration* and *Climate Intervention: Reflecting Sunlight to Cool Earth.* Washington, DC: The National Academies. Accessed on May 25, 2015 at https://nas-sites.org/americasclimatechoices/other-reports-on-climate-change/2015-2/climate-intervention-reports/; some commentators were skeptical both of the rhetorical strategies used in the NAS reports and the plans to stop changes in the Earth's climate without stopping the causes of climate change; see Hamilton, Clive. 2015. "Geoengineering Is Not a Solution to Climate Change." *Scientific American* (March). Accessed on May 25, 2015 at www.scientificamerican.com/article/geoengineering-is-not-a-solution-to-climate-change/; Bagley, Katherine. 2015. "National Academy: Geoengineering No Substitute for Carbon Cuts." *Inside Climate News* (February 10). Accessed on May 26, 2015 at http://insideclimatenews.org/news/10022015/national-academy-geoengineering-no-substitute-carbon-cuts.

[107] Blackstone, Jason J., and Jane C.S. Long. 2010. "The Politics of Geoengineering." *Science*, Vol. 327, No. 5965:527.

[108] For a discussion of some possible dynamics of competitive geoengineering reminiscent of the Cold War's Mutually Assured Destruction (MAD) scenario, see Schnellnhuber, Hans Joachim. 2011. "Geoengineering: The Good, the MAD, and the Sensible." *Proceedings of the National Academy of Sciences*, Vol. 108, No. 51:20,277–20,278.

6
GENDER AND CLIMATE CHANGE SKEPTICISM

The next two chapters focus on two very different political responses to climate change. This chapter explores the gendered, ideological, and economic basis of climate change "skepticism" or "denialism." The next chapter examines the gendered landscape of climate change policy. Climate change skepticism is an organized movement funded by conservative groups and foundations. Many of these funders have links to industries (e.g. fossil fuel producers) with an interest in avoiding environmental and economic regulations designed to slow the causes of climate change. Just as climate science is dominated by men, climate skeptics are predominantly male, and as we shall see in Chapter 7, so are climate change policymakers. As in previous chapters, in the first sections of the chapter we will examine the characteristics and extent of climate change skepticism generally. In the second half of the chapter, we will focus specifically on the place of gender in climate change denialism.

Legislating Away Climate Change

In 2010, the North Carolina Science Panel on Coastal Hazards issued a *Sea Level Rise Assessment Report* based on data from four North Carolina coastal research studies and the Intergovernmental Panel on Climate Change (IPCC).[1] The report found that North Carolina coastal sea levels could rise as much as 39 inches by 2100:

> All of the historical tide gauge records over the last century and geologic evidence over the last several centuries offer undisputable evidence that sea level has been steadily rising in North Carolina, and based on multiple indicators suggesting that global climate is warming, the [NC Science] Panel believes that an acceleration in the rate of SLR [sea level rise] is likely.[2]

The implications of a 3-foot rise in sea level for North Carolina's coastal development and real estate values alarmed the "NC-20," a group of mainly male state legislators representing coastal counties.[3] They took issue with the report's prediction, and introduced legislation mandating new sea level rise measurement rules.[4] The legislation limited official estimates of 21st-century sea level rise to 8 inches, contradicting the findings of the North Carolina scientists and the IPCC:

> [Sea level rise] rates shall only be determined using historical data, and these data shall be limited to the time period following the year 1900. Rates of sea level rise may be extrapolated linearly to estimate future rates of rise but shall not include scenarios of accelerated rate of sea level rise.[5]

The legislation was passed into law in 2012, flying in the face not only of the scientific consensus, but also the realities of encroaching coastal waters that North Carolina had grappled with for decades. For instance, in 1999, North Carolina's famous Cape Hatteras Light Station had to be "relocated from the spot on which it had stood since 1870 [b]ecause of the threat of shoreline erosion," which had slowly devoured the original 1500 feet of beach separating it from the sea.[6] In 2011, the mayor of Ocean Isle Beach, North Carolina estimated that because of high tides, storm surges, and seasonal flooding, "repairs, property losses and protective measures along Shallotte Inlet have cost $62 million in private and public money in the past decade."[7]

Sea level rise is costing North Carolinians and their insurers hundreds of millions of dollars in property damage repair, beach erosion management, and structure relocations:

N.C. insured-property losses from hurricanes averaged $10.6 million a year (in 2005 dollars) from 1949 to 1988 ... [and] as development grew and hurricane activity intensified, average losses between 1989 and 2005 soared to $296 million a year.[8]

The sea has been a boon that now threatens to bust North Carolina's estimated $20 billion tourism industry.[9] In light of the state's ongoing beachfront maintenance costs, battles have intensified over who will pay for its disappearing beaches – state or federal tax payers, coastal communities, insurance companies, or property owners? No one expects the seas to retreat, not even the state legislature.

Why, then, did North Carolina attempt to legislate away sea level rise? Critics of the legislation pointed out that the law couldn't stop sea level rise, but it could allow realtors in the "lucrative North Carolinian oceanfront property market" to stop talking about it:

> Prior to the passage of this bill, real estate brokers were required to disclose this information to potential buyers. Post passage, brokers are not required to disclose anything about rising sea levels as the science behind this is now legally considered to be unfounded.[10]

The primary sponsor of the North Carolina law was Republican Representative Pat McElraft, one of the few women involved in the legislative effort and the only woman on the NC-20 Board of Directors in 2014. McElraft, a real estate broker, shared a common business background with the men advocating for the legislation and, like many of her male colleagues, enjoyed the financial support of real estate developers who stood to lose if sea level rise became a big public issue:

> Development interests have played a key role in financing McElraft's political career. Since McElraft was first elected to the General Assembly in 2007, real estate has been the top industry contributor to her campaign ... Her single biggest contributor has been the N.C. Association of Realtors, followed by the N.C. Home Builders Association.[11]

The role of economic interests in challenging climate change reports and sponsoring climate change legislation is, on its face, gender neutral, although many fewer women are involved in political efforts to deny the effects of climate change. This kind of climate politics is not unique to North Carolina. Nor is the state alone in its efforts to legislate against climate change or the procedures for studying it. In 2011 Montana House Bill No. 549 was introduced in the state legislature, declaring that:

> (a) global warming is beneficial to the welfare and business climate of Montana; (b) reasonable amounts of carbon dioxide released into the atmosphere have no verifiable impacts on the environment; and (c) global warming is a natural occurrence and human activity has not accelerated it.[12]

In 2014 the US House of Representatives passed a bill "that would require United States weather agencies to focus more on predicting storms and less on climate studies."[13]

Not only have there been legislative efforts to deny the existence, extent, or dangers of climate change, there are campaigns to regulate the teaching of climate change. In 2000, the conservative American Legislative Exchange Council (ALEC), whose slogan is "limited government, free markets, federalism," drafted model legislation known as the "Environmental Literacy Improvement Act." The legislation required environmental education programs in schools, universities, and agencies to "provide a range of perspectives presented in a balanced manner," governed by a council of experts in economics, education, and natural sciences, but specifically "not environmental science."[14] In 2012, observers reported:

> Texas and Louisiana have introduced education standards that require educators to teach climate change denial as a valid scientific position. South Dakota and Utah passed resolutions denying climate change. Tennessee and Oklahoma also have introduced legislation to give climate change skeptics a place in the classroom.[15]

Colorado and Arizona joined the one-fifth of US state houses introducing the Environmental Literacy Improvement Act, and in 2014 Wyoming's Board of Education blocked the implementation of national

"Next Generation Science Standards" because they included a section on anthropogenic climate change. Wyoming's *Casper Star-Tribune* editorialized against the action: "Facts aren't always convenient. But that doesn't make them any less factual and ignoring them doesn't make them go away."[16] The use of ALEC-type legislative and official efforts to regulate the classroom presentation of scientific findings led the President of the National Center for Science Education to conclude that "climate change education is where evolution was 20 years ago."[17]

ALEC is headquartered in Washington, DC, and has been labeled a "stealth business lobbyist" by the *New York Times*; *Bloomberg Businessweek* declared:

> It's a bill laundry. Corporations suggest a bill to a state legislator, then bring it to ALEC's attention, where, after a complicated process ... the bill becomes "model legislation," which the corporations can then suggest to other state legislators. In one case ... the corporations actually wrote the bullet points of the initial piece of legislation themselves. There's nothing illegal about this, but it does look bad. ALEC creates the fiction that these bills grow wild in the fertile, democratic loam of America's state legislatures.[18]

Many prominent corporations have contributed to ALEC, including ExxonMobil and McDonalds; in 2010 "AT&T, Pfizer and Reynolds American each contributed $130,000 to $398,000."[19] Controversies over some of ALEC's legislative foci (e.g. promoting Florida-type "stand your ground" gun legislation) and the credibility of its Internal Revenue Service (IRS) status as a 501(c)(3) public charity have led to the exodus of a number of corporate and foundation paid members including Walmart, Walgreens, Proctor & Gamble, Wendy's, PepsiCo, Amazon, CocaCola, General Motors, Intuit, the Gates Foundation, Google, Visa, Facebook, and Kraft Foods.[20]

Climate Change Skepticism and the Scientific Consensus

Despite an amazing list of past and present sponsors and an active anti-environmental regulation campaign, as we shall see later in this chapter, ALEC is only a minor player in the organized climate change skepticism game. Before examining the political and social organization of climate change skepticism, we need to take a look at the demography of skepticism: who is skeptical and who is not, and what is the role of gender in climate skepticism? To clarify, "climate change skepticism" refers to a range of opinions that share in common the *denial*, "both of the reality of climate change and[/or] of its status as a problem deserving amelioration."[21] It is important to distinguish this "denialist" position from scientific skepticism that is part of the scientific method.

By and large, scientists are trained to be skeptical iconoclasts. They are quick to challenge research approaches, demand verification of claims, seek independent duplication of results, respect only peer-reviewed findings, and even then, often argue and vehemently disagree with one another. A recent example is the debate over whether accelerated Arctic warming caused changes in the behavior of the northern polar jet stream, displacing the "polar vortex," and bringing subzero temperatures to large sections of North America in 2014.[22] Science is not without its flaws, as I have argued throughout this book. And there have been relatively rare instances in history when the scientific consensus has been shown to be wrong.[23] The fact that the scientific consensus can be overthrown affirms the self-correcting nature of scientific skepticism, and it is why I am convinced by the science documenting the reality and gravity of climate change.

How strong is the scientific consensus on the existence and seriousness of climate change? In 2004, before there was widespread knowledge outside of scientists and environmentalists about climate change, a researcher analyzed 928 abstracts of articles on climate change published in refereed scientific journals 1993–2003. Three-quarters of the papers supported the consensus position reflected by the IPCC's position that Earth's climate is changing due to human activities. One-quarter of the papers addressed methods or other topics and took no position on anthropogenic climate change. Not one of the 928 papers disagreed with the consensus position.[24]

In the past decade these findings have been confirmed in multiple studies. In 2013 a research team examined 11,944 climate science abstracts 1991–2012 addressing "global warming" or "climate change" in order to assess the extent to which the papers agreed with the scientific consensus on anthropogenic global warming (AGW). The researchers rated the papers, and to check their interpretations, they asked the authors also to rate their own papers to determine the extent to which they supported the AGW scientific consensus. Using both methods they found near-universal agreement:

> Among abstracts expressing a position on AGW, 97.1% endorsed the consensus position that humans are causing global warming. In a second phase of this study, we invited authors to rate their own papers ... Among self-rated papers expressing a position on AGW, 97.2% endorsed the consensus.[25]

These results are summarized in Figure 6.1.

Despite impressive levels of agreement among scientists whose training and culture encourages questioning and disagreement, there is a widespread public perception that there is a scientific "debate" about global warming and climate change. In a 2010 survey of US

Figure 6.1 Climate Science Research Papers Supporting Anthropogenic Global Warming[26]

adults, researchers found that half of Americans believed that there was significant disagreement among scientists over global warming. Specifically 45 percent responded "there is a lot of disagreement among scientists about whether or not global warming is happening," and 5 percent responded that "most scientists think that global warming is not happening."[27]

The public perception that scientists disagree about climate change has important consequences. For instance, researchers found that respondents who believed there was no scientific consensus about global warming also opposed public policies to address climate change.[28]

> It seems that the debate on the authenticity of global warming and the role played by human activity is largely nonexistent among those who understand the nuances and scientific basis of long-term climate processes. The challenge, rather, appears to be how to effectively communicate this fact to policymakers and to a public that continues to mistakenly perceive debate among scientists.[29]

The Demographics of Climate Change Skepticism

The gap between very high levels of scientific *agreement* about global warming and the perception that there are high levels of scientific *disagreement* among a significant proportion of the US population has led researchers to look into who among the public believes there is scientific debate. The first place social scientists look to understand population trends is differences in age, race, class, and gender. When researchers asked respondents in a 2009/2010 national survey whether they believed that global warming was happening, 57 percent answered "yes," 20 percent answered "no," and 23 percent said they didn't know. When those data were broken down by age, there were no significant differences among various age groups.[30] When the same respondents were asked about the scientific consensus on global warming, 34 percent reported that "most scientists think global warming is happening," 40 percent reported that "there is a lot of disagreement," 5 percent reported that "most scientists think global warming is not happening," and 21 percent didn't know enough to say either way. Once again, age did not matter much in determining Americans' assessment of the scientific consensus.[31]

If age is not a determinant of belief in global warming or in the assessment of the scientific consensus, then what about race? In a 2010 survey of Americans, researchers asked if global warming is happening, do you think it is caused mostly by human activities, natural changes in the environment, some combination of human and natural changes, or "neither because global warming isn't happening."[32] The majority of Americans (57 percent) reported that global warming was caused mostly by human activities and hardly any (4 percent) believed that global warming wasn't happening. When Hispanics, blacks, whites, and all other races were compared, researchers found no significant difference about the causes of global warming or its existence. The same lack of racial and ethnic difference was true when respondents were asked about the scientific consensus.[33] This uniformity of opinion about climate change was somewhat puzzling since there is likely differential vulnerability among ethnic and racial groups to the effects of climate change:

> The impacts of climate change are likely to be felt disproportionately by those who face socioeconomic inequalities. In the United States this includes many Hispanics, African Americans and other racial and ethnic groups who are likely to be more vulnerable to heat waves, extreme weather events, environmental degradation, and subsequent labor market dislocations.[34]

If race and ethnicity are not determinants of belief in global warming or the extent of scientific consensus about global warming, then what about class? Income and education are the two most commonly used indicators of social class. In a 2008 study using Gallup Poll data, researchers found that level of education was positively associated with belief in climate change and its human causes as well as recognition of the scientific consensus, i.e. more educated respondents were more likely to agree that climate change was happening and that scientists were in agreement about it. The opposite was true of income, which tended to be negatively associated with beliefs about climate change and the scientific consensus, i.e. higher-income respondents were *less* likely to agree that climate change was happening or that scientists were in agreement about it.[35] These findings are consistent with a 2006 study that also found a reverse relationship between income and education and their relationship to environmental attitudes and behavior:

> While more education and higher income tend to go together, the effect of higher income sometimes is different from that of education [on environmental issues] ... Richer people ... tend to be more conservative politically, which is associated with lesser support for government policies intended to improve the environment ... more education and higher income appear to have different, sometimes conflicting, effects on environmental behaviors. More education tends to lead to more environmentally-positive behavior but higher income has more mixed effects.[36]

Gender and Climate Change Skepticism

The only missing piece of our demographic puzzle is gender. How does gender fit into the emerging picture of the age, race, and class dimensions of climate change attitudes and skepticism? Research consistently shows that women express more concern than men about environmental issues generally.[37] Perhaps this is because women are more knowledgeable about environmental matters. In a study using Gallup Poll data from 2001 to 2008, a researcher compared the extent of women's and men's knowledge about climate change and their concern about it. They found that women knew more and worried more than men about climate change, and that women also were more modest about their knowledge:

> Contrary to expectations from scientific literacy research, women convey greater assessed scientific knowledge of climate change than do men. Consistent with much existing sociology of science research, women underestimate their climate change knowledge more than do men.[38]

The researchers also found that men and women differed on questions of global warming, its human causes, and the scientific consensus. On all three issues women were more likely to answer positively:

[A] greater percentage of women than men believe that global warming is happening now (59% to 54%) and is primarily caused by human activities (64% to 56%). Also, a greater percentage of women than men (66% to 60%) agree that most scientists believe global warming is happening.[39]

The gender gap in beliefs about climate change reported in this study is corroborated by a large body of research on the gender gap in environmental knowledge and attitudes generally:

A widespread and consistent finding reveals that women as compared to men, demonstrate higher levels of awareness and response to environmental problems ... Gender differences have been reported in pro-environmental attitudes, concern for the environment, knowledge levels regarding climate change, and willingness to take action to improve environmental problems. How can we understand these and related differences?[40]

How *can* we understand the differences between women's and men's belief and disbelief in climate change, the gender gap in environmental attitudes and activism, or the disjuncture between male and female levels of climate change knowledge compared to their levels of confidence about their knowledge? Researchers offer several possible explanations for women's pro-environmental attitudes, knowledge, and actions, and for men's lesser enthusiasm for environmental issues, less knowledge (but more confidence in their knowledge) about environmental matters, and greater skepticism about climate change.

One set of explanations focuses on men's and women's different social roles and socialization. The research cited above finds little support for the gender role hypothesis that women's home-centered duties make them more environmentally aware or more likely to believe in global warming.[41] Socialization arguments seem to hold more promise: "compared to males, females [in this study] had higher levels of socialization to be other oriented and socially responsible," leading researchers to believe that women have the potential to "be influential in future environmental activism, policy development, and political leadership."[42]

Another explanation centers on women's relative vulnerability to some aspects of climate change (as we discussed in Chapters 2 and 3) and their feelings of responsibility to protect their children from the negative consequences of climate change. Risk is a prominent feature of explanations comparing men's and women's risk-taking and perception of risk, sometimes called the "white male effect," because "risks tend to be judged lower by men than by women and by white people than by people of colour."[43] A 2013–2014 global risks perception survey found that women consistently scored higher than men in estimation of risk relating to a wide number of issues (e.g. state collapse, oil price shock, data fraud/theft), especially on climate-related risks (e.g. climate change, biodiversity loss and ecosystem collapse, extreme weather events).[44]

Some researchers attribute men's relative skepticism about climate change and their disregard of the risks of climate change to their insulated lives. That is, many men share a worldview that stresses their relative invulnerability to all kinds of risks (illness, crime, climate change), a view that is based on their privileged social position as men.[45] The next section examines this claim and adds an additional gender-related factor in climate change attitudes: politics.

Gender and the Politics of Climate Change Skepticism

Men are more likely than women to be politically conservative. To the extent that political party affiliation is related to liberalism and conservatism, a 2011 study of politics and global warming attitudes found differences in the gender composition of the respondents' identification with political parties. Those respondents who identified their political affiliation as "Democrat" were more likely to be women than men (59 percent were women compared to 41 percent of men). Of those who identified themselves as "Independent," 48 percent were women versus 52 percent of men. "Tea Party" affiliates were more likely to be men (44 percent of women versus 56 percent of men). The one exception was self-identified "Republicans," which included 51 percent of women and 49 percent of men.[46] This study found that political affiliation had implications for belief in global warming and recognition of the scientific consensus:

> Majorities of Democrats (78%), Independents (71%) and Republicans (53%) believe that global warming is happening. By contrast, only 34 percent of Tea Party members believe global warming is happening, while 53 percent say it is not happening ... A majority of Democrats (55%) say that most scientists think global warming is happening, while majorities of Republicans (56%) and Tea Party members (69%) say that there is a lot of disagreement among scientists about whether or not global warming is happening.[47]

Figure 6.2 divides beliefs about global warming into six categories: Alarmed, Concerned, Cautious, Disengaged, Doubtful, and Dismissive.[48] Researchers charted political party identification within each of these categories. The Tea Party was not part of this analysis.[49] The thickness of each bar indicates the proportion of respondents holding that belief. As the figure shows, political party affiliation maps in a fairly linear fashion across the bars, with 56 percent of Democrats in the "Alarmed" category and 64 percent of Republicans in the "Dismissive" category.

In a further analysis of the politics of global warming attitudes, in 2011 a research team analyzed Gallup Poll public opinion data from 2001 to 2010. They examined the role of gender, class, race, and political ideology on respondents' answers to five questions, about: the likelihood of global warming, whether it is human-caused, the extent of the scientific consensus, whether the seriousness of global warming is exaggerated, and how worried they were about global warming.[51] Researchers then compared respondents' answers to their political attitudes ("very conservative, conservative, middle of the road, liberal, very liberal"). They also asked respondents how confident they were about their understanding of global warming. When they combined scores on global warming attitudes, political ideology, and confidence in knowledge about climate change, researchers found that, compared to all other adults, conservative white males were far more likely to deny

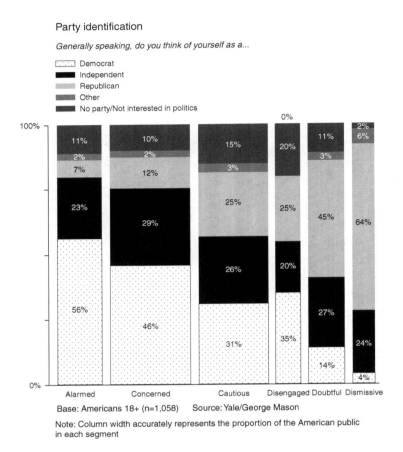

Party identification

Generally speaking, do you think of yourself as a...

- Democrat
- Independent
- Republican
- Other
- No party/Not interested in politics

Figure 6.2 Political Party Identification and Attitudes Toward Global Warming[50]

global warming and to express high confidence in their knowledge about it. This is despite the fact that other research shows men to be less informed than women about climate change.

Specifically, these researchers found that conservative white men were four times as likely as other respondents to believe that global warming will *never* happen; 1.8 times as likely to believe that humans were *not* the cause of recent temperature increases; 1.7 times as likely to believe that there is *no* scientific consensus about global warming;

2.2 times as likely to think that the seriousness of global warming is exaggerated; and 2.7 times as likely *not* to worry at all about global warming.[52] When researchers examined the scores of conservative white male respondents who considered themselves very confident about their knowledge, their denial scores were even higher, doubling on some items, especially "the effects of global warming will never happen."[53] When one of these researchers compared skeptical responses from conservative men and women, he found that conservative men were twice as likely to see global warming as a fiction: "14.9 percent of conservative women believe the effects of global warming will never happen [compared] to 29.6 percent of their male counterparts."[54]

What is it about conservative white males that makes them so likely to deny climate change? One researcher coined the phrase "smart idiot effect" to refer to the paradox that the more educated and knowledgeable conservatives [thought they] were, the more likely they were to refuse to believe scientific findings that challenged their political beliefs, a phenomenon that was confirmed in a 2015 Gallup Poll that found "Republicans with higher levels of education are more likely … to say that the seriousness of global warming is 'generally exaggerated'":[55]

> What accounts for the "smart idiot" effect? For one thing, well informed or well educated conservatives probably consume more conservative news and opinion, such as by watching Fox news. Thus they are more likely to know what they're supposed to think about the issues – what people like them think – and be familiar with arguments for reasons for holding these views. If challenged, they can then recall and reiterate these arguments. They've made them a part of their identities, a part of their brains, and in doing so, they've drawn a strong emotional connection between certain "facts" or claims, and their deeply held political views.[56]

Many social scientists agree that "it is impossible to understand current responses to the environmental crisis, as well as gendered differences in these responses, without taking into consideration the impact of social and psychological processes," such as cognitive barriers to sorting out conflicting messages, emotional overload associated with seemingly unsolvable global problems, discomfort with uncertainty, attachment to habits, or unwillingness to "hear" bad news.[57] There is also simple self-interest – a desire to defend the status quo, especially when it benefits the defender.

Researchers have referred to a cluster of attitudes associated with protecting one's social position as "system justification," which refers to "the social psychological motivation to defend, bolster, and justify aspects of the status quo."[58] Individuals scoring high on system justification tend to agree with statements like, "If people work hard, they almost always get what they want," "Most policies serve the greater good," and "In general, the American political system operates as it should."[59] Men consistently score higher on measures of system justification than women, a fact that is not surprising in light of US men's relatively greater levels of income and political power. Researchers conclude that "higher system justification among men would account for their greater denial of [troublesome] environmental realities in comparison with the less privileged social status of women":[60]

> These findings ... have direct implications for explaining gender differences in environmentalism [and climate change skepticism]. The motivation to justify the system is related to an individual's status within society. Occupying a privileged position within a hierarchical social order yields many benefits. Women, minorities, and the poor are often in a situation of disadvantage, while groups who control material resources exploit those lacking resources.[61]

The researchers whose work on gender and climate change attitudes is cited above conclude that economic interests play a major role in climate change skepticism, particularly among those with the most to lose if carbon emissions are regulated. The result is not simply isolated conservative white men holding private attitudes about climate change. They point to uniformities in the skeptical message and its mainly male messengers as indicators of an organized "denialist" movement dominated by conservative white men:

A growing body of recent scholarship has analyzed the strategies, techniques, and effectiveness of fossil fuels (and other) industry organizations, conservative think tanks, contrarian scientists, and conservative Republican politicians in promoting climate change denial in the United States. Even casual observers of denialist activities likely notice an obvious pattern; with rare exceptions, the most prominent denialists are conservative white males. This is true for contrarian scientists (e.g. Patrick Michaels and Fred Singer), media pundits (e.g. Rush Limbaugh and Glenn Beck), think tank representatives (e.g. Joseph Bast and William O'Keefe), and politicians (e.g. Senator James Inhofe and Representative Joe Barton). Within the ranks of elites, climate change denialists are overwhelmingly conservative white males.[62]

Men not only are the primary articulators of persons for climate change skepticism, they set the agenda, provide the funding, and are the main supporters of organized climate change denialism. In the next section we profile some of the founding fathers of climate change skepticism, and examine the gendered nature of organized denialist attacks on climate science and scientists.

The Social Organization of Climate Change Skepticism

The George C. Marshall Institute is a conservative organization whose motto is "science for better public policy."[63] One of the Marshall Institute's five major foci is climate change, which it describes as "the subject of current scientific debate" characterized by data and models that are "uncertain." The skeptical tone of the Marshall Institute's stance on climate change reflects the position of three of its founding members: Frederick Seitz, Robert Jastrow, and William Nierenberg – all men and all physicists who were influential government advisors during the Second World War and the Cold War; all became vocal climate skeptics in their later years. One researcher attributed their embrace of climate skepticism as a reaction against the rise of environmental science and the relative marginalization of the formerly high status field of physics.[64] But at least one of these men had a history of scientific skepticism. Frederick Seitz's 2008 *New York Times* obituary described him as "a renowned physicist who led both the National Academy of Sciences and Rockefeller University." It went on to note that:

> From 1978 to 1988, Dr. Seitz was a member of the medical research committee of the R.J. Reynolds Tobacco Company. His work for the company was the subject of a 2006 article in *Vanity Fair* magazine that criticized what it called an "overlap" between scientists who deny climate change and "tobacco executives who denied the dangers of smoking."[65]

In 2010, former Vice President Al Gore wrote an editorial in the *New York Times* pointing out similarities between the economic interests opposed to regulating greenhouse gases (GHGs) and the tobacco industry's role in promoting skepticism about the link between tobacco exposure and lung cancer:

> Over the years, as the science has become clearer and clearer, some industries and companies whose business plans are dependent on unrestrained pollution of the atmospheric commons have become ever more entrenched. They are ferociously fighting against the mildest regulation – just as tobacco companies blocked constraints on the marketing of cigarettes for four decades after science confirmed the link of cigarettes to diseases of the lung and the heart.[66]

In their 2010 book, *Merchants of Doubt: How a Handful of Scientists Obscured the Truth on Issues from Tobacco Smoke to Global Warming*, researchers show how some of the same actors, organizations, and strategies that were involved in the campaigns against the regulation of tobacco now are spearheading the fight against climate science and the regulation of carbon dioxide (CO_2).[67] In the 1980s, Seitz and the Marshall Institute were enlisted in efforts to refute the scientific research supporting the harmful effects of environmental tobacco smoke ("secondhand smoke"), as was Fred Singer, another contrarian physicist who also challenged the science linking the use of chlorofluorocarbons (CFCs) and the depletion of the ozone layer, the damaging

effects of acid rain, and, as we shall see below, the existence and negative effects of climate change.[68]

Merchants of Doubt authors argue that organized climate change
skepticism follows the same "playbook" used by organized tobacco skepticism. Both denial campaigns were built on links among a relatively
few scientists, conservative organizations, industry representatives, and
sympathetic politicians, typically from states whose economies depend
on those industries producing products linked to climate change. They
also found a parallel role for the media, which presented "the scientific
debate over tobacco as unsettled long after scientists had concluded
otherwise."[69]

The Marshall Institute is one of several dozen non-profit foundations and organizations involved in what one researcher has named,
the "climate change counter-movement (CCCM)."[70] Among the leading voices denying the existence or importance of climate change are
the Heritage Foundation, Heartland Institute, American Enterprise
Institute, and Americans for Prosperity Foundation. Climate change
denial is not the only issue on the plate of these and other CCCM
organizations. Most, like the Cato Institute, Reason Foundation, and
ALEC, described at the start of this chapter, are involved in free market
and small government advocacy. Underlying many of these organizations' messages about climate change is an argument against government intervention in the economy to regulate GHGs. Their rhetoric,
however, extends beyond calls for limited governmental response to climate change. They deny the scientific facts and consensus about climate
change and question the credibility of climate scientists themselves.

The Nongovernmental International Panel on Climate Change
(NIPCC), founded by physicist and leading climate skeptic, Dr. Fred
Singer, is an example of a denial organization with ties to the Heartland
Institute, whose mission is to "discover, develop, and promote
free-market solutions to social and economic problems."[71] The NIPCC
does not take the usual scientific position of separating research from
advocacy. Although its "namesake," the IPCC divides its scientific analysis and policy recommendations into different reports, the NIPCC
states:

Because we are not predisposed to believe climate change is caused by human greenhouse gas emissions, we are able to look at evidence the Intergovernmental Panel on Climate Change (IPCC) ignores. Because we do not work for any governments, we are not biased toward the assumption that greater government activity is necessary.[72]

The NIPCC's website is hosted by another skeptic organization, which also publishes NIPCC reports on its own website: the Center for the Study of Carbon Dioxide and Global Change, whose founders argue that increases in CO_2 are unrelated to global warming, "are a boon to the biosphere ... [and] Atmospheric CO_2 enrichment brings growth and prosperity to man and nature alike."[73] This common skeptic claim that elevated levels of atmospheric CO_2 will benefit humans, animals, and plants has been widely challenged in the scientific literature.[74]

In light of the focus of this book on gender and climate change, it is important to point out again that men dominate the climate skepticism universe. This is true not only in the US, but elsewhere. Researchers studying Sweden's much smaller climate skeptic movement reported that almost all skeptics were "elderly men with influential positions in academia or large private companies." They found that these denialists were unconvinced about the extent of the problem and opposed any proposed CO_2 reduction solutions to climate change, and they linked the men's opposition to not only their economic interests, but their vision of themselves as powerful men in a world they had created:

[T]heir arguments are intertwined with a masculinity connected to industrial modernisation, natural science and engineering rationality. We argue that for these climate sceptics it was not the environment that was threatened, it was a certain kind of modern industrial society built and dominated by their form of masculinity.[75]

In both Sweden and the US, all of the founders and most of the spokespersons for the organizations championing climate denial are men, as are most contrarian scientists and skeptic bloggers. We have seen earlier in this book that climate science itself is also a predominantly male enterprise. But, as underrepresented as women are in climate science, they are far more visible in climate research publications and presentations than are the many fewer women climate change skeptics.[76]

Gender and the Climate Change "Counter-Movement"

Researchers investigating the social organization of climate change skepticism argue that the information, some say "disinformation," that climate skeptic organizations provide about anthropogenic climate has contributed to the gap between the scientific consensus and the general public's knowledge about climate change.[77] CCCM organizations seek a voice and are invited to speak as part of the US mass media's quest for "balanced" news reporting.[78] This focus on balance has provided an "equal time" platform for the voices of the small skeptical minority, and the result is the distortion of public opinion about climate change. As the US National Research Council notes in its 2011 report, *America's Climate Choices*:

> Most people rely on secondary sources for information, especially the mass media; and some of these sources are affected by concerted campaigns against policies to limit CO_2 emissions, which promote beliefs about climate change that are not well supported by scientific evidence. US media coverage sometimes presents aspects of climate change that are uncontroversial among the research community as being matters of serious scientific debate. Such factors likely play a role in the increasing polarization of public beliefs about climate change, along lines of political ideology.[79]

Many climate change denialists seek not only to discredit established climate science, they often participate in virulent attacks on the reputations of climate researchers who challenge their point of view.[80] For instance, all five authors of a 2013 article on efforts by denialists to intimidate climate scientists published in the Association for Psychological Science's *Observer*, reported being harassed by

> cyber-bullying and public abuse; harassment by vexatious freedom-of-information (FOI) requests, complaints, and legal

threats or actions; and perhaps most troubling, by the intimidation of journal editors who are acting on manuscripts that are considered inconvenient by deniers.[81]

These authors represented a variety of disciplines (psychology, paleoclimatology, public health, and cognitive science). Their experience and that of colleagues working in the field of climate science led them to conclude that "The uniformity with which these attacks are pursued across several disciplines suggests that their motivation is not scientific in nature."[82]

In 2012, critical comments by conservative commentator and climate change denier Rush Limbaugh launched a particularly destructive assault by his supporters and skeptical bloggers on the author of *Living in Denial: Climate Change, Emotions, and Everyday Life.*[83] The relentlessness of skeptics' abusive emails resulted in the need to shut down the researcher's university email account. *Time* magazine came to her and other targets' defense, noting that:

> Climate scientists have described death threats, threats to their safety, and the safety of their children. The bullying is coming from the highest levels of government: Senator Inhofe – R, Oklahoma, and self-described "planet's number one worst enemy" – has sought to criminalize and prosecute 17 leading climate scientists … The bullying and intimidation tactics have gotten so out of hand that a donor-funded climate science legal defense fund has been established to help defray the costs of fighting the bullies.[84]

Like Rachel Carson, a generation earlier, women climate scientists find themselves under attack not only for their research, but also for their gender. After she appeared on a television series focusing on climate change, one woman scientist reported that she became the object of misogynistic abuse:

> [M]uch of the internet harassment she receives focuses on her gender … According to … women who have been targeted for their climate change research, more than 90 percent of the harassing emails they receive are from men and often include gender-specific abuse. Some emails tell them to get back in the

kitchen. A few are more threatening. "I've filed a police report before," [reported one woman scientist] after emails made her feel unsafe or threatened her family.[85]

Another type of attack on climate scientists was the 2009 so-called "climategate scandal," in which hacked email exchanges among climate scientists were publicly released in an effort to show that they were distorting their findings in order to inflate the threat of climate change. The charges against, in this case, male scientists were investigated in 2010 by the American Geophysical Union, American Association for the Advancement of Science, UK House of Commons Science and Technology Committee, American Meteorological Society, Pennsylvania State University, US Environmental Protection Agency, Inspector General of the US Department of Commerce, and National Science Foundation, among others. No agency found misconduct on the part of the scientists, though several decried the hacking of private emails. That did not end the matter – in 2011 many of the scientists' emails were hacked and published again.[86]

When two CCCM organizations, Competitive Enterprise Institute and the conservative publication, *National Review*, compared climate scientist Michael Mann to convicted child molester, Jerry Sandusky,[87] Mann filed a defamation lawsuit against both of them and two of their journalists:

> Dr. Mann is a climate scientist whose research has focused on global warming. Along with other researchers, he was one of the first to document the steady rise in surface temperatures during the 20th Century and the steep increase measured in temperatures since the 1950s. As a result of this research, Dr. Mann and his colleagues were awarded the Nobel Peace Prize … The defendants, for business and other reasons, assert that global warming is a "hoax" and have accused Dr. Mann of improperly manipulating the underlying data to reach his conclusions … Unsatisfied with their lacerations of his professional reputation, defendants have also maliciously attacked Dr. Mann's personal reputation with the knowingly false comparison to a child molester.[88]

The defamation lawsuit's reference to "business" reasons underlying skeptical attacks on climate science is consistent with the data presented above linking relatively high income survey respondents to an increased likelihood of denying the importance of climate change and the scientific consensus. Both suggest that there is an economic motive underlying both individual and organizational climate change denial. The attempt to legislate away sea level rise in North Carolina discussed at the start of this chapter was seen by some observers as an attempt to protect real estate, economic development, and tourism interests. Efforts to restrict the teaching of climate science in several states used model legislation drafted by the conservative ALEC, which was identified by a business magazine as a "bill laundry" for corporate interests – in this case to build public support against the need to regulate carbon.[89]

In 2014, a researcher used 2003–2010 IRS data and the budget reports of 140 different foundations to trace the sources of funding going to 91 of the major climate change skeptic organizations in the US CCCM.[90] Climate change was only one item on the agenda of most of these conservative organizations, so the author was less interested in the total amount of funding received by these organizations than in identifying the sources of support for the CCCM.[91] He found that "the overwhelming majority of the philanthropic support comes from conservative foundations," and saw an increase in funding over time from "donor directed" foundations such as "Donors Trust" and "Donors Capital," organizations that are able to conceal the identities of their donors.[92] Financial support to CCCM groups from these two anonymous donor foundations increased from less than 5 percent in 2003 to nearly 25 percent in 2010.[93] This trend toward anonymous donors has made it increasingly difficult to document fossil fuel or other economic interest group support from such corporate donors as Koch Industries and ExxonMobil. For instance, the researcher found that traceable funding to CCCMs from "Koch Affiliated Foundations, which peaked at 9% in 2006, declined to 2% [by 2010]. The ExxonMobil Foundation effectively stopped publicly funding CCCM organizations in 2007."[94] The author concludes that climate denialist funding has not stopped, rather it has gone underground in order to hide its economic motivation.

Conservative climate skeptics are not the only groups mobilizing around climate change. In 2014, partially in response to concerns about increased funding to skeptical organizations due to the US Supreme Court's "Citizens United" decision to strike down the overall limit on how much individuals can give candidates and political parties, the League of Conservation Voters and the Natural Resources Defense Council Action Fund joined together to form LeadingGreen, "a collaboration that will steer donations to federal candidates and enlist the help of major donors and lobbying elected officials" about climate change, energy, and environmental issues.[95]

Conclusion

The 2013/2014 publication of the three-volume IPCC's Fifth Assessment Report (AR5) shows that climate change is occurring faster than previously predicted in earlier reports:

> [G]lobal emissions of greenhouse gases have risen to unprecedented levels despite a growing number of policies to reduce climate change. Emissions grew more quickly between 2000 and 2010 than in each of the three previous decades ... "Climate policies in line with the two degrees Celsius goal need to aim for substantial emission reductions ... There is a clear message from science: To avoid dangerous interference with the climate system, we need to move away from business as usual.[96]

The message is not getting across. Americans' attitudes toward climate change have continued to be shaped less by science than by the "conservative consensus" that climate change is not real. Public opinion data show an increase of skepticism by the majority of those polled. A 2012 study of the US public's concern about climate change from 2002 to 2010 found that:

> Weather extremes have no effect on aggregate public opinion. Promulgation of scientific information to the public on climate

change has a minimal effect. The implication would seem to be that information-based science advocacy has had only a minor effect on public concern, while political mobilization by elites and advocacy groups is critical in influencing climate change concern.[97]

A nationally representative Gallup Poll data showed that public skepticism about global warming seems to be increasing among conservatives and men. Political conservatives polled who agreed that "the effects of global warming are already occurring," declined from 50 percent in 2008 to 30 percent in 2010. Liberals' agreement with the same statement rose only 2 percent. Both men's and women's agreement also dropped during the two years. Men's agreement with the statement that global warming is already occurring fell from 58 percent in 2008 to 42 percent in 2010, and women's agreement fell from 64 percent in 2008 to 56 percent in 2010.[98] Again, we see evidence of men's more skeptical stance, but we also see the American public's skepticism unaffected by increases in extreme weather events and CO_2 levels.[99]

The vociferous claims of an organized climate change skeptic movement that continues to deny the existence of a clear scientific consensus about the dangers of climate change has led one researcher to ask: "Is climate science disinformation a crime against humanity?"[100] It will be up to policymakers to bridge the gap between the challenge of climate change to the planet and its inhabitants and the well-funded mobilized skeptics' refusal to acknowledge climate change science. Their work is cut out for them. The next chapter examines the role of gender in the workings of climate change policy.

Notes

[1] Intergovernmental Panel on Climate Change (IPCC). 2007. Fourth Assessment Report. Geneva – North Carolina Coastal Resources Commission, 2010. North Carolina Sea-Level Rise Assessment Report (March). Accessed on March 31, 2014 at www.ncleg.net/documentsites/committees/LCGCC/Meeting%20Documents/2009-2010%20Interim/March%2015,%202010/Handouts%20and%20Presentations/2010-0315%20T.Miller%20-%20DCM%20NC%20Sea-Level%20Rise%20Rpt%20-%20CRC%20Science%20Panel.pdf, pp. 7–10.

2   North Carolina Coastal Resources Commission. 2010, op. cit., p. 12.
3   NC-20. 2014. "Twenty Counties ... One Voice." Accessed on March 31, 2014
     at www.nc-20.com/board.htm.
4   Lee, Jane J. 2012. "Update: Revised North Carolina Sea Level Rise Bill
     Goes to Governor." *Science* (July 3). Accessed on March 31, 2014 at http://
     news.sciencemag.org/climate/2012/07/update-revised-north-carolina-sea-
     level-rise-bill-goes-governor.
5   General Assembly of North Carolina, Session 2011. *House Bill 819: An Act to
     Study and Modify Certain Coastal Management Policies.* Accessed on March 31,
     2014 at www.nccoast.org/uploads/documents/CRO/2012–5/SLR-bill.pdf.
6   US National Park Service. 2014. "Moving the Cape Hatteras Lighthouse."
     Accessed on March 31, 2014 at www.nps.gov/caha/historyculture/movingth-
     elighthouse.htm; for a photographic survey of US national monuments thre
     atened by climate change, including the Statue of Liberty, see Hilaire, Eric, and
     Sajid Shaikh. 2014. "Landmark Sites in US at Risk from Climate Change –
     in Pictures." *The Guardian* (May 20). Accessed on May 21, 2014 at www.
     theguardian.com/environment/gallery/2014/may/20/us-landmark-sites-
     climate-change-statue-of-liberty; my thanks to Ebenezer Obadare for bring-
     ing this to my attention.
7   Henderson, Bruce. 2011. "As North Carolina Beaches Erode, Debate
     Rises." *Charlotte Observer* (April 1). Accessed on March 31, 2014 at www.
     charlotteobserver.com/2011/02/27/2095721/as-beaches-erode-debate-rises.
     html#.UztMvPldVIE.
8   Ibid.
9   Ibid.
10 Andres, Joe. 2014. "Global Warming Illegal? North Carolina Makes House
     Bill 819, Banning Science." *The Michigan Tech Lode* (March 25). Accessed on
     March 31, 2014 at www.mtulode.com/2014/03/05/global-warming-illegal-no
     rth-carolina-makes-house-bill-819-banning-science/.
11 Sturgis, Sue. 2012. "The Big Money behind the Assault against Sea Level Rise
     Science in North Carolina." *Facing South.* The Institute for Southern Studies.
     Accessed on April 14, 2014 at www.southernstudies.org/2012/07/the-big-
     money-behind-the-assault-against-sea-level-rise-science-in-north-carolina.
     html; for details of McElraft's contributors, see the report on the non-partisan,
     non-profit National Institute on Money in State Politics' website: fol-
     lowthemoney.org. Accessed on April 14, 2014 at www.followthemoney.org/
     database/uniquecandidate.phtml?uc=7964.
12 Montana 62nd Legislature. 2011. *House Bill No. 549: An Act Stating Montana's
     Position on Global Warming.* Accessed on December 11, 2014 at http://open-
     states.org/mt/bills/2011/HB549/; the bill died in committee; another bill was
     introduced in the same Montana legislative session, *House Bill No. 550: An
     Act Prohibiting the State from Implementing Any Federal Greenhouse Gas
     Regulatory Program.* Accessed on December 11, 2014 at http://openstates.
     org/mt/bills/2011/HB550/; the bill was passed by the Montana House of
     Representatives, but also died in committee.

13 Reuters. 2014. "Bill Puts Predicting Weather Before Studying Climate." *New York Times* (April 1). Accessed on April 2, 2014 at www.nytimes. com/2014/04/02/us/bill-puts-predicting-weather-before-studying-climate. html?ref=climateandenergylegislation&_r=0.

14 American Legislative Exchange Council. 2013. *Environmental Literacy Improvement Act.* Accessed on April 2, 2014 at www.alec.org/model-legislation/environmental-literacy-improvement-act/; for a contrasting approach to environmental literacy, see North American Association for Environmental Education. 2011. *Developing a Framework for Assessing Environmental Literacy.* Accessed on April 2, 2014 at www.naaee.net/sites/default/files/framework/DevFramewkAssessEnvLitOnlineEd.pdf.

15 Banerjee, Neela. 2012. "Climate Change Skepticism Seeps into Science Classrooms." *Los Angeles Times* (January 16). Accessed on April 2, 2014 at http://articles.latimes.com/2012/jan/16/nation/la-na-climate-change-school-20120116.

16 Star-Tribune Editorial Board. 2014. "Suppressing Science Education Standards Is Irresponsible." *Casper Star-Tribune* (March 20). Accessed on April 30, 2014 at http://trib.com/opinion/editorial/editorial-board-suppressing-science-education-standards-is-irresponsible/article_9ab88089-1b9d-5275-b462-e4986cdec711.html.

17 Ibid.

18 Greeley, Brendan. 2012. "What Occupy Wall Street Gets Wrong about ALEC." *Bloomberg Businessweek* (March 1). Accessed on April 14, 2014 at www.businessweek.com/articles/2012-03-01/what-occupy-wall-street-gets-wrong-about-alec; MacIntire, Mike. 2012. "Conservative Nonprofit Acts as a Stealth Business Lobbyist." *New York Times* (April 21). Accessed on April 14, 2014 at www.nytimes.com/2012/04/22/us/alec-a-tax-exempt-group-mixes-legislators-and-lobbyists.html?pagewanted=all&_r=0.

19 Ibid.

20 Greeley, Brendan. 2012. "ALEC's Secrets Revealed; Corporations Flee." *Bloomberg Businessweek* (May 3). Accessed on April 14, 2014 at www.businessweek.com/articles/2012-05-03/alecs-secrets-revealed-corporations-flee; Mendoza, Menchie. 2014. "Facebook, Just Like Google, Will Withdraw Support for ALEC." *Tech Times* (September 26). Accessed on December 11, 2014 at www.techtimes.com/articles/16360/20140926/facebook-just-like-google-will-withdraw-support-for-alec.htm; Jackman, Molly. 2013. "ALEC's Influence over Lawmaking in State Legislatures." Brookings (December 6). Accessed on April 12, 2014 at www.brookings.edu/research/articles/2013/12/06-american-legislative-exchange-council-jackman; see also Hertel-Fernandez, Alexander. 2013. "Alec Has Tremendous Influence in State Legislatures. Here's Why." *Washington Post* (December 9). Accessed on April 12, 2014 at www.washington post.com/blogs/monkey-cage/wp/2013/12/09/alec-has-tremendous-influence-in-state-legislatures-heres-why/; for a clickable map of ALEC's state legislator membership and model bills introduced and enacted in each state, see the "ALEC's Influence in Your State." Brookings (December 12). Accessed on April 12, 2014 at www.brookings.edu/research/interactives/2013/map-alec-in-your-state.

21 McCright, Aaron M., and Riley E. Dunlap. 2011. "Cool Dudes: the Denial of Climate Change among Conservative White Males in the United States." *Global Environmental Change*, Vol. 21, No. 4:1163–1172, p. 1163.

22 Kintisch, Eli. 2014. "Into the Maelstrom." *Science*, Vol. 344, No. 6181:250–153; Liu, J.P., J.A. Curry, H.J. Wang, M.R. Song, and R.M. Horton. 2012. "Impact of Declining Arctic Sea Ice on Winter Snowfall." *Proceedings of the National Academy of Sciences*, Vol. 109, No. 11:4074–4079; National Research Council. 2014. *Linkages between Arctic Warming and Mid-Latitude Weather Patterns: Summary of a Workshop*. Washington, DC: National Academies Press.

23 Kuhn, Thomas S. 1962. *The Structure of Scientific Revolutions*. Chicago, IL: University of Chicago Press.

24 Orestes, Naomi. 2004. "The Scientific Consensus on Climate Change." *Science*, Vol. 306, No. 5702:1686.

25 Cook, John, Dana Nuccitelli, Sarah A. Green, Mark Richardson, Barbel Winkler, Rob Paintin, Robert Way, Peter Jacobs, and Andrew Skuce. 2013. "Quantifying the Consensus on Anthropogenic Global Warming in the Scientific Literature." *Environmental Research Letters*, Vol. 8, No. 2 (no page numbers – doi:10.1088/1748–9326/8/2/024024). Accessed on August 3, 2014 at http://iopscience.iop.org/1748–9326/8/2/024024/pdf/1748-9326_8_2_024024.pdf.

26 Ibid., Figure 3.

27 Ding, Ding, Edward W. Maibach, Xiaoquan Zhao, Connie Roser-Renouf, and Anthony Leiserowitz. 2011. "Support for Climate Policy and Societal Action Are Linked to Perceptions about Scientific Agreement." *Nature Climate Change*, Vol. 1, No. 9:462–466.

28 Ibid.

29 Doran, Peter T., and Maggie Kendall Zimmerman. 2009. "Examining the Scientific Consensus on Climate Change." *Eos, Transactions American Geophysical Union*, Vol. 90, No. 3:22–23.

30 Feldman, Lauren, Matthew C. Nisbet, Anthony Leiserowitz, and Edward Maibach. 2010. "The Climate Change Generation? Survey and Analysis of the Perceptions and Beliefs of Young Americans." New Haven, CT: Yale Project on Climate Change (March 2), p. 6. Accessed on April 16, 2014 at http://environment.yale.edu/climate-communication/files/YouthJan2010.pdf.

31 Ibid., p. 7.

32 Leiserowitz, Anthony, and K. Akerlof. 2010. "Race, Ethnicity and Public Responses to Climate Change." New Haven, CT: Yale Project on Climate Change, p. 25. Accessed on April 16, 2014 at http://environment.yale.edu/climate-communication/files/Race_Ethnicity_and_Climate_Change_2.pdf.

33 Ibid.

34 Ibid., p. 4.

35 Dunlap, Riley E., and Aaron M. McCright. 2008. "A Widening Gap: Republican and Democratic Views on Climate Change." *Environment: Science and Policy for Sustainable Development*, Vol. 50, No. 5:26–35.

36 Patchen, Martin. 2006. "Public Attitudes and Behavior about Climate Change." Purdue Climate Change Research Center, PCCRC Outreach Publication

0601 (October). Accessed on April 16, 2014 at www.purdue.edu/discovery-park/climate/assets/pdfs/Patchen%20OP0601.pdf.

37 Xiao, Chenyang, and Aaron M. McCright. 2015. "Gender Differences in Environmental Concern: Revisiting the Institutional Trust Hypothesis in the USA." *Environment and Behavior,* Vol. 47, No. 1:17–37.

38 McCright, Aaron M. 2010. "The Effects of Gender on Climate Change Knowledge and Concern in the American Public." *Population and Environment,* Vol. 32, No. 1:66–87, p. 66.

39 Ibid., p. 76.

40 Goldsmith, Rachel E., Irina Feygina, and John T. Jost. 2013. "The Gender Gap in Environmental Attitudes: A System Justification Perspective." In Alston, M., and K. Wittenbury (eds.), *Research, Action, and Policy: Addressing the Gendered Impacts of Climate Change.* New York: Springer, pp. 159–171, pp. 159–160; see also, Arnocky, Steven, and Mirella Stroink. 2010. "Gender Differences in Environmentalism: The Mediating Role of Emotional Empathy." *Current Research in Social Psychology,* Vol. 16, No. 9:1–14.

41 McCright, op. cit., pp. 81–82.

42 Zelezny, Lynnette C., Poh-Pheng Chua, and Christina Aldrich. 2000. "Elaborating on Gender Differences in Environmentalism." *Journal of Social Issues,* Vol. 56, No. 3:443–457, pp. 443 and 455; McCright, op. cit., pp. 83–84

43 Finucane, Melissa L., Paul Slovic, C.K. Mertz, James Flynn, and Theresa A. Satterfield. 2000. "Gender, Race, and Perceived Risk: The 'White Male' Effect." *Health, Risk & Society,* Vol. 2, No. 2:159–172, p. 159; Palmer, Christina G.S. 2003. "Risk Perception: Another Look at the 'White Male' Effect." *Health, Risk & Society,* Vol. 5, No. 1:71–83.

44 World Economic Forum. 2014. *Global Risks 2014.* Geneva: World Economic Forum. Accessed on April 29, 2014 at www3.weforum.org/docs/WEF_GlobalRisks_Report_2014.pdf, p. 18. My thanks to Robert Antonio for bringing this report to my attention.

45 Kahan, Dan M., Donald Braman, John Gastil, Paul Slovic, and C.K. Mertz. 2007. "Culture and Identity-Protective Cognition: Explaining the White Male Effect in Risk Perception." *Journal of Empirical Legal Studies,* Vol. 4, No. 3:465–505.

46 Leiserowitz, A., Maibach, E., Roser-Renouf, C., and Hmielowski, J.D. 2011. "Politics & Global Warming: Democrats, Republicans, Independents, and the Tea Party." New Haven, CT: Yale Project on Climate Change Communication, p. 24. Accessed on April 16, 2014 at http://environment.yale.edu/climate/files/PoliticsGlobalWarming2011.pdf; prior to the rise of the Tea Party, more men than women identified themselves as "Republican."

47 Ibid., p. 4. European men are less concerned about climate change than European women, especially men whom researchers classify as "right wing in their political outlook," but the climate change gender gap is much larger in the United States; see European Commission and the European Parliament. 2009. "Europeans' Attitudes toward Climate Change." *Special Eurobarometer Report,* No. 313 (July), p. 18. Accessed on May 7, 2014 at http://ec.europa.eu/public_opinion/archives/ebs/ebs_313_en.pdf.

[48] Leiserowitz, A., Maibach, E., Roser-Renouf, C., Feinberg, G., and Howe, P. 2013. "*Global Warming's Six Americas.*" New Haven, CT: Yale Project on Climate Change Communication, pp. 5–6. Accessed on August 3, 2014 at http://environment. yale.edu/climate-communication/files/Six-Americas-September-2012.pdf.

[49] For a discussion of climate change ideological "orthodoxy" in the Tea Party, see Broder, John M. 2010. "Climate Change Doubt Is Tea Party Article of Faith." *New York Times* (October 20). Accessed on May 19, 2014 at www.nytimes. com/2010/10/21/us/politics/21climate.html?_r=0.

[50] Leiserowitz, *et al.*, op. cit., p. 42.

[51] McCright and Dunlap, op. cit., p. 1166.

[52] Ibid., p. 1167.

[53] Ibid.

[54] Pyper, Julia, and ClimateWire. 2011. "Why Conservative White Males Are More Likely to Be Climate Skeptics." *Scientific American* (October 5). Accessed on April 3, 2014 at www.scientificamerican.com/article/why-conservative-white-maes-are-more-likely-climate-skeptics/

[55] Newport, Frank, and Andrew Dugan. 2015. "College-Educated Republicans Most Skeptical of Global Warming." Gallup (March 26). Accessed on June 1, 2015 at www.scientificamerican.com/article/why-conservative-white-maes-are-more-likely-climate-skeptics/

[56] Mooney, Chris. 2012. *The Republican Brain: The Science of Why They Deny Science – and Reality.* New York: Wiley & Sons, pp. 48–49.

[57] Goldsmith *et al.*, op. cit., p. 160; Norgaard, Kari Marie. 2011. *Living in Denial: Climate Change, Emotions, and Everyday Life.* Cambridge, MA: Massachusetts Institute of Technology Press.

[58] Jost, John T., and Erin P. Hennes. 2010. "The Mind of the Climate Change Skeptic." *Association for Psychological Science Observer,* Vol. 26, No. 4. Accessed on April 17, 2014 at www.psychologicalscience.org/index.php/ publications/ observer/2013/april-13/the-mind-of-the-climate-change-skeptic.html.

[59] Jost and Hennes, op. cit.

[60] Ibid., p. 165.

[61] Ibid., p. 164.

[62] McCright and Dunlap, 2011, op. cit., p. 1163.

[63] The George C. Marshall Institute. 2014. Accessed on April 17, 2014 at http:// marshall.org/.

[64] Lahsen, Myanna. 2008. "The Experience of Modernity in the Greenhouse: A Cultural Analysis of a Physicist 'Trio' Supporting the Backlash against Global Warming." *Global Environmental Change*, Vol. 18, No. 4:204–219.

[65] Hevesi, Dennis. 2008. "Frederick Seitz, Physicist Who Led Skeptics of Global Warming, Dies at 96." *New York Times* (March 6). Accessed on March 17, 2014 at www.nytimes.com/2008/03/06/us/06seitz.html?_r=0; see also Hertsgaard, Mark. 2006. "While Washington Slept." *Vanity Fair* (May). Accessed on April 17, 2014 at www.vanityfair.com/politics/features/2006/05/warming200605?cur rentPage=all.

[66] Al Gore. 2010. "We Can't Wish Away Climate Change." *New York Times* (February 27). Accessed on April 18, 2014 at www.nytimes.com/2010/02/28/opinion/28gore.html?pagewanted=all.

[67] Oreskes, Naomi, and Erik M. Conway. 2010. *Merchants of Doubt: How a Handful of Scientists Obscured the Truth on Issues from Tobacco Smoke to Global Warming.* New York: Bloomsbury Press.

[68] Ibid., p. 148.

[69] Ibid., p. 242; recent research extends this analysis to the National Football League's slow response to the scientific evidence of the role of concussion in brain injury and disease among football players; Fainaru-Wada, Mark, and Steve Fainaru. 2013. *League of Denial: The NFL, Concussions and the Battle for Truth.* New York: Crown Archetype.

[70] Brulle, Robert J. 2014. "Institutionalizing Delay: Foundation Funding and the Creation of US Climate Change Counter-movement Organizations." *Climatic Change*, Vol. 122, No. 4:681–694.

[71] The Heartland Institute. 2014. "About the Heartland Institute." Accessed on April 17, 2014 at https://heartland.org/about.

[72] Nongovernmental International Panel on Climate Change. 2013. "About the NIPCC." Accessed on April 17, 2014 at www.nipccreport.org/about/about.html.

[73] Center for the Study of Carbon Dioxide and Global Change. 2014. "Carbon Dioxide and Global Warming: Where We Stand on the Issue." Accessed on April 17, 2014 at www.co2science.org/about/position/globalwarming.php.

[74] For a summary of such claims and critiques of them, see Svoboda, Michael. 2013. "Uprooting the 'Carbon Dioxide Is Plant Food' Argument. "Yale Forum on Climate Change in the Media (July 24). Accessed on April 18, 2014 at www.yaleclimatemediaforum.org/2013/07/uprooting-the-carbon-dioxide-is-plant-food-argument/; LePage, Michael. 2007. "Climate Change: A Guide for the Perplexed." *New Scientist* (May). Accessed on April 18, 2014 at www.newscientist.com/article/dn11462-climate-change-a-guide-for-the-perplexed.html#.U1GEM_ldXh5.

[75] Anshelm, Jonas, and Martin Hultman. 2014. "A Green *Fatwa*? Climate Change as a Threat to the Masculinity of Industrial Modernity." *NORMA: International Journal for Masculinity Studies*, Vol. 9, No. 2:84–96, p. 85.

[76] There are some established women scientists who are skeptical of aspects of established climate science, but they often chafe at being referred to as "denialists" or "skeptics." They include Tamsin Edwards, University of Bristol (http://blogs.plos.org/models/author/models/), Judith Curry, Georgia Institute of Technology (http://judithcurry.com/), and Lucia Liljegren, Iowa State University (http://rankexploits.com/musings/2014/bleg-timeline-software/); two non-scientist women climate skeptic bloggers are Donna Laframboise (http://nofrakkingconsensus.com/) and Joanne Nova (http://joannenova.com.au/); my thanks to Stephen Egbert, University of Kansas Geography Department, for bringing these women to my attention.

[77] Union of Concerned Scientists. 2013. "Global Warming Skeptic Organizations." Accessed on April 18, 2014 at www.ucsusa.org/global_warming/solutions/fight-misinformation/global-warming-skeptic.html.

78 Antilla, Liisa. 2005. "Climate of Skepticism: US Newspaper Coverage of the Science of Climate Change." *Global Environmental Change*, Vol. 15, No. 4:338–352.

79 National Research Council. 2011. *America's Climate Choices*. Washington, DC: National Academies Press. Accessed on April 17, 2014 at www.nap.edu/download.php?record_id=12781.

80 For a list of tactics used by climate change denial organizations which include personal and professional attacks, see Dunlap, Riley E., and Aaron M. McCright. 2013. "The Climate Change Denial Campaign." Scholars Strategy Network. Accessed on April 14, 2014 at www.scholarsstrategynetwork.org/sites/default/files/ssn_key_findings_dunlap_and_mccright_on_climate_change_denial.pdf.

81 Lewandowsky, Stephen, Michael E. Mann, Linda Bauld, Gerard Hastings, and Elizabeth F. Loftus. 2013. "The Subterranean War on Science." *Association for Psychological Science Observer*, Vol. 26, No. 9. Accessed on April 17, 2014 at www.psychologicalscience.org/index.php/publications/observer/2013/november-13/the-subterranean-war-on-science.html; my thanks to Robert Brulle for bringing this article to my attention.

82 Ibid.

83 The Rush Limbaugh Show. 2012. "Environmentalist Wacko: Climate Change Skeptics Are Sick." April 12. Accessed on April 17, 2014 at www.rushlimbaugh.com/daily/2012/04/02/environmentalist_wacko_climate_change_skeptics_are_sick.

84 Browning, Dominique. 2012. "When Grown-Ups Bully Climate Scientists." *Time* (April 10). Accessed on April 17, 2014 at http://ideas.time.com/2012/04/10/when-grownups-bully-climate-scientists/.

85 Theel, Shauna. 2014. "Eighty-Five Percent of Climate Change Guests Are Men." *Media Matters for America* (April 21). Accessed on April 25, 2014 at http://mediamatters.org/blog/2014/04/21/report-eighty-five-percent-of-climate-change-gu/198955.

86 For an overview of the investigations and findings as well as continued email account hacking, see Marshall, Michael. 2011. "Climategate 2: Hacked Emails Released." *New Scientist* (November 23). Accessed on April 17, 2014 at www.newscientist.com/article/dn21203-climategate-2-hacked-emails-released.html#.U1Bj4PldXh4; see also the anti-skeptic blog, Skeptical Science. 2014. "What Do the 'Climategate' Hacked CRU Emails Tell Us?" Accessed on April 17, 2014 at www.skepticalscience.com/Climategate-CRU-emails-hacked.htm.

87 Steyn, Mark. 2012. "Football and Hockey." *National Review* (June 15). Accessed on June 1, 2015 at www.nationalreview.com/corner/309442/football-and-hockey-mark-steyn; see also Mann, Michael E. 2012. *The Hockey Stick and Climate Wars: Dispatches from the Front Lines*. New York: Columbia University Press.

88 Fox News. 2012. "Michael Mann vs. National Review, Competitive Enterprise Institute." Accessed on April 18, 2014 at www.foxnews.com/science/interactive/2012/10/23/michael-mann-vs-national-review-competitive-enterprise-institute/.

[89] Greeley, March 1, 2012, op. cit.

[90] Brulle, op. cit.

[91] Robert Brulle, personal communication, April 15, 2014.

[92] Ibid., p. 687.

[93] Ibid., p. 691.

[94] Ibid., p. 690; see also Fischer, Douglas. 2013. "'Dark Money' Funds Climate Change Denial Effort." *Scientific American* (December 23). Accessed on April 18, 2014 at www.scientificamerican.com/article/dark-money-funds-climate-change-denial-effort/.

[95] Eilperin, Juliet. 2014. "Two Environmental Groups to Create Political Alliance." *Washington Post* (April 14). Accessed on April 16, 2014 at www.wa of him and shingtonpost.com/blogs/post-politics/wp/2014/04/14/two-environmental-groups-to-create-political-alliance/.

[96] IPCC. 2014. "Greenhouse Gas Emissions Accelerate despite Reduction Efforts; Many Pathways to Substantial Emissions Reductions Are Available." IPCC Press Release (April 13). Accessed on May 18, 2014 at www.ipcc.ch/pdf/ar5/pr_wg3/20140413_pr_pc_wg3_en.pdf.

[97] Brulle, op. cit., p. 690; see also Brulle, Robert J., Jason Carmichael, and J. Craig Jenkins. 2012. "Shifting Public Opinion on Climate Change: An Empirical Assessment of Factors Influencing Concern over Climate Change in the US, 2002–2010." *Climatic Change*, Vol. 114, No. 2:169–188; other researchers confirmed that the availability of scientific evidence about climate change does not increase public interest or change public opinion, see Anderegg, William R., and Gregory R. Goldsmith. 2014. "Public Interest in Climate Change Over the Past Decade and the Effects of the 'Climate Gate' Media Event." *Environmental Research Letters*, Vol. 9, No. 5:1–8.

[98] Jones, Jeffrey M. 2010. "Conservatives' Doubts about Global Warming Grow." Gallup (March 11). Accessed on April 18, 2014 at www.gallup.com/poll/126563/conservatives-doubts-global-warming-grow.aspx.

[99] Saad, Lydia. "U.S. Views on Climate Change Stable After Extreme Winter." Gallup (March 25). Accessed on June 1, 2015 at www.gallup.com/poll/182150/views-climate-change-stable-extreme-winter.aspx?utm_source=CATEGORY_CLIMATE_CHANGE&utm_medium=topic&utm_campaign=tiles.

[100] Brown, Donald A. 2010. "Is Climate Science Disinformation a Crime against Humanity?" *The Guardian* (November 1). Accessed on May 19, 2014 at www.theguardian.com/environment/cif-green/2010/nov/01/climate-science-disinformation-crime.

7
GENDER AND CLIMATE CHANGE POLICY

In previous chapters we have examined the gender dimensions of climate change impacts, science, and skepticism. We have seen some areas where gender matters, and some where it does not. Both men and women struggle in the face of climate change-related disasters, but research has shown that women are more likely to die in greater numbers than men. Some effects of climate change pose greater threats to men (wildfires), while others have disproportionately negative outcomes for women (heat waves). Both men and women work as scientists, but men far outnumber women in the fields that dominate climate science. A major funder of US science, the Department of Defense (DOD), has a long history of predominantly male membership, an entrenched culture that valorizes masculinity, and research priorities that emphasize security and militarize scientific inquiry. American men and women are the least likely in the global North to recognize that there is a scientific consensus about climate change or acknowledge its seriousness. Greater numbers of men deny the existence of climate change, and male voices dominate the discourse of climate skepticism in politics, news media, blogs, and nonprofit organizations. In this chapter we will shine a gender spotlight on the last piece of the gender and climate change puzzle: climate change policy.

"Where Are the Women [and the Men]?"

During the past 25 years, a well-known feminist political scientist repeatedly has asked this question about many aspects of the field of International Relations (IR): "Where are the women?"[1] IR is a discipline with a quintessentially masculine history of diplomats, governments, treaties, and wars. It is well-established that these government officials and generals have been men. But it is worth noting that the countries they represent have women living in them, and these women are affected by the men's decisions. An example is the history of US–Latin American political and economic relations:

> [So-called] "banana republics" were those Central American countries which came to be dominated by the United Fruit Company's monoculture, the US Marines and their hand-picked dictators ... Yet these political systems, and the international relationships which underpin them, have been discussed as if women scarcely existed. The principal actors on all sides have been portrayed ... as if their being male was insignificant. Thus the ways in which their shared masculinity allowed agribusiness entrepreneurs to form alliances with men in their own diplomatic corps and with men in Nicaraguan and or Honduran societies have been left unexamined.[2]

The point being made here is: not only are the women invisible in much classical international relations research, so are the men – that is, they are invisible as "men." By looking for women, you also can find men. This discovery allows you to see who the men are, what they think, whom they represent, and what they are up to ... as men. The search for women *and* men in the human dimensions of climate change has guided our explorations throughout the past chapters, and is the reason this book is entitled "Gender and Climate Change," not "Women and Climate Change."

Our focus in this chapter is the gendered dimensions of climate change policy: Where are the women (and the men) in climate change international policy organizations and negotiations? Before beginning our gender quest, we need to map the international climate change policy landscape, which is located mainly within the realm of governmental, intergovernmental, and nongovernmental organizations (NGOs), especially the United Nations (UN). The next section will provide an overview of climate policymaking organizations and processes, followed by a discussion of the places of women and men in climate change policy.

The International Climate Change Policy Terrain

The United Nations Framework Convention on Climate Change (UNFCCC) is one of three "Rio Conventions" adopted at the 1992 UN-sponsored "Earth Summit" in Rio de Janeiro.[3] The other two Rio Conventions are the UN Convention on Biological Diversity and the UN Convention to Combat Desertification.[4] The UNFCCC is an international treaty established to address increasing global temperatures and their impact on the planet. Five years after the Rio Summit, in 1997, the Kyoto Protocol was adopted and linked to the UNFCCC to legally bind signatory countries (known as "parties") to greenhouse emission reduction targets.[5] Establishing these emissions standards required scientific information; that is the role of the Intergovernmental Panel on Climate Change (IPCC). The IPCC's First Assessment Report provided baseline scientific data for the 1992 Earth Summit.[6]

Since it was established in 1988, the IPCC has issued assessment reports approximately every six years (1990, 1995, 2001, 2007, 2013) to inform the public about findings in climate change science and about climate change's progress, impacts, vulnerabilities, adaptation, and mitigation. These IPCC reports have served as a basis for discussions at the annual meetings of the "Conference of the Parties" (COP) to the UNFCCC treaty. COP meetings are held in a different host country each year to facilitate climate change negotiations among the 194 countries that are parties to the UNFCCC treaty.[7] Since 2005, parties to the Kyoto Protocol also have met at the COP meetings.[8]

The agendas of annual COP meetings contain lists of decisions to be made, resolutions to be passed, and negotiations to be conducted. In addition to voting members, there are hundreds of national representatives and world leaders, and thousands of other attendees, including scientific experts, representatives of the media, and members of intergovernmental and nongovernmental organizations, such as the International Atomic Energy Agency, Organization for Economic Co-operation and Development, World Wildlife Fund, World Coal Association, and Pew Charitable Trusts.[9]

In December, 2009, Denmark hosted the COP15 meeting in Copenhagen with the ambitious goal of achieving a comprehensive international climate agreement which included a plan to reduce global warming and create a mechanism for wealthy countries to finance climate change adaptation efforts in the global South:

> The Copenhagen Climate Change Conference raised climate change policy to the highest political level. Close to 115 world leaders attended the high-level segment, making it one of the largest gatherings of world leaders ever outside UN headquarters in New York. More than 40,000 people, representing governments, nongovernmental organizations, intergovernmental organizations, faith-based organizations, media, and UN agencies applied for accreditation [to attend the meeting].[10]

The meeting concluded by announcing the "Copenhagen Accord," which included a long-term goal of limiting global warming to 2°C above pre-industrial levels. "There was, however, no agreement on how to do this in practical terms," and even the mainly symbolic agreement did not satisfy vulnerable poorer countries who had demanded an agreement to limit the global temperature increase to 1.5 °C.[11]

After the 2009 Copenhagen COP meeting, the climate science consensus continued to grow and the IPCC issued special reports urging action, such as *Managing the Risks of Extreme Events and Disasters to Advance Climate Change Adaptation.*[12] The COP met year after year, but in the years after Copenhagen they were not successful in establishing viable plans to limit greenhouse gas (GHG) emissions. There was little progress on designing strategies for low carbon development in emerging and growing economies such as India and China, and the effort stalled to find funding for adaption measures in countries in the global South who were suffering damage from climate change at levels far disproportionate to their contribution, if any, to the problem.

"Call in the Women"

The failure of the COP meetings to generate binding decisions about how to address the causes and consequences of climate change, the general ineffectiveness of the UN, and the fact that both the COPs and the UN are dominated by men, led one researcher to conclude that it was time to "call in the women":

> The current landscape of industries, governments and other bodies with a say in climate change issues – including transport, energy, waste management, architecture and city planning – is predominantly male. In the [2007] Intergovernmental Panel on Climate Change (IPCC), only 5 of the 31 chairs, co-chairs and vice-chairs are women. Perhaps surprisingly, this dearth of female faces extends to nongovernmental organizations and campaign groups. In my eight years as chair of the UK-based Women's Environmental Network, I was struck by the machismo of much of the environmental campaigning sector.[13]

An interdisciplinary team of climate researchers further documented the absence of women in major climate change meetings by reviewing the gender composition of presenters at the March 2009 Copenhagen Climate Congress. The Congress was attended by "more than 2500 delegates from nearly 80 countries," with a goal of updating the 2007 IPCC's Fourth Assessment Report in the lead-up to the Copenhagen COP15 meeting later that year.[14] The researchers examined 590 abstracts from the oral presentations made at the Congress, and found that the gender of the presenters mirrored the gender composition of climate science generally:

> Less than a third of oral presentations were from women. This was especially pronounced in the geosciences, where less than 20% of presentations were from women, contrasting with more than 40% within the social sciences.[15]

The research team also analyzed the content of the presentations to understand the dominant message and approach of the presenters. They found very limited consideration of gender in the abstracts in favor of an almost exclusive emphasis on the natural environmental aspects of climate change:

> [A]n epistemological hierarchy exists in the framing of climate change whereby the geosciences disproportionately influence the representation of climate change as primarily an environmental issue. Developed country and male contributions also disproportionately influence this framing. We argue that simply carrying out more physical science – and framing climate change as an awaited future catastrophe – will not enable political leaders to win the case for large-scale, transformative social change.[16]

To understand the reasons for and implications of viewing climate change as an issue mainly involving the natural environment with an emphasis on catastrophic outcomes, the researchers looked for the men and their agenda by drawing on the work of gender scholars who argue that:

> [T]he lack of attention to gender issues in climate change reflects a more general misunderstanding of the social sciences within mainstream climate framing ... the mainstream framing [i]s stereotypically "masculine" in its discourse of technological innovation, large-scale economic instruments, and climate modeling ... such discourses [are] inherently gender-inequitable: for example, women's restricted access to resources such as land, credit, and information hinders them from playing an equitable role in climate-mitigation market instruments.[17]

The exclusion of women's voices and perspectives from the 2007 IPCC Fourth Assessment Report (and earlier reports) and the 2009 Copenhagen Climate Conference represents business as usual not only in climate science, but in climate negotiations and policymaking as well as in other arenas of national and international politics. In 2015, women represented only 22 percent of members of all parliamentary structures in the world's national governments (women were 19 percent of US House of Representatives and 20 percent of the US Senate), and of the 194 countries party to the UNFCCC, only 24 (12 percent) were headed by women (thus far none of the 43 US presidents have been women).[18]

Women and the UN: Decades of Dithering

Even though none of the eight UN Secretary-Generals have been female, women's marginalization in UN activities might be seen as odd, since the UN established its Commission on the Status of Women (CSW) in 1946, less than a year after its founding. It would be an understatement to say that progress on women's rights and inclusion has been slow since that time. Although the commission hired a number of women and busied itself with measuring women's health, education, and political status during its first decades, women's groups frequently complained about the CSW's limited results, complaints that presaged current feminist criticisms of the UN, UNFCCC, IPCC, and the COP process.

Half a century after the establishment of the UN Commission on the Status of Women, there remained deep dissatisfaction with the conditions of women's lives around the world and their lack of representation in the UN. In 1995 women's issues were front and center at the UN's Fourth World Conference on Women in Beijing, which issued the Beijing Declaration and Platform for Action, with its "agenda for women's empowerment" advocating the removal of all obstacles to:

> women's active participation in all spheres of public and private life through a full and equal share in economic, social, cultural and political decision-making. This means that the principle of shared power and responsibility should be established between men and women at home, in the workplace and in the wider national and international communities.[19]

Five years later, in 2000, the 23rd special session of the UN General Assembly (Bejing+5) was convened to discuss progress, gaps, and emerging issues in the pursuit of gender equality and the empowerment of women. Climate change was not a prominent topic. Women's rights also were on the agenda at the 2000 United Nations Millennium Summit, where one of the eight Millennium Development Goals (MDGs) was "to promote gender equality and empower women."[20] Again, climate change was not ranked high among the MDGs, and women remained on the margins of the UNFCCC's annual COP meetings and IPCC's assessment activities.

As the decade progressed, women's organizations denounced the UN's glacial pace and, some said, casual disregard of gender considerations in climate change and sustainable development priorities. Activists demanded that women and their interests be included in formal UN climate change meetings and deliberating bodies. What had been a largely behind-the-scenes organizing movement for women's rights in climate change matters exploded into public view at the 2007 COP13 meeting in Bali, Indonesia. In response to these public pressures, the Indonesian Ministry for the Environment "expressed their commitment to support women's involvement in the conference as well as the desire for integrating gender equality in the deliberations."[21]

Indonesia's Environment Ministry was not successful in "mainstream[ing] gender into the Bali Outcomes."[22] In fact, after the public spotlight dimmed following the COP13 meeting, the ministry quickly seemed to lose interest in women's issues, and did not place gender on the Indonesian agenda at the next COP meeting in Poland in 2008, nor was gender included in Indonesia's National Council for Climate Change established that same year.[23] Despite Indonesia's short gender attention span, the Bali COP meeting provided fertile grounds for the creation of influential women-and-climate-change organizations. For instance, in 2008 the NGO GenderCC – Women for Climate Justice was created to establish a clear link between climate change and gender interests and inequalities, and call for fundamental changes beyond including women in the climate change establishment. Their slogan: *No Climate Justice without Gender Justice!*

> The challenges of climate change and gender injustice resemble each other – they require whole system change: not just gender mainstreaming but transforming gender relations and societal

structures. Not just technical amendments to reduce emissions, but real mitigation through awareness and change of unsustainable life-styles and the current ideology and practice of unlimited economic growth.[24]

Mobilizing for Change

Following the COP13 in Bali, GenderCC and other women's organizations began to document the systematic underrepresentation of women in the activities of the UNFCCC. A 2008 study of governmental delegations to the first 13 annual COP meetings found that women's representation ranged from a low of 15 percent at COP3 in 1997 to a high of 28 percent at COP9 in 2003.[25]

The mobilized atmosphere that followed in the wake of the Bali meeting generated a flurry of reports and policy studies of women and climate change.[26] The UN was discovering women (but not yet men) all over the climate change issue, and longstanding women's interest groups were turning their attention toward climate change. In 2009 the "Beijing Agenda" expanded to include climate change in its "International Conference on Gender and Disaster Risk Reduction," but the focus was mainly on women's vulnerability to disasters, with only lip service paid to "gender mainstreaming" (the inclusion of gender in policy and planning), since very little had been done in most countries to make women equal partners in disaster preparedness, response, or recovery.[27]

In 2010, a decade after the start of the UN Millennium Summit, an assessment of its MDGs found that not only was "there an inherent conflict between the development agenda and required [climate change] mitigation actions," but in the developing world "women are more vulnerable against climate change impacts. Overcoming gender disparities is an important factor to reduce vulnerability of societies against these impacts."[28] Besides women's vulnerabilities, UN documents repeatedly reminded readers of women's value though there were few concrete plans to remove persisting institutional barriers to including them in decision-making:

[W]omen are not only vulnerable to climate change but they are also effective actors or agents of change in relation to both mitigation and adaptation. Women often have a strong body of knowledge and expertise that can be used in climate change mitigation, disaster reduction and adaptation strategies. Furthermore, women's responsibilities in households and communities, as stewards of natural and household resources, positions them well to contribute to livelihood strategies adapted to changing environmental realities.[29]

Even UN Secretary-General Ban Ki-moon seemed to be getting the message. In the run-up to the 2009 Copenhagen COP15 meeting, he stressed the importance of making space for women in climate change negotiations:

[We must create] an environment where women are key decision-makers on climate change, and play an equally central role in carrying out these decisions. We must do more to give greater say to women in addressing the climate challenge.[30]

In a classic instance of "actions speaking louder than words," five months after this affirmation, in February 2010, the Secretary-General contradicted his statements by appointing a 19-member *male-only* "Climate Change Financing" group to "study the potential sources of revenue for financing mitigation and adaptation in developing countries, and to make progress on this key issue in the course of 2010."[31] The exclusion of women from this important UN committee outraged women's groups, who demanded that women be included on the committee and that women's issues be added to the agenda. The response from the UN did nothing to calm the waters:

According to Ban's spokesperson Ari Gaitanis, a multitude of factors, such as nominations by governments, geographical representation and balance between developed and developing countries, influenced the decision-making. Mentioning also the time constraint, Gaitanis admits that these factors precluded appropriate attention to the gender balance.[32]

As a "concession," Ban accepted the French government's offer to replace its French appointee with a woman.[33] One analyst wondered how much any woman single-handedly could be expected to change the direction of a group favored and selected by an entrenched "boy's club" like the UN:[34]

> In March 2010, a coalition of women's environmental groups challenged the all-male nominations to the UN's High Level Advisory Group on Climate Change Financing. One woman, Christine Lagarde, the French minister of economic affairs, industry and employment, replaced a man in the advisory group, although alone she is unlikely to be able to make significant changes. Similarly, the May 2010 appointment of Christiana Figueres, a former government minister and environmental negotiator from Costa Rica, as the new executive secretary of the UN Framework Convention on Climate Change is encouraging, but alone it might not be enough.[35]

At the end of 2010, the UN was still lamenting gender disparities and their implications for climate change vulnerability, and its mainly male national negotiating teams were still ineffective at brokering an international climate change agreement. That year an article appeared in the journal *Nature*, announcing that it was time to "call in the women."[36]

The "Doha Miracle?"

By 2012, at the COP18 meeting in Doha, Qatar, the mobilization of women's groups seemed to be paying off. The COP made an official decision to try to reverse the UNFCCC's gender exclusionary course:

> In decision 23/CP.18, the COP agreed to promote gender balance and improve the participation of women in UNFCCC negotiations, and adopted a goal of gender balance in bodies established under the Convention and the Kyoto Protocol to ... inform more effective climate change policy that addresses the needs of women and men equally.[37]

UNFCCC Executive Secretary Christiana Figueres pronounced decision 23/CP.18 the "Doha Miracle," because it reflected an official commitment to include women in UNFCCC activities, and because it required that data on gender participation be collected and made public. The lack of public gender data prior to 2012 made it very difficult for researchers and policy analysts to document gender representation in many UN bodies, including the UNFCCC. For instance, in order to determine the extent of women's participation in the COP process, researchers had to pore over the UNFCCC participant list for each meeting and hand count the number of women whose names appeared on the list. They found that the average participation by women on UNFCCC national delegations 2008–2012 was 32 percent.[38] Because of the Doha COP18 decision to require UNFCCC gender participation records be kept, it was much easier for me to find that the proportion of women delegates to the 2013 COP19 meeting in Poznań, Poland, had not increased.[39]

The IPCC also has begun to report the number of women on most of its assessment report Chapter Teams. There were three Working Group reports in the IPCC's Fifth Assessment Report (AR5): Working Group I: The Physical Science Basis, Working Group II: Impacts, Adaptation, and Vulnerability, and Working Group III: Mitigation of Climate Change. In 2013/2014, women comprised 18.4 percent of AR5 Working Group I's Chapter Teams, 28 percent of Working Group II's Chapter Teams and 18.6 percent of Working Group III's Chapter Teams.[40] These percentages were not appreciably different from past Assessment Reports.

The women had been called in, but clearly they had not yet arrived in substantially increased numbers. Women's representation on COP delegations a year after Doha at COP19 in Poznań in 2013 (29 percent) was virtually the same as their presence a decade earlier at COP9 in Milan in 2003 (28 percent). That underrepresentation combined with the low rate of female representation on the 2013/2014 IPCC AR5 chapter teams to raise doubts about the transformative power of the so-called Doha Miracle.[41]

Should we care if the canonization of Doha is premature? Does it matter that women remain minority voices in climate change research, policymaking, and international negotiations? How convincing are the arguments that male researchers are focusing too much on technical science issues that are low on the agendas of many non-scientists and women's groups? Is it a real concern that men are failing to negotiate effective international climate change agreements to slow the increase of GHG emissions? The rest of this chapter will search for answers to these questions and evaluate the utility of calling in the women to save the planet.

General Issues in Climate Change Ethics

Climate change is not only a scientific, or environmental, or political problem; it also is an ethical problem. There are issues of *blame* (Who is causing the problem?), *harm* (Who is being injured by climate change?), *justice* (How are the injured being compensated?), *responsibility* (Who will compensate and assist the injured?), and *representation* (Who gets to decide the answers to these questions?). The issues raised by these and other moral questions associated with climate change have led some researchers to refer to climate change as a "perfect moral storm."[42] Their argument rests on several aspects of climate change that "encourage moral corruption or the propensity among those who cause climate change to ignore their duties, responsibilities, and obligations" for enacting just and ethical climate change responses.[43] Those aspects of climate change that challenge morality are: 1) the global nature of the problem – what happens in one place affects those in other places, 2) the intergenerational timescale on which climate change takes place – the need to pay in advance for the problems facing future generations, and 3) the inadequacy of contemporary ethical and political systems – theories and institutions are not prepared for nor do they have the authority to ethically guide policies or design and enforce binding regulations addressing climate change and other complex sustainability issues, especially when they span national borders.[44]

Table 7.1 CO_2 Emissions and GDP Per Capita of Top 25 GHG Emitters, 2009–2011[47]

COUNTRY	CO_2 EMISSIONS IN MILLIONS OF METRIC TONS 2011	PERCENT OF GLOBAL CO_2 EMISSIONS	CO_2 EMISSIONS PER CAPITA 2009	GDP PER CAPITA IN CURRENT US$ 2011
China	8715.3	26.8	5.8	5447
United States	5490.6	16.9	17.7	49,854
Russia	1788.1	5.5	11.2	13,284
India	1725.8	5.3	1.4	1540
Japan	1180.6	3.6	8.6	46,135
Germany	748.5	2.3	9.3	44,355
Iran	624.9	1.9	6.9	7006
Korea, South	611.0	1.9	10.9	22,388
Canada	552.6	1.7	16.0	50,578
Saudi Arabia	513.6	1.6	18.6	24,116
United Kingdom	496.8	1.5	8.4	39,186
Brazil	475.4	1.5	2.1	12,576
Mexico	462.3	1.4	4.0	9717
South Africa	461.6	1.4	9.2	7790
Indonesia	426.8	1.3	1.7	3471
Italy	400.9	1.2	7.0	36,180
Australia	392.3	1.2	19.6	62,081
France	374.3	1.1	6.3	42,560
Spain	318.6	1.0	7.1	31,118
Poland	307.9	0.9	7.4	13,382
Ukraine	304.4	0.9	5.6	3576
Turkey	296.3	0.9	3.3	10,605
Taiwan	293.3	0.9	12.7	20,030
Thailand	269.6	0.8	3.8	5192
Netherlands	253.0	0.8	14.9	49,886
World	32,578.6	–	4.5	12,700

An example of the challenge of determining moral responsibility and ethical action in response to climate change involves the issue of location – *where* are the activities producing GHG emissions, and *where* are the effects of those emissions? A number of agencies track the greenhouse emissions of individual countries, and researchers compile climate observations and make projections to indicate where the damage from climate change is occurring now and into the future.[45] Table 7.1 shows total and per capita carbon dioxide (CO_2) emissions from the consumption of energy (coal, oil, gas) in 2011 and 2009 respectively and gross domestic product (GDP) per capita in 2011 for the 20 major CO_2-emitting countries.[46]

As the table shows, the top five CO_2-emitting countries in 2011 were China, the US, Russia, India, and Japan, in that order. Together these five countries produced nearly three-fifths (58 percent) of global CO_2 emissions in 2011.[48] Historically, the US has led the world in CO_2 emissions, accounting for more than a quarter of global emissions in 2005. In 2006, China moved ahead of the US as the world leader in CO_2 emissions.[49] By 2011, China contributed 26.8 percent of global CO_2 emissions, and the US global share had dropped to 16.9 percent.

Considering these total emissions data alone, China, the US, and the other top CO_2 emitters bear the greatest ethical responsibility for reducing CO_2 emissions to slow associated global warming. They also are morally accountable for compensating low-emitting countries for damages done to them by climate change. The moral certainty wavers, however, when CO_2 emissions are put in historical and demographic contexts.

Until 2006, the world's industrial countries were the major source of CO_2 emissions. CO_2 added to the atmosphere since the beginning of the Industrial Revolution and especially during the period from 1950 to the present largely has come from industrial country emissions. Only in the last decade have the emerging economies of Asia, Latin America, and Eastern Europe begun to contribute significantly to global CO_2 emissions. Much of the economic growth and associated CO_2 emissions in emerging economies result from industrial production that has been outsourced from the developed world: US, European, and rich Asian countries' consumption is pushing up China's and India's emissions as they burn more coal to run their factories to produce goods for us to buy:

> [C]ritics say blaming China for its rampant pollution is unfair, given all the manufacturing the world's developed countries outsource to Chinese companies. Qin Gang, China's foreign ministry spokesman, refers to China as the "world's factory" and

says: "A lot of what you use, wear and eat is produced in China … On the one hand, you increase production in China; on the other hand you criticize China on the emission reduction issue." Yang Ailun of Greenpeace China agrees: "All the West has done is export a great slice of its carbon footprint to China and make China the world's factory."[50]

As Table 7.1 shows, most of the world's wealthiest economies, as measured by GDP per capita, appear on the list of 20 highest CO_2 emitters. This is part of the demographic aspect of the moral responsibility question. Who is more responsible for China's CO_2 emissions? Is it the US and other wealthy national consumers of its industrial products, or is it China, for producing those products in an effort to raise the standard of living of its people? Another demographic aspect can be seen in per capita emissions. The US GDP per capita is more than nine times greater than China's GDP per capita, and US emissions per capita are more than three times greater than China's. Should China be asked to reduce its emissions and slow or stall improvement in its people's lives, or should Americans and other wealthy consumer economies be asked to find ways to more sustainably maintain our standard of living? Is there no moral responsibility in consumer societies to develop alternative energies, increase energy efficiencies, or use our vast technical capacity to reorient our economies from a dependency on growth to an emphasis on sustainability?

Population – its growth and regulation – is another demographic factor that raises an interesting set of ethical and policy issues involving gender and responsibility. While women produce children, men participate, and often exert significant control over women's reproductive choices.[51] In many countries and communities there are official, religious, social, and interpersonal forces regulating women's and men's access to and use of contraceptives and abortion. In some cases, access is restricted or defined in moral terms (e.g. Catholic Church doctrine and abortion restrictions in the US, Ireland, and other countries).[52] In other cases, reproduction technologies are mandatory or imposed (e.g. China's one-child policy, involuntary sterilizations of American Indian women).[53] The debate about population can devolve into blaming women for not effectively managing their fertility. Aside from many women's limited control over childbearing, some researchers argue that it is not simply a question of how many humans are on the planet, but how much they are consuming:

> World Watch names "population" as a major cause of environmental degradation, and in fact, the climate debate has brought old style environmental talk about population back into fashion. This removes the need to examine capitalist over-production and consumption – mostly in the industrialised North, by placing responsibility for climate destabilisation onto politically voiceless women – mostly in the global South. Yet what kind of arithmetic is involved in this correlation between emissions and population? If 60 per cent of humanity is responsible for only 1 per cent of carbon emissions – why talk about population?[54]

As the cases of China's emissions and population control illustrate, climate change justice often is framed in regional and national terms: which countries produce the greatest harm; which countries will be harmed the greatest? If we look for the men and the women in these national settings, we can discover that there is a gender element in this moral calculus of blame and harm. The next section engenders climate change ethics.

Three Reasons to Call in the Women: Ethics, Effectiveness, Economics

Researchers and women's interest groups offer several logics for involving women in climate change research, policymaking, and negotiation. They can be summarized as the "3-Es" of women's participation: including women in climate change matters is *ethical, effective,* and *economical.*[55] The sections below review the literature supporting these 3-E reasons for calling in the women.

Gender, Ethics, and Climate Change

When gender enters into discussions of climate change morality, it raises different questions about who is responsible for CO_2 emissions and consumption. Research was presented in Chapter 4 that measured men's and women's ecological footprints in developed societies such as the US, Canada, and Sweden. Those researchers concluded that men's participation in economic activities and consumption linked to higher GHG emissions made them more responsible than women for the problems associated with climate change.[56]

Added to the issue of a gendered environmental footprint is gendered responsibility stemming from men's power. Historically men have ruled national governments, directed national economies, and exercised control over the lives of women and their families. Emissions increases associated with the Industrial Revolution and 20th-century economic growth happened on men's watch. As the rulers of countries, captains of industry, and masters of their castles at home, men can be judged to be mainly to blame for the current state of the planet. Will calling in the women generate success where men have failed in the politics of climate change? Only a changing of the gender guard will answer that question definitively, but we review some evidence about women's effectiveness in the next section.

Related to ethics is the question of equality. The current global political ethos stresses one person, one vote. That is the basis of equitable participation in the UN and other international bodies, and in most national and local governments. This democratic rule may not always be followed, but equal representation is the moral basis for contemporary systems of governance. Women and men are declared to be equal in UN documents and in virtually all national constitutions. Yet, inequality between the genders is an economic, political, and social universal around the world – whether in developing countries or in the developed world.

Women are not equally represented in governments, economies, or societies in any country in the world. We already have reviewed data on women's unequal representation in national governments, the UN, UNFCCC, and IPCC. It is true that women can vote in all countries (though they still can't drive everywhere), but in many places that is the extent of their equality. Around the world, including in industrial countries, women are paid less than men, have less access to land, and are vastly underrepresented in national governments and on the governing boards of major economic institutions.[57]

One measure of women's unequal worth is their vulnerability to physical attack. Men's violence against women in domestic settings as well as in conflict zones is widespread, and the details of women's suffering mainly at the hands of men shock the conscience.[58] Around the world, women are objects of sexual assault, including rape, torture, mutilation, enslavement, and homicide. These acts occur not only in developing nations, where women's lesser status often is the subject of international condemnation, but also in developed countries, where rates of sexual abuse in private homes, educational institutions, churches, and the military are far from sources of national pride.[59]

When it comes to climate change, women do not equally generate GHG emissions, nor are they equally represented in the negotiations to control them. But women are more than equal when it comes to bearing the negative effects of climate change.[60] Gender is not the only basis for raising ethical and equity questions about climate change impacts and decisions, but it is an important one.

Gender, Effectiveness, and Climate Change

Men have a demonstrably poor track record when it comes to global climate change agreements, but what is to be gained by opening the doors to women? The answer is, quite a bit. Research shows that gender balance is linked to successful outcomes in groups, businesses, and governments. The presence and/or leadership of women have been found to influence success rates in group decision-making, corporate management effectiveness, business company performance, environmental outcomes, and political negotiations.

In a 2010 article on "collective intelligence" published in *Science*, researchers reported the results of two studies involving 699 people working in groups of two to five; their goal was to understand why some groups consistently tend to make better decisions and reach more accurate conclusions than other groups or individuals performing the same task. They found that three factors accounted for the greatest group successes: "the average social sensitivity of group members, the equality in distribution of conversational turn-taking, and the proportion of females in the group" (which had an independent effect, but was related to social sensitivity).[61] This research suggests that the presence of significantly increased numbers of women at climate change negotiations holds the promise of improving the likelihood of reaching emissions reduction agreements.

Gender balance (including a critical mass of women in decision-making bodies) also has been found effective in achieving organizational goals. In a 2003 study of the success of recycling efforts in waste management programs in the UK and Ireland, researchers compared program performance by analyzing various aspects of the composition and leadership of management decision-making teams. They found that broadening participation in general led to more success in community recycling:

> We found that the local authorities with the highest recycling rates had a higher percentage of women managers than average. They also tended to include fewer engineers and more decision-makers from diverse backgrounds, including education.[62]

Analysis of data from a 2007/2008 United Nations Development Programme study showed that female representation in elected national governments was a factor in reducing countries' carbon emissions levels.

> Out of the 70 most developed countries in the world, only 18 reduced or stabilized their overall carbon emissions between 1990 and 2004. Fourteen of these had a greater-than-average percentage of female elected representatives ... [T]hat doesn't prove causation, but it hints that gender balance and more sustainable decision-making may go hand in hand.[63]

Another aspect of gendered decision-making – consensus building – might be part of the reason for women's policy and legislative successes. In a 2013 study of women lawmakers in the US Congress from 1973 to 2008, researchers found that women in the minority party were more likely to build coalitions to bring about new policies, whereas men in the minority party more often chose to obstruct and delay and were less successful in their legislative efforts.[64] This was consistent with previous research showing that female lawmakers differed from their male counterparts "by engaging more fully in consensus building activities."[65] Researchers also found, however, that women in the majority party did not do as well as their minority party sisters and performed about the same as male majority party members in legislative effectiveness. This finding led researchers to conclude that women's position in governing bodies affects their legislative approach and success:

> Taken together, these findings suggest that the key to female lawmakers' effectiveness lies at the intersection of behavioral traits (i.e. being consensus oriented) and institutional positioning (i.e. being in the minority party, where such traits are necessary and valuable) ... To the extent that women generally pursue different policy agendas than men, our research stands as an essential step toward understanding whether increasing numbers of women in legislatures will yield significantly different policy outcomes than would occur in their absence.[66]

Gender, Economics, and Climate Change

Women's success in political decision-making has been found by researchers to extend to the economic sector. Studies of women's performance in business settings in the US and Europe indicate that women's participation is good for the economic bottom line. A 2007 study ranked 520 Fortune 500 companies in 2001–2004 according to the average percentage of women on their governing boards; researchers examined the companies' performance on a variety of financial measures (return on equity, return on sales, and return on invested capital);[67] they found that boards with at least three women performed better on all three measures.[68]

These findings were similar to another 2007 report that reviewed the evaluations of 115,000 employees in 231 public and private companies and non-profit organizations to identify the factors related to a company's financial performance. Researchers found that companies' financial success was linked to high scores on nine criteria of organizational excellence, and that organizational excellence was linked to women's representation on governing boards:

> [C]ompanies with three or more women in senior management functions score more highly, on average, for each organizational criterion than companies with no women at the top. It is notable that performance increases significantly once a certain critical mass is attained: namely, at least three women on management committees for an average membership of 10 people. Below this threshold, no significant difference in company performance is observed.[69]

In a related study, researchers examined the records of 89 companies listed on the European stock exchange with the highest level of gender diversity in top management posts. They found that these companies outperformed other companies in their sector during the period from 2005–2007 on three measures of financial performance: return on equity (11.4 percent versus an average 10.3 percent), earnings before interest and taxes (11.1 percent versus 5.8 percent), and stock price growth (64 percent versus 47 percent).[70]

The economic value of women's presence on governing boards of companies was confirmed in a 2011 study of the financial performance of Dutch companies with and without women on their boards. The researcher offered several explanations for the differential advantage of companies with women in the boardroom:

> [O]ur results may add support to the idea that having women on the board is a logical consequence of a more innovative, modern, and transparent enterprise where all levels of the company achieve high performance. The results may also support the notion that companies with women on their boards have a better connection with the relevant stakeholders at all levels of the company, which also improves the company's reputation ... [Female] employees at companies with women on boards are more motivated to excel because they all see that they can reach the top. Companies with women on board could be more successful because people are promoted on the basis of their capabilities and not on the basis of demographic characteristics and

the companies are more successful in making use of the whole talent pool for competent directors instead of only half of the talent pool.[71]

In another effort to understand why women might outperform men on corporate boards and corporate performance, in 2013 researchers surveyed 624 board directors (75 percent male; 25 percent female), and measured their reliance on three reasoning methods for making decisions: personal interest, normative, and complex moral reasoning (CMR):

> The results showed that female directors achieved significantly higher scores than their male counterparts on the complex moral reasoning dimension which essentially involves making consistently fair decisions when competing interests are at stake. Since directors are compelled to make decisions in the best interest of their corporation while taking the viewpoints of multiple stakeholders into account, having a significant portion of female directors with highly developed CMR skills on board would appear to be an important resource for making these types of decisions and making them more effectively.[72]

At the most basic level, the economics of women's inclusion in climate policymaking might seem attractive simply because women work for less money than men around the world. In 2014 there was no country in the world in which women earned, on average, more than men. A 2013 "global gender gap" report ranked 130 countries in terms of women's and men's wages for similar work. In the most equal country, Malaysia, the female-to-male (FTM) ratio was 0.81; in the least equal country, Mauritania, ranked 130, the FTM ratio was 0.43. The US was in the middle of the pack, with a FTM ratio of 0.65, ranking 67 out of 130.[73]

In addition to the "cost savings" associated with hiring women to do the same work as men, there is another economic logic to including women, one that has a double edge. Christine Lagarde, Managing Director of the International Monetary Fund, argues that "more women at work means good news for the global economy."[74] She provides several rationales for this optimism:

1. Women help economic growth because increasing female labor force participation boosts the level of GDP per capita.
2. Men's reckless financial risk taking was at the heart of the 2008 global financial crisis, and "women bring a better balance of risk and reward in business and finance."
3. Women control two-thirds of discretionary consumer spending globally, and their participation in economic decision-making should be increased, since "it is simply good business and good policy to understand the market."
4. Women invest more in future generations by spending on health and education, which contributes to "building human capital to fuel future growth and savings to finance it."
5. Women can be seen as agents of change, since, as managers, "women tend to be more open to diverse perspectives more likely to sponsor and develop new talent, and more inclined to encourage collaboration."[75]

Might as Well Face It…

We're addicted to growth. Lagarde's first reason above for the "win-win" of embracing gender equality in the economic sphere is women's potential for increasing economic growth:

> In many countries, growth could be much higher if more women were in paid employment. In Japan, for example, raising female labor force participation to northern European levels would permanently raise per capita GDP by 8 percent. Increasing women's employment rates in line with those of men would boost the level of GDP 4 percent in France and Germany by 2020, and up to 34 percent in Egypt.[76]

This reasoning is problematic in that it implicitly frames what is good for women as something that might be bad for the climate, and thus bad for the planet. Many analysts believe that economic growth is one of the main drivers of CO_2 emissions and climate change.[77] The argument that women's labor force equality is a means to growth can have the unintended implication that holding back women is one way to save the planet. During the past three decades, the World Bank, International Monetary Fund, and most international financial institutions have embraced the "Washington consensus" – sometimes known as neoliberalism – that stresses tax reduction, deregulation, trade liberalization, and the privatization of government functions. These principles were defined by advocates as "necessary elements of 'first stage policy reform' that all countries should adopt to increase economic growth."[78]

While these principles may reflect a Washington consensus, there is widespread disagreement about the economic benefits to developing countries from this approach, and a growing critique based on doubts about the sustainability of perpetual economic growth.[79] One researcher summarizes the dangers of the "there is no alternative" (TINA) argument, which sees economic growth as the only path to economic development:

> TINA is a suicidal but seductive philosophy, especially alluring in the United States, based as it is on the truth that capitalist economies can be powerful engines of seemingly unlimited growth, profit, and individualism. But those very capitalist attributes – and the rejection of limits in itself – are part of what makes the US capitalist model systemically dangerous for the environment and a leading cause of climate change.[80]

How will gender equality fare in the policy debate over economic restructuring on the path to development? As is the case with climate policy, women will have to struggle to make their voices heard. In the Conclusion we will review some recommendations for engendering climate change.

Notes

1   Enloe, Cynthia. 2004. *The Curious Feminist: Searching for Women in a New Age of Empire*. Berkeley, CA: University of California Press.
2   Enloe, Cynthia. 1990. *Bananas, Beaches, and Bases: Making Feminist Sense of International Politics*. Berkeley, CA: University of California Press, p. 133; quotes added.
3   United Nations. 2014a. "Background on the UNFCCC: The International Response to Climate Change." *United Nations Framework Convention on*

Climate Change. Accessed on May 8, 2014 at https://unfccc.int/essential_back-ground/items/6031.php.

4   United Nations. 1992. *The Convention on Biological Diversity.* Accessed on May 9, 2014 at www.cbd.int/convention/; United Nations. 1992. *United Nations Convention to Combat Desertification.* Accessed on May 9, 2014 at www.cbd.int/convention/.

5   United Nations, 2014a, op. cit.

6   Intergovernmental Panel on Climate Change (IPCC). 1990. *Climate Change: The IPCC First Assessment Report.* Accessed on May 12, 2014 at www.ipcc.ch/publications_and_data/publications_ipcc_first_assessment_1990_wg1.shtml.

7   For a list of COP meetings, see United Nations. 2014. "Meetings." *United Nations Framework Convention on Climate Change.* Accessed on May 9, 2014 at https://unfccc.int/meetings/items/6240.php.

8   United Nations. 2014b. "Status of Ratification of the Kyoto Protocol". *United Nations Framework Convention on Climate Change.* Accessed on May 9, 2014 at http://unfccc.int/kyoto_protocol/status_of_ratification/items/2613.php; the US is a party to, but has not ratified, the Kyoto Protocol, and Canada withdrew from the Kyoto Protocol in 2012 in order to avoid an estimated \$14 billion in penalties for exceeding CO_2 emission standards set by the treaty; see CBC News. 2011. "Canada Pulls out of Kyoto Protocol." Accessed on May 9, 2014 at www.cbc.ca/news/politics/canada-pulls-out-of-kyoto-protocol-1.999072.

9   For a list of admitted NGOs to UNFCCC COP meetings, see United Nations. 2014c. "Admitted NGO." Accessed on May 9, 2014 at http://maindb.unfccc.int/public/ngo.pl?mode=wim&search=A.

10 United Nations. "Copenhagen Climate Change Conference – December 2009." *United Nations Framework Convention on Climate Change.* Accessed on May 9, 2014 at https://unfccc.int/meetings/copenhagen_dec_2009/meeting/6295.php.

11 Ibid.

12 IPCC. 2012. *Managing the Risks of Extreme Events and Disasters to Advance Climate Change Adaptation.* Accessed on May 9, 2014 at www.ipcc-wg2.gov/SREX/.

13 Buckingham, Susan. 2010. "Call in the Women." *Nature,* Vol. 468, No. 7323:502.

14 O'Neill, Saffron J., Mike Hulme, John Turnpenny, and James A. Screen. 2010. "Disciplines, Geography, and Gender in the Framing of Climate Change." *Bulletin of the American Meteorological Society,* Vol. 91, No. 8:997–1002, p. 998.

15 Ibid., p. 1001.

16 Ibid.

17 Ibid; see also Terry, Geraldine. 2009. *Climate Change and Gender Justice.* Warwickshire, United Kingdom: Practical Action Publishing.

18 PARLINE. 2015. "Women Parliamentarians." Inter-Parliamentary Union. Accessed on May 25, 2015 at www.ipu.org/parline-e/WomenInParliament.asp?REGION=All&typesearch=1&LANG=ENG; Worldwide Guide to Women in Leadership. 2014. "Current Women Leaders." Accessed on May 25, 2015 at www.guide2womenleaders.com/Current-Women-Leaders.htm.

[19] United Nations. 1995. "Platform for Action." Beijing: Fourth World Conference on Women. Accessed on May 12, 2014 at www.un.org/women-watch/daw/beijing/platform/plat1.htm#statement.

[20] United Nations. 2014c. "Goal 3: Promote Gender Equality and Empower Women." UN Millennium Development Goals and Beyond 2015. Accessed on May 12, 2014 at www.un.org/millenniumgoals/gender.shtml.

[21] Röhr, Ulrike, and Minu Hemmati. 2008. "A Gender-Sensitive Climate Regime?" GenderCC – Women for Climate Justice. Accessed on May 9, 2014 at www.gendercc.net/fileadmin/inhalte/Dokumente/UNFCCC_conferences/Conclusions_COP13.pdf.

[22] Ibid.

[23] When asked why gender considerations had been dropped from the Indonesian agenda in 2008, the Indonesian State Minister of Environment responded: "There are many women already among the Staff or decision-makers in the State Ministry of environment." Soentoro, Tea. 2014. "No Climate Justice without Gender Justice: A Perspective to Engender Climate Change Talks among Ourselves and with the Climate Regime." *NGO Forum on* ADB Accessed on May 13, 2014 at www.forum-adb.org/inner.php?sec=13&ref=extras&id=184.

[24] GenderCC. 2010. "Vision." GenderCC – Women for Climate Justice. Accessed on May 9, 2014 at www.gendercc.net/about-gendercc.html; see GenderCC's founding document at www.gendercc.net/fileadmin/inhalte/Dokumente/Network/GenderCC-statutes-en.pdf

[25] Hemmati, Minu. 2008. "Gender Perspective on Climate Change." UN Commission on the Status of Women, Fifty-second Session (February 25–March 7). Accessed on May 12, 2014 at www.un.org/womenwatch/daw/csw/csw52/panels/climatechangepanel/M.Hemmati%20Presentation%20Climate%20Change.pdf, p. 7.

[26] United Nations Educational, Scientific and Cultural Organization. 2008. "Fourth Forum – The Gender Dimensions of Climate Change." Accessed on May 12, 2014 at www.unesco.org/new/en/unesco/themes/gender-equality/features/unesco-forum-on-gender-equality/4th-forum/; United Nations Development Programme. 2008. "Gender and Climate Change: Impact and Adaptation." Negomo, Sri Lanka (September 24–26). UNDP Asia-Pacific Gender Community of Practice Annual Learning Workshop. Accessed on May 12, 2014 at www.undpcc.org/undpcc/files/docs/publications/submitted/look%20at%20forword%20for%20summary%20UNDP%20REP-colombo.pdf; Isatou, Gaye, and Josue Dione. 2009. "Gender and Climate Change: Women Matter." Addis Ababa: UN Economic Commission for Africa. Accessed on May 12, 2014 at www.uneca.org/sites/default/files/publications/gender-and-climate-change.pdf United Nations Environment Program. 2009. "Consultation: Impact of Climate Change on Women and Gender Relations." United Nations Foundation. Accessed on May 12, 2014 at www.rona.unep.org/documents/publications/Gender_Report_20091218.pdf; United Nations Development Program. 2009. *Resource Guide on Gender*

and Climate Change. Accessed on May 12, 2014 at www.un.org/womenwatch/downloads/Resource_Guide_English_FINAL.pdf.

27   United Nations Office for Disaster Risk Reduction. 2009. "Beijing Agenda for Global Action on Gender Sensitive Disaster Risk Reduction." International Conference on Gender and Disaster Risk Reduction. Accessed on May 12, 2014 at http://capwip.org/Beijing%20Agenda%20%20for%20Global%20Action%20on%20Gender%20Sensitive%20DRR22.04.09.pdf; "Gender Mainstreaming Is the (Re)Organization, Improvement, Development and Evaluation of Policy Processes, so that a Gender Equality Perspective Is Incorporated in all policies at all Levels and at all Stages, by the Actors Normally Involved in Policymaking." Dankelman, Irene. 2010. *Gender and Climate Change: An Introduction.* Sterling, VA: Earthscan, p. 12; this definition is attributed by Dankelman to Council of Europe. 1998. *Gender Mainstreaming: Conceptual Framework, Methodology and Presentation of Good Practice.* Strasbourg: Council of Europe, p. 15.

28   Sönke Kreft, Sven Harmeling, Christoph Bals, Winfried Zacher, Klemens van de Sand. 2010. *The Millennium Development Goals and Climate Change: Taking Stock and Looking Ahead.* Berlin: Germanwatch

29   United Nations. 2009. "Women, Gender Equality and Climate Change." UN WomenWatch. Accessed on May 13, 2014 at www.un.org/womenwatch/feature/climate_change/downloads/Women_and_Climate_Change_Factsheet.pdf.

30   Rust, Selina. 2010. "Climate Change: The UN's Boys' Club." *Inter Press Service News Agency* (March 18). Accessed on May 7, 2014 at www.ipsnews.net/2010/03/climate-change-the-uns-boys-club/.

31   United Nations. 2010. "Secretary-General Names Members of High-Level Advisory Group on Mobilizing Climate Change Resources." UN Department of Public Information (March 4). Accessed on May 13, 2014 at www.un.org/News/Press/docs/2010/sga1223.doc.htm.

32   Rust, op. cit.

33   Bhanoo, Sindya. 2010. "New UN Climate Change Group Is All Male." *New York Times* (March 11). Accessed on May 13, 2014 at http://dotearth.blogs.nytimes.com/2010/03/11/new-u-n-climate-change-group-is-all-male/?_php=true&_type=blogs&_php=true&_type=blogs&_php=true&_type=blogs&_php=true&_type=blogs&_r=3.

34   Rust, op. cit.

35   Buckingham, op. cit.

36   Ibid.

37   United Nations Framework Convention on Climate Change. 2013. "Provisional Agenda." *Workshop on Gender, Climate Change and the UNFCCC.* Accessed on May 13, 2014 at http://unfccc.int/files/adaptation/application/pdf/in_session_workshop_agenda_web.pdf.

38   Burns, Bridget. 2013. "Women's Participation in UN Climate Negotiations." *Women's Environment and Development Organization.* Accessed on May 13, 2014 at www.wedo.org/wp-content/uploads/WomenUNFCCCParticipation 2008-2012FINAL2013.pdf; to get a sense of the kind of hand calculations required to determine women's participation, see the COP9 participant list at

http://unfccc.int/resource/docs/cop9/inf01.pdf (accessed on May 15, 2014); it is difficult to discern the gender of many of the named participants, so further research is required to identify each participant's gender.

[39] United Nations. 2013. "Report on Gender Composition." *United Nations Framework Convention on Climate Change.* Accessed on May 12, 2014 at http://unfccc.int/resource/docs/2013/cop19/eng/04.pdf, p. 7.

[40] IPCC. 2013. "AR5 Contributors." *Working Group I – Climate Change 2013: The Physical Science Basis.* Accessed on May 13, 2014 at www.climatechange2013.org/contributors/; "AR5 Contributors." *Working Group II – Climate Change 2014: Impacts, Adaptation, and Vulnerability.* Accessed on May 13, 2014 at http://ipcc-wg2.gov/AR5/contributors/; "Authors." *Working Group III – Climate change 2014: Mitigation of Climate Change.* Accessed on May 13, 2014 at www.ipcc-wg3.de/assessment-reports/fifth-assessment-report/Authors; oddly, the number of authors in the Working Group III report were not calculated, so we had to go back to the old pre-"Doha Miracle" method of counting names chapter-by-chapter for all 14 chapters of the report and looking up pictures to determine the gender of those names we did not recognize as men or women. My thanks to Natalie Parker for her assistance in this gender count task.

[41] Hone, Katharina. 2013. "The 'Doha Miracle'? Where Are the Women in Climate Change Negotiations?" *E-International Relations* (January 18). Accessed on May 5, 2014 at www.e-ir.info/2013/01/18/the-doha-miracle-where-are-the-women-in-climate-change-negotiations/.

[42] Gardiner, Stephen M. 2011. *A Perfect Moral Storm: The Ethical Challenge of Climate Change.* New York: Oxford University Press; Brown, Donald A. 2013. *Climate Change Ethics: Navigating the Perfect Moral Storm.* New York: Routledge.

[43] Brown, op. cit., p. 7.

[44] Ibid., p. 8.

[45] For example, the European Energy Agency keeps track of European Union member states' GHG emissions and the US Energy Information Administration tracks global emissions country-by-country; the World Bank identifies nations at risk from "the five main threats arising from climate change: droughts, floods, storms, rising sea levels, and greater uncertainty in agriculture"; World Bank. 2009. *Convenient Solutions to an Inconvenient Truth: Ecosystem-based Approaches to Climate Change.* World Bank Environment Department. Accessed on May 16, 2014 at www.irinnews.org/pdf/convenient_solutions_to_an_inconvenient_truth.pdf.

[46] Data are more widely available for CO_2 emissions, so Table 7.1 focuses on CO_2; for total GHG emissions by Annex I country, see United Nations. 2013. *National Greenhouse Gas Inventory Data for Period 1990–2011.* United Nations Framework Convention on Climate Change, Table 5. Accessed on May 16, 2014 at http://unfccc.int/resource/docs/2013/sbi/eng/19.pdf; for three main GHG emissions by Annex II country, see United Nations. 2013. *Sixth Compilation and Synthesis of Initial National Communications from Parties Not Included in Annex I to the Convention.* United Nations Framework Convention

on Climate Change, Table 3, Accessed on May 16, 2014 at http://unfccc.int/resource/docs/2005/sbi/eng/18a02.pdf.

47   CO₂ emissions data from US Energy Information Administration. 2014. "International Energy Statistics: Total Carbon Dioxide Emissions from the Consumption of Energy." Accessed on May 15, 2014 at www.eia.gov/cfapps/ipdbproject/IEDIndex3.cfm?tid=90&pid=44&aid=8; GDP per capita data from World Bank. 2014. "GDP Per capita, PPP (current international $)." *World Bank: Data*. Accessed on May 16, 2014 at http://data.worldbank.org/indicator/NY.GDP.PCAP.PP.CD; Taiwan GDP per capita data from International Monetary Fund. 2014. "Gross Domestic Product per Capita." *IMF World Economic Outlook (April)*. Accessed on May 16, 2014 at http://knoema.com/IMFWEO2014Apr/imf-world-economic-outlook-april-2014; for a critical analysis of CO₂ emissions data, see Rogers, Simon, and Lisa Evans. 2011. "World Carbon Dioxide Emissions Data by Country: China Speeds Ahead of the Rest." *The Guardian* (January 31). Accessed on May 15, 2014 at www.theguardian.com/news/datablog/2011/jan/31/world-carbon-dioxide-emissions-country-data-co2#data.

48   Ibid., US Energy Information Administration.

49   Rosenthal, Elisabeth. 2008. "China Increases Lead As Biggest Carbon Dioxide Emitter." *New York Times* (June 14). Accessed on May 15, 2014 at www.nytimes.com/2008/06/14/world/asia/14china.html?_r=0.

50   Earth Talk. 2009. "Is the World Outsourcing Its Greenhouse Emissions to China?" *Scientific American* (November 5). Accessed on May 16, 2014 at www.scientificamerican.com/article/earth-talks-outsourcing-greenhouse-china/; for a general discussion of these and related issues, see also Cuomo, Chris J. 2011. "Climate Change, Vulnerability, and Responsibility." *Hypatia*, Vol. 26, No. 4:691–714.

51   For a broad-ranging discussion of population and climate change, see Guzman, Jose Miguel, George Martine, Gordon McGranahan, Daniel Schensul, and Cecilia Tacoli. 2009. *Population Dynamics and Climate Change*. United Nations Population Fund and International Institute for Environment and Development. Accessed on June 20, 2014 at www.unfpa.org/public/home/publications/pid/4500.

52   Pope Paul VI. 1968. *Humanae Vitae: Encyclical of the Supreme Pontiff Paul VI on the Regulation of Birth*. Encyclical Letter (July 25). Accessed on May 28, 2014 at www.vatican.va/holy_father/paul_vi/encyclicals/documents/hf_p-vi_enc_25071968_humanae-vitae_en.html; Ralston, Michelle, and Elizabeth Podrebarac. 2008. "Abortion Laws around the World." Pew Research Religion and Public Life Project. Accessed on May 28, 2014 at www.vatican.va/holy_father/paul_vi/encyclicals/documents/hf_p-vi_enc_25071968_humanae-vitae_en.html; www.pewforum.org/ 2008/09/30/abortion-laws-around-the-world/.

53   Kane, Penny, and Ching Y. Choi. 1999. "China's One Child Family Policy." *BMJ* (*British Medical Journal*), Vol. 319, No. 7215:992–994; Jian, Ma. 2013. "China's Brutal One-Child Policy." *New York Times* (May 21).

Accessed on May 28, 2014 at www.nytimes.com/2013/05/22/opinion/chinas-brutal-one-child-policy.html?_r=0; Lawrence, Jane. 2000. "The Indian Health Service and the Sterilization of Native American Women." *American Indian Quarterly*, Vol. 24, No. 3:400–419.

54   Salleh, Ariel. 2010. "Climate Strategy: Making the Choice between Ecological Modernization or Living Well." *Journal of Australian Political Economy*, Vol. 66 (December):118–143, p. 121.

55   For an expanded rationale for including women, see United Nations Division for the Advancement of Women. 2005. *Equal Participation of Women and Men in Decision-Making Processes, with Particular Emphasis on Political Participation and Leadership.* Accessed on May 20, 2014 at www.un.org/womenwatch/daw/egm/eql-men/FinalReport.pdf, pp. 8–9.

56   In addition to the research cited in Chapter 4, see van Dyke, Amanda, and Stephney Dallmann. 2013. "Mining for Talent: A Study of Women on Boards in the Mining Industry." Women in Mining and PwC (PricewaterhouseCoopers). Accessed on May 20, 2014 at www.womeninmining.org.uk/wordpress/wp-content/uploads/2013/02/Mining-for-talent-FINAL-report-20131.pdf.

57   Grossman, Samantha. 2014. "This Map Shows Just How Big the Wage Gap between Men and Women Is." *Time* (March 6). Accessed on May 16, 2014 at http://time.com/14153/global-gender-pay-gap-map/; for an overview of gender inequality around the world see World Bank. 2014. "Gender." *World Bank: Data.* Accessed on May 16, 2014 at http://data.worldbank.org/topic/gender?display=graph; for quantitative analyses of women's representation in a wide range of economic and business sectors, see Catalyst. 2014. "By the Numbers." Accessed on May 19, 2014 at www.catalyst.org/knowledge/by-the-numbers.

58   Amnesty International. 2013. *Violence against Women Information.* Accessed on May 17, 2014 at www.amnestyusa.org/our-work/issues/women-s-rights/violence-against-women/violence-against-women-information; United Nations. 2014. "Facts and Figures: Ending Violence against Women." United Nations Entity for Gender Equality and the Empowerment of Women. Accessed on May 17, 2014 at www.unwomen.org/en/what-we-do/ending-violence-against-women/facts-and-figures.

59   World Health Organization. 2013. *Global and Regional Estimates of Violence against Women.* Accessed on May 17, 2014 at www.who.int/reproductivehealth/publications/violence/9789241564625/en/; European Union Agency for Fundamental Rights. 2014. *Violence against Women: An EU-Wide Survey.* Accessed on May 17, 2014 at http://fra.europa.eu/sites/default/files/fra-2014-vaw-survey-main-results_en.pdf; US Department of Defense. 2014. Sexual Assault Prevention and Response: Reports to Congress. Accessed on May 17, 2014 at www.sapr.mil/index.php/annual-reports.

60   Roberts, Maryam. 2009. "War, Climate Change, and Women." *Race, Poverty & the Environment*, Vol. 16, No. 2:39–41.

61   Woolley, Anita Williams, Christopher F. Chabris, Alex Pentland, Nada Hashmi, and Thomas W. Malone. 2010. "Evidence for a Collective Intelligence Factor in the Performance of Human Groups." *Science*, Vol. 330, No. 6006:686–688, p. 686.

[62] Buckingham, op. cit.; see also Buckingham, Susan, Dory Reeves, and Anna Batchelor. 2005. "Wasting Women: The Environmental Justice of Including Women in Municipal Waste Management." *Local Environment*, Vol. 10, No. 4:427–444.

[63] Ibid.; see also United Nations Development Program. 2008. "Fighting Climate Change: Human Solidarity in a Divided World." *Human Development Report – 2007/2008*. Accessed on May 19, 2014 at http://hdr.undp.org/sites/default/files/reports/268/hdr_20072008_en_complete.pdf, pp. 310–313 (Table 24: Carbon Dioxide Emissions) and pp. 330–333 (Table 29: Gender Empowerment Measure).

[64] Volden, Craig, Alan E. Wiseman, and Dana E. Wittmer. 2013. "When Are Women More Effective Lawmakers Than Men?" *American Journal of Political Science*, Vol. 57, No. 2:326–341.

[65] Ibid., p. 326.

[66] Ibid., p. 338.

[67] Return on Sales (ROS): the pre-tax net profit divided by revenue. Return on Invested Capital (ROIC): the ratio of after-tax net operating profit to invested capital. Return on Equity (ROE): the ratio of after-tax net profit to stockholders' equity; Carter, Nancy M., and Harvey M. Wagner. 2011. "The Bottom Line: Corporate Performance and Women's Representation on Boards (2004–2008)." *Catalyst Research Report* (March 1). Accessed on April 29, 2014 at http://catalyst.org/knowledge/bottom-line-corporate-performance-and-womens-representation-boards-20042008, p. 3.

[68] Ibid. Their findings were statistically significant for two out of the three indicators of corporate performance (return on sales and return on invested capital), p. 2.

[69] Desvaux, Georges., Sandrine Devillard-Hoellinger, and Pascal Baumgarten. 2007. *Women Matter: Gender Diversity, A Corporate Performance Driver.* McKinsey and Company. Accessed on May 19, 2014 at www.europeanpwn.net/files/mckinsey_2007_gender_matters.pdf

[70] Ibid., p. 14.

[71] Luckerath-Rovers, Mijntje. 2013. "Women on Boards and Firm Performance." *Journal of Management and Governance*, Vol. 17, No. 2:491–509.

[72] Bart, Chris, and Gregory McQueen. 2013. "Why Women Make Better Directors." *International Journal of Business Governance and Ethics*, Vol. 8, No. 1:93–99, p. 93.

[73] World Economic Forum. 2013. *The Global Gender Gap Report, 2013*. Table D2: Wage equality survey, p. 50. Accessed on May 21, 2014 at www3.weforum.org/docs/WEF_GenderGap_Report_2013.pdf.

[74] Lagarde, Christine. 2013. "Dare the Difference." *Straight Talk*. International Monetary Fund, Vol. 50, No. 2. Accessed on May 21, 2014 at www.imf.org/external/pubs/ft/fandd/2013/06/straight.htm.

[75] Ibid.; see also Nellemann, C., R. Verma, and L. Hislop. 2011. *Women at the Front Lines of Climate Change: Gender Risks and Hopes*. United Nations Environment Programme. Accessed on May 15, 2014 at www.grida.no/files/publications/women-and-climate-change/rra_gender_screen.pdf.

[76] Ibid.; see also, Hewlett, Sylvia Ann. 2012. "More Women in the Workforce Could Raise GDP by 5%." *Harvard Business Review*, HBR Blog Network

(November 1). Accessed on June 20, 2014 at http://blogs.hbr.org/2012/11/more-women-in-the-workforce-could-raise-gdp/.

77 Stern, Nicholas. 2006. *The Stern Review on the Economics of Climate Change.* London: HM Treasury. Accessed on December 17, 2014 at http://webarchive.nationalarchives.gov.uk/+/http:/www.hm-treasury.gov.uk/independent_reviews/stern_review_economics_climate_change/stern_review_report.cfm; both the Stern Review and many investment analysts conclude there is a reverse connection between economic growth and climate change, for instance, see Scott, Mike. 2014. "Climate Change Threatens Economic Growth – UN Report. How Should Investors React?" *Forbes* (April 3). Accessed on December 17, 2014 at www.forbes.com/sites/mikescott/2014/04/03/climate-change-threatens-economic-growth-un-report-how-should-investors-react/.

78 World Health Organization. 2014. "Washington Consensus." WHO: Trade, Foreign Policy, Diplomacy and Health Glossary of Globalization. Accessed on May 21, 2014 at www.who.int/trade/glossary/story094/en/.

79 Stiglitz, Joseph. 2003. *Globalization and Its Discontents.* New York: W.W. Norton & Company.

80 Derber, Charles. 2010. *Greed to Green: Solving Climate Change and Remaking the Economy.* Boulder, CO: Paradigm Publishers, p. 6.

CONCLUSION
Engendering Global Climate Change

The goal of this book has been to answer the question, "Why gender and climate change?" We have examined the gendered impacts of two main dimensions of climate change: global warming and sea level rise. While research points to women's relatively greater vulnerabilities, we have seen that men, too, can fall victim to the effects of climate change.

Climate change portends major disruptions in virtually all global systems, but its causes and consequences follow some fairly predictable gendered patterns. Just as men dominate the sciences generally, they also dominate climate science. The gender imbalance in climate science is not neutral. Men set the research agenda, which focuses more on the operation of macro-scale natural and physical systems than on the impacts on human health and well-being. The partnership of two masculine systems – science and the military – has the consequence of militarizing climate change by emphasizing security threats and large-scale technical and engineering solutions more consistent with military missions than with empowering women and men to develop sustainable strategies for mitigation and adaptation.

Even when men do not speak with one voice, as in the case of climate skepticism, which pits mostly male climate scientists against mostly male climate change deniers, women and their viewpoints remain on the margins. Both men and women climate scientists are targeted by denier activists seeking to discredit their work or besmirch their characters. When women climate scientists become targets, they are specially treated to demeaning, sometimes vicious, sexist depictions and threats.

Climate change policy and negotiations also are gendered realms. Men occupy a disproportionate number of power positions in governments and the organizations tasked with setting climate change policy and negotiating climate change agreements. Despite promises to include women, United Nations (UN) organizations responsible for climate change research and policymaking have been slow to act on their stated commitments to gender equality. Women have had to launch activist campaigns to move the UN forward toward including women and gender-related issues in climate change studies and diplomacy.

How to Achieve Gender Parity?

Even in the face of entrenched systems of male privilege, women have made progress, gaining access to male-dominated arenas in science, government, business, and international policymaking. But the sluggish pace of their gains has led a number of organizations and countries to adopt more robust strategies in pursuit of gender parity – i.e. women's and men's equal representation. One approach to increasing women's participation has been to mandate a specified degree of women's proportional representation (quotas) in some local and national governments and government-run organizations (e.g. in France, Algeria, India, Argentina, Slovenia, and Belgium).[1] For instance, in 2003 Norway passed legislation requiring 40 percent women on corporate boards of public limited, state-owned, and inter-municipality companies by 2008. Researchers found that the mandate succeeded in increasing women's representation and did not generate significant resistance. In fact, the mandate opened a national and local dialogue about women's equality. Researchers concluded that without the mandate, corporate boards would not have pursued a goal of gender inclusion.

> The Norwegian experience reveals that a quota is the key to a successful implementation. Not only does it create the pressure needed for fundamental change but it also triggers a public debate at the core of which are questions of gender equality in wider society.[2]

A 2013 study reviewed some of the organizational consequences of Norway's corporate board quota system. Researchers found that despite the presence of significantly more women members who were overall more qualified than their male counterparts, men still dominated as corporate board chairs.[3] They reported, however, that the presence of women board members was positively related to the appointment of female board chairs and female CEOs. They concluded that although male privilege and networks are quite durable, quotas work and can have a snowball effect, creating new mentorship networks and building momentum for increasing the presence and leadership of women:

> Talented female executives need mentors and sponsors to help them climb the career ladder, but male senior managers may be reluctant to support young women because such relationships could be misconstrued [as sexual]. A gender quota may break this vicious cycle by putting more women on senior management teams, who can then function as role models and support other women.[4]

In 2011, researchers compared the effects of gender quota systems for political positions and corporate board membership in Norway and India, and found that quotas were successful in both countries. They offered three reasons for their effectiveness in moving organizations toward gender equality:

> First, quotas can and do increase female leadership in politics and the corporate sphere. This provides prima facie evidence that the primary constraint on female leadership is not a lack of interest in leadership positions by women. Second, female

leadership influences policy outcomes. The evidence for this is clearer in the policy arena where it reflects gender differences in economic status and work responsibilities ... Third, gender quotas do not seem to create a sustained backlash among citizens – rather, evidence from political quotas suggests that voters use new information about how female leaders perform to update their beliefs about women.[5]

No Climate Justice Without Gender Justice!

At the Fourth World Conference on Women in Beijing in 1995, then-First Lady Hillary Clinton spoke before an audience of thousands: "If there is one message that echoes from this conference, let it be that human rights are women's rights and women's rights are human rights, for once and for all." A commentator at the time called Clinton's remarks "the speech that launched a movement ... [that] remains the defining battle cry for women."[6]

That movement was still underway two decades later. In 2014, at a UN commemoration of International Women's Day under the banner "Equality for Women Is Progress for All," Clinton commented that equality for women "remains the great unfinished business of the 21st century."[7] That same year, the European Union's (EU's) Organization for Economic Co-operation and Development declared that "financing the unfinished business of gender equality and women's rights [are] priorities for the post-2015 [development] framework."[8]

As we have seen throughout this book, gender equality – as it relates to climate change or virtually any sector of social, economic, or political life – is indeed far from finished business. It is possible to mandate women's equal representation in business or government. It is also possible to legislate women's equal rights and write them into constitutions and legal codes. But in homes, streets, schools, workplaces, churches, temples, mosques, government agencies, or many other aspects of social and interpersonal relations, women's equality cannot be accomplished simply by decree. Nonetheless, mandating women's representation is a first and important step.

Figure 8.1 Protesters in Bangkok, Thailand, 2009. Photo credit: Mongkhonsawat Leungvorapant/ Oxfam[9]

The 1995 Beijing Women's Conference Platform for Action defined two objectives for advancing women's participation in power and decision-making – access and capacity. Both objectives remain unfulfilled two decades later:

- ensure women's equal access to and full participation in power structures and decision-making;
- increase women's capacity to participate in decision-making and leadership.[10]

Quotas, legislation, and constitutionally-enshrined women's rights can offer women "equal access," but cannot guarantee their "full participation in power structures and decision-making." Women's "capacity to participate" depends on their full and equal participation in families, schools, workplaces, and social life in general. Equal access is a necessary, but not sufficient, condition for full participation. The "capacity to participate in decision-making and leadership" is the other necessary condition for women to take advantage of the promise of equal access.

Women's capacity to participate equally in society depends not only on legal gender equality, but also on gender justice. "Gender justice means equal treatment and equitable value of the sexes," and the right to fair and equal recourse when injustice occurs.[11] There is no gender justice for hundreds of millions of women globally who are treated as inferior to men without access to a means to change their status. Gender injustice is experienced by women whose lives are restricted to the home out of view of the world, who are forbidden or threatened from attending school, who are forcibly married at a young age, who have no freedom of movement except with their father's or husband's permission, who have no rights of inheritance or land ownership, who are ignored or shunned when they become victims of sexual assault, and who can be murdered with impunity by a jealous husband, dissatisfied family, or because they are from the wrong social or ethnic group.

Engendering Climate Change Justice

Gender mandates to achieve gender parity are a first step toward including women's interests, perspectives, and knowledge in climate change research and policy. Guaranteed membership on a climate change advisory panel, negotiating team, scientific research group, or policymaking committee will help many, but will provide only limited realistic opportunities for women whose lives are without gender justice:

> In the context of climate change, gender justice is critical. Women and men experience the effects and impacts of climate change differently due to the roles and responsibilities they normally fulfill in their public and private lives. Therefore, gender-differentiated effects and impacts have to be taken into account when designing policies and programmes to adapt to the effects of climate change and to mitigate those anticipated to occur in the future.[12]

Not only does climate change affect women and men differently, they also are differently positioned to take advantage of opportunities to shape climate policy. There are practical considerations related to the living conditions of many women around the world that must be acknowledged by climate change policymakers – whether they are male or female. When climate disruptions occur:

- women typically have less ability to move elsewhere, as they have less access to credit;
- women may face discrimination in food distribution and have less say in decisions about crop production;
- women are more likely to be excluded from community decision-making and higher-level policymaking;
- low carbon technologies often fail to connect with women's needs.[13]

The last point above – about the fit between women's needs and efforts to address the causes of climate change by adopting low carbon technologies – is illustrated by two studies of alternative energy and their impact on women in the communities where they were adopted. The first study examined a solar lighting project in Bangladesh designed to produce a low-carbon source of light to empower women by allowing them to earn extra money by working at home. A major consequence of developing this new source of nighttime light was to extend women's workday:

[T]he solar lighting extended women's working hours till 11pm, when the solar home system went off … women felt that they needed to seize this opportunity to work hard in the evening, in order to make more money for their families. The system also created a sense of competition among female villagers who felt they lagged behind their neighbours. As a result, the new technological intervention has, unwittingly, increased women's working hours and exerted an extra burden on their already-tired bodies. Men made use of the solar lighting to pursue leisure activities in the evening, such as watching television, reading religious books, or gathering together for a chat … many men went to bed long before the solar systems were turned off at 11pm. They said that they were tired after working so hard … in the day. They supported their wives to carry out income-generating activities because they thought women could combine their domestic duties and income generation at home.[14]

In this project women were both [em]powered, but also exploited by the pressure to work harder and longer for their families and other project-related demands. When women were tasked with collecting the fees for sustaining this lighting system (because they were seen by project organizers to have better social skills), they found themselves sources of friction. When only some families could afford to keep paying for the power (often because the women worked at night), the pressure on women grew:

> [L]ighting [became] a visible symbol of status and wealth … those mothers whose electricity supplies were disconnected felt guilty because their children were deprived of the [study time] opportunity that the lighting could bring.[15]

The second study illustrating the potential disconnect between alternative energies and the role of women in responding to climate change focused on the "bio-fuel frenzy" in Asia and Africa.[16] The land needed for the large-scale production of palm nuts and other oil seeds for bio-fuel production is displacing traditional agriculture, historically the province of women farmers. Since women have limited or no control over land use, their agricultural plots are being transformed into corporate or state-run energy production for a global market. The result is the disruption of food production and an undermining of women's already low position in the local economy in favor of benefits to national and multinational business interests. Their lack of education, property rights, and political power has marginalized women from decision-making about whether their traditional farm land would be used to plant trees for fuel crop production or carbon sequestration. The result is a "trade-off between food and fuel":

> [Women] are typically not participants in the discussions and decisions around monetary aspects of land use and value. What keeps them from being persuasive and forceful advocates on

behalf of securing communal revenues from carbon sequestration of their forest lands is their lack of information, insights, and engagement in the evolving carbon market and the emerging economic value proposition of ecosystems and bio-diversity.[17]

Saving the Planet by Changing Women's Lives

There often are unintended consequences for women from climate change mitigation and adaptation programs such as those described above and the REDD+ forestation project described in Chapter 4. The inclusion of women in designing and implementing these and other efforts to reduce greenhouse gas (GHG) emissions is critical to their sustainability. Women's capacity to gain access to decision-making and policy formation must be a goal in climate change mitigation and adaptation projects. That means that researchers, project designers, and policymakers must push local and national governments to address women's inequality in their homes, education, workplaces, and government.[18]

Research has shown that countries with greater levels of women's equality are more capable of grappling with climate change. For instance, a 2012 study of the relationship between women's political status and carbon dioxide (CO_2) emission levels found that women's support of environmental protection was more likely to be enacted into law when women had political power:

> We find that CO_2 emissions per capita are lower in nations where women have higher political status, controlling for GDP per capita, urbanization, industrialization, militarization, world-system position, foreign direct investment, the age dependency ratio, and level of democracy. This finding suggests that efforts to improve gender equality around the world may work synergistically with efforts to curtail global climate change and environmental degradation more generally.[19]

Even when they are relatively disadvantaged vis-à-vis their male counterparts, women have been reported to play an important role in climate-related disaster planning and response. Women can be a valuable resource, both in terms of their labor and their knowledge of the local community and landscape, but they tend not to be recognized as a resource. For instance, women were critical in recovery efforts following Hurricane Mitch in 1998 in Central America: "Local women made up the core of the Red Cross volunteers working on the project and, as such, were both its implementers and main beneficiaries."[20] Women worked alongside men clearing debris and roads, rescuing people stranded by high waters, organizing women-only work crews. Some men recognized women's contribution, though others saw the women as "helping them," and not essential to the recovery efforts. When men and women were paid by relief agencies, longstanding gender role behaviors emerged:

> When we were working, he received his money, drank part of it and spent it on women. Me, I invested my money in my children, in my own things, because everyone holds on to their own money. Sometimes mine runs out first because a woman has more costs. Even when they're older the children are constantly asking "Mum, you don't have five pesos...?" and so your money disappears, while his doesn't.[21]

Based on lessons learned from women's participation in the response to Hurricane Mitch and other disasters, one study recommends empowering women by "earmark[ing] resources to contract women from the country concerned" in disaster planning or recovery efforts and for "financing for gender projects that focus more on women's strategic needs than on their practical needs" since "being the beneficiary of material reconstruction resources does not change the existing system of domination and therefore does not guarantee that women will have control of the ... resources."[22]

An example of paying women directly for their climate change mitigation and adaptation work is a United Nations Development Programme-sponsored nationwide sand encroachment effort in Niger, in which women grew and planted deep-rooted mesquite plants to block desertification:

> The women were paid per plant and earned about US $800 over the course of five months, which they used to feed their household and take care of their children. They also receive meals on-site from the World Food Programme, which co-sponsored the project.[23]

Another strategy, from South Africa, features nongovernmental organization (NGO)-sponsored climate change adaptation workshops attended
by local men, women, and children. Together, participants learn, share
experiences, collect information from small-scale experiments and climate
monitoring, and plan strategies:

> Men and women propose small adaptation projects on their
> farms ... The equal access of men and women to funding for
> adaptation projects is important and supports an approach that
> includes the entire community and draws on the strength of
> its members ... Women who want to play a larger role and be
> involved in the farmers' co-operative have been able to establish
> themselves as voices of authority.[24]

As we read in Chapter 3, women are particularly vulnerable to seasonal
and storm-related flooding in Bangladesh. With the assistance of government and religious NGOs, Bangladeshi women worked together
to provide financial assistance for flooding recovery. They formed a
cooperative to provide loans to other women to buy livestock and other
income improvements. The women's cooperative became the vehicle for
NGO-sponsored flooding prevention improvements:

> [They] identified 17 of the village's poorest households and
> decided to raise the foundational platform, or plinth, of their
> houses by four feet to protect them from the flood waters. A few
> other households, after seeing the benefits of such raised plinths,
> in turn made their own investments to raise the plinths of their
> houses. With their agricultural lands inundated for months,
> many households in the area also use a floating bed of com-
> pacted water hyacinths to grow vegetables, locally known as
> *baira*. These floating gardens fall and rise with the water level
> and can allow households to grow vegetables for consumption
> when the flood waters are high. [Project managers] have devised
> ways to improve the design of such *bairas* to make them lighter
> and stay afloat for longer periods of time.[25]

These and many other small-scale projects focused on empowering women are important examples of capacity-building for women's

empowerment. Alone these projects cannot overturn centuries of patri-archy and women's subjugation, nor can they stop climate change. To successfully engender climate change will require local efforts such as these working in concert with national level legislation, expanded edu-cational opportunities, outreach and mentoring of women at all lev-els of society, and guarantees of women's representation in national and international organizations. Since women are not a homogenous group within or across countries, diversity of advisors, participants, and approaches will be essential to any strategy – a diversity that must expand gender to include men.

Men are critical allies for transforming women's lives and working with them to save the planet. A central tenet of this book has been that climate change research and policies – and indeed, climate change itself – reflects men's universal and longstanding power, perspectives, and preferred pursuits. Like women, men are not homogenous, though their relative wealth and status set them above women in most organ-izational and national settings. Like women, however, men are at risk and must confront the problems of climate change – causes and consequences:

> [Although] men in most societies enjoy the benefits of male privilege, they may share with women in their lives simi-lar experiences of indignity, subordination, and insecurity as a result of discrimination or social and economic oppression. So rather than discounting men in gender analyses of climate change as if they were somehow non-gendered and impervious to the harsh impacts of environmental degradation and context of economic or social marginalization, we need to find spaces within gender and climate change frameworks to acknow-ledge and communicate the vulnerabilities that some men also experience.[26]

A multifaceted approach is required to address the multifaceted real-ities of gender and climate change. Recognizing and embracing this intersectional complexity is an important step in engendering climate change to meet the challenges of the 21st century.

Notes

[1] Dahlerup, Drude. 2009. "About Quotas." *Quota Project: Global Database of Quotas for Women.* Accessed on May 21, 2014 at www.quotaproject.org/about-quotas.cfm.

[2] Storvik, Aagoth, and Mari Teigen. 2010. *Women on Board: The Norwegian Experience.* Berlin: Friedrich-Ebert-Stiftung International Policy Analysis.

[3] Wang, Mingzhu, and Elisabeth Kelan. 2013. "The Gender Quota and Female Leadership: Effects of the Norwegian Gender Quota on Board Chairs and CEOs." *Journal of Business Ethics,* Vol. 17, No. 3:449–466, p. 460.

[4] Ibid., p. 463.

[5] Pande, Rohini, and Deanna Ford. 2011. "Gender Quotas and Female Leadership: A Review." World Bank: Background Paper for the World Development Report on Gender. Accessed on May 21, 2014 at http://scholar.harvard.edu/files/rpande/files/gender_quotas_-_april_2011.pdf.

[6] Fuller, Jaime. 2014. "Hillary Clinton Says Equality for Women Is the 'Great Unfinished Business of the 21st Century'." *Washington Post* (March 7). Accessed on May 23, 2014 at www.washingtonpost.com/blogs/post-politics/wp/2014/03/07/hillary-clinton-says-equality-for-women-is-the-great-unfinished-business-of-the-21st-century/.

[7] Ibid.

[8] Treussart, Teresita Kelly Lopez. 2014. "Financing the Unfinished Business of Gender Equality and Women's Rights: Priorities for the Post-2015 Framework." Organization of Economic Co-operation and Development (March). Accessed on May 23, 2014 at www.oecd.org/dac/gender-development/Long%20version%20-%20Financing%20the%20unfinished%20business%20of%20gender%20equality.pdf.

[9] Women's March, UN Intersessional Conference on Climate Change, Bangkok, Thailand, October, 2009. Accessed on July 16, 2015 at www.flickr.com/photos/oxfam/3971297063/in/album-72157622369065993/; photo credit: Mongkhonsawat Leungvorapant/Oxfam.

[10] United Nations Division for the Advancement of Women. 2005. *Equal Participation of Women and Men in Decision-Making Processes, with Particular Emphasis on Political Participation and Leadership.* Accessed on May 22, 2014 at www.un.org/womenwatch/daw/egm/eql-men/FinalReport.pdf, p. 7.

[11] African Women's Development and Communication Network. 2012. "What Is Gender Justice in the Context of Climate Change?" Accessed on May 22, 2014 at http://femnet.co/index.php/en/introduction-gender-and-climate-justice/177-what-is-gender-justice-in-the-context-of-climate-change.

[12] Ibid.

[13] Höne, Katharina. 2012. "COP18: Negotiating Climate Change. Where Are the Women?" Diplo. Accessed on May 22, 2014 at www.diplomacy.edu/blog/cop18-negotiating-climate-change-where-are-women.

[14] Wong, Sam. 2009. "Climate Change and Sustainable Technology: Re-linking Poverty, Gender, and Governance." *Gender and Development,* Vol. 17, No. 1: 95–108, p. 103.

[15] Ibid., p. 105.
[16] Tandon, Nidhi. 2009. "The Bio-fuel Frenzy: What Options for Rural Women? A Case of Rural Development Schizophrenia." *Gender and Development*, Vol. 17, No. 1:109–124.
[17] Ibid., p. 112.
[18] Gender-blindness in recent research underlines the continuing need to remind climate change scholars and policymakers that women's lives matter in climate policy and adaptation; vast evidence of inattention to gender can be found in prominent climate change journals, even in articles addressing the social aspects of climate change; for examples, see Matthew, Richard. 2014. "Integrating Climate Change into Peacebuilding." *Climatic Change*, Vol. 123, No. 1:83–93 or Shindell, Drew T. 2015. "The Social Cost of Atmospheric Release." *Climatic Change*, Vol. 130, No. 2:313–326.
[19] Ergas, C., and Richard York. 2012. "Women's Status and Carbon Dioxide Emissions: A Quantitative Cross National Analysis." *Social Science Research*, Vol. 41, No. 4:965–976.
[20] International Federation of Red Cross and Red Crescent Societies. 2002. "Housing Reconstruction in Honduras and Nicaragua." Accessed on May 23, 2014 at www.recoveryplatform.org/assets/submissions/200909010435_honduras_hurricanemitch_shelter.pdf.
[21] Bradshaw, Sarah. 2001. "Dangerous Liaisons: Women, Men, and Hurricane Mitch." Managua, Nicaragua: Fundación Puntos de Encuentro, pp. 17–18. Accessed on May 23, 2014 at http://worldbank.mrooms.net/file.php/349/references/dangerous_liaisons-power_relations_hurricane_mitch-_Sarah.pdf.
[22] Ibid., pp. 23, 26.
[23] United Nations Development Programme. 2014. "In Niger, Groups of Women Fight against Sand Encroachment." UNDP Women's Empowerment. Accessed on May 23, 2014 at www.undp.org/content/undp/en/home/our-work/womenempowerment/successstories/in-niger–groups-of-women-fight-against-sand-encroachment-.html.
[24] Annecke, Wendy, and Bettina Koelle. 2011. "Including Women in Adaptation Processes." *JotoAfrica*, No. 6 (March). Accessed on May 23, 2014 at www.eldis.org/vfile/upload/1/document/1104/JotoAfrika_Issue%206.pdf.
[25] Dixit, Aarjan. 2011. "Adapting to Climate Change in Bangladesh." World Resources Institute (April 14). Accessed on May 23, 2014 at www.wri.org/blog/2011/04/adapting-climate-change-bangladesh.
[26] Mearns, Robin, and Andrew Norton. 2008. *Social Dimensions of Climate Change: Equity and Vulnerability in a Warming World.* New York: World Bank, p. 140.

INDEX